"Once in a while, a book comes alon[g] ... human spirit at a whole new level—t[...] to understand a new way to be free, you must read *The Drama-Free Way*. Thank you, Jennifer, for offering up all of your insight from your own internal exploration as well as the research from so many others. Here's to a drama-free life!"

—**Rick Tamlyn, Hay House author,** *Play Your Bigger Game*

"Jennifer Ally Kern covers a plethora of valid explanations on how and why our personal pain commonly leads us down the addictive, destructive, and deceptive path of believing we need drama to feel alive. She lays out a thought-provoking and excellent approach to consciously thrive drama-free!"

—**Claudia Church, actress, singer, model, and coauthor of** *The Masterpiece Within*

"*The Drama-Free Way* brilliantly provides a blueprint for understanding the drama paradigm within ourselves and those around us. Jennifer Ally Kern provides masterful insight, perspective, and practical application, paving a path out of emotional destruction to a life of peace and deep fulfillment."

—**Nova Wightman, Spiritual Alignment founder and author of** *Awake and Aligned*

"*The Drama-Free Way* will resonate with anyone seeking a path to true emotional freedom. In this impactful book, author Jennifer Ally Kern provides a roadmap to that freedom, combining inspiring real-life stories with practical examples and tools. A wonderful book with a powerful message and beautiful vision for how to better the world one person at a time. Don't miss it."

—**Karen Kimsey-House, coauthor of bestselling** *Co-Active Coaching* **and** *Co-Active Leadership*, **cofounder of the Coaches Training Institute**

"Jennifer Ally Kern has managed to pack much wisdom and insight into a very readable book. Her personal anecdotes and fresh, direct style make for a valuable resource for reflection and personal growth."

—**Dominic Longo, PhD, Assistant Professor, Department of Theology; Co-Director, Muslim-Christian Dialogue Center, University of St. Thomas**

"In *The Drama-Free Way*, Jennifer Ally Kern candidly reveals the wounds of her being to illustrate the tools we need to embrace, heal, and love our own. By incorporating the daily practices Jennifer suggests for GRATE-full living, there is a clear path for all human beings to give each other the love, acceptance, and forgiveness we desire and deserve. Jennifer's mind-full daily practice rhythmically turns each day into a bountiful feast of joy. If you are hungry for daily living that leaves you feeling joyful and fulfilled, *The Drama-Free Way* will become your pocket companion for THRIVING your way through each and every day!"

—**Megan K. MacLaughlin-Barck, attorney, CEO, wife and mother**

"I loved *The Drama-Free Way* because it gave me an opportunity to look at my own life and where and how I can create more ease and peace for myself and others. When applied collectively, this book can help us create a world that is more reflective and self-aware. An important book to stopping the blame game."

—**Ursula Pottinga, Certified NeuroTransformation Coach, cofounder and COO of BEabove Leadership**

"Jennifer Ally Kern has written a beautiful, thoughtful, and realistic guide to managing the drama inside your head. Her time-tested tools give readers clear ways to create a more peaceful, intentional life. When my inner drama queen comes out to play, I'm reaching for *The Drama-Free Way*!"

—**Jacquelyn B. Fletcher, author of *Dear You: Messages from Your Heart***

NATIONAL AWARD-WINNING AUTHOR

JENNIFER ALLY KERN

The
Drama-*Free*
Way

AUTHENTIC *THRIVING*
IN A CHAOTIC WORLD

I have tried to recreate events, locales and conversations from my memories of them. In order to maintain their anonymity in some instances I have changed the names of individuals and places, I may have changed some identifying characteristics and details such as physical properties, occupations, and places of residence.

This book is not intended as a substitute for the medical advice of physicians. The reader should regularly consult a physician in matters relating to his/her health and particularly with respect to any symptoms that may require diagnosis or medical attention.

ISBN 13: 978-1-63489-382-4
eISBN: 978-1-63489-011-3

Library of Congress Catalog Number: 2015950348
Printed in the United States of America
Second Edition: 2021
25   24   23   22   21   6   5   4   3   2

Cover photograph © Depositphotos.
Interior design by Lift Creative.

Wise Ink Creative Publishing
807 Broadway St. NE, Suite 46
Minneapolis, Minnesota 55413
wiseink.com

For those who bear the burden of wound-based drama,
may your healing ensue and the true essence of your Soul be free to shine
through;

for Mi-Chi, Elias Zen, Sacha, Max & McKenzie, Nora-Amora and Cassialinda
in the hopes of contributing to a harmonious "new earth" for you to enjoy,
explore, and peacefully grow within for decades to come;

and

for my family,
with infinite gratitude for the miracle of your steadfast, unconditional love, and
all that I have learned and become as a result of it.

Table of Contents

Author's Note

Since the original writing of this book in 2014–2015, the drama in our world has continued to increase. In 2020, in particular, we have seen unprecedented worldwide changes—independent of culture, race, gender, language, nationality, or other distinguishing characteristics that make us humans believe we're separate from one another. Humanity is being pushed to its thresholds and change is no longer an option—it is *mandatory*.

But change in the outer world has to begin on the inside. *As within, so without*. It's not enough to identify the problems or even brainstorm solutions, if we are not *also* taking responsibility for the energy we infuse into the world at large by way of our thoughts and emotions. I'll develop this concept further in the introduction.

As my note to you, Dear Reader, first of all, thank you for being here. If you've found your way to this book, there is something of value for you in these pages. Trust that, get curious, take the ideas that resonate for you into your daily living, and enjoy! Second of all, the edits here are subtle—a little "nip and tuck", but most of the revision is in the introduction. Truth be told, I could completely redo this book, given new learning, insights, and my own personal development since the original writing. But we'll just save that for future books.

One significant update since the initial publication is that I was married at that time—and then I got *un*married. There are stories in this book that reference "my husband", which was true and current when I wrote the first edition. I have left those stories intact because they serve an illustrative purpose that is still relevant and useful. But know that they are not an accurate reflection of my present-day reality and are not meant to be misleading.

My intention with this second edition is to draw a higher level of awareness to what's going on within your personal inner world, so you are empowered to take charge of it. *Thoughts become things. What you focus on expands. Energy flows where attention goes.* You are truly the "manifestor" of all things in your individual life. And collectively, we are all partaking in the co-creation of our planet and its unfolding path. As each individual takes greater responsibility for the quality of energy they are exuding, we gradually elevate the trajectory of humanity and the world we are cultivating for our children, and all future generations.

There's no more time to wait. This is the era of awakening and claiming our authentic *thriving*. I hope this book will serve you in your journey.

With high regard and deep reverence,
Jennifer ALLY
October, 2020

Are You Steeped in the DRAMA Paradigm?

L et me paint a picture for you of life on planet earth.

The environment is flourishing. Air is pure, waters are clean, forests are burgeoning. Everyone in the animal kingdom is exactly where they belong, and the temperature is *just right*.

People are prospering. Everyone has access to whatever they need and desire, it always shows up "on time" . . . and they've come to *expect* this. Children are boundless in their self-expression, romping about in their curious nature and learning to be human. They are receiving a holistic education that prepares them for what their unique souls came here to be, do, and have. Teenagers are carefree, growing in collaboration with one another, discovering the truth of Who They Really Are and boldly bringing their talents to the world. Adults are gliding effortlessly through the process of life, following their hearts' callings and joyfully striving toward the manifestation of their greatest visions. Elders are cared for with dignity and respect. And there's more than enough love, support, and encouragement for *everyone*.

The economy is multifaceted and no longer hinged on money alone. In fact, money isn't even an issue; people understand that it's *just energy*, and that it's not the only form of currency or exchange. They know that there are infinite possibilities for how to get the things they desire—and they allow these to just come to them. People are also unattached to material belongings; *stuff* doesn't define them. They enjoy an object for as long as they need, and then pass it on.

Relationships are harmonious and easy to navigate. The physical body is thriving and chronic disease is a thing of the past. Governments are free to serve the people, sans political strife. Countries honor peaceful accords. Social inclusion is the norm and all individuals are valued for who they are. They feel good and safe within their tribes. In fact, they feel good in life overall—*and they don't rely on anyone or anything outside of themselves to give it to them.*

Now, it may sound like this book is about creating a utopian sort of society, but it's not. With the drama our world is steeped in today, we're too far away from that. However, *the children being born aren't.* They could see this in their lifetimes . . . *if* we lay the groundwork for them now. We are at a critical point in our trajectory—a point that will determine the future timeline of humanity and our beautiful earth home. Our choices today are paving the path for subsequent generations. It can't happen all at once, but we can set things into motion. This book is about making that *pivot.*

In order to select a higher path, we have to start focusing our efforts in the right place. While great things are achieved with persistent action, that's not where the achievement actually begins. Napoleon Hill did not say "whatever a man does, he achieves." He said, "whatever the mind of man can *conceive* and *believe,* it can achieve." Conceiving happens in *thought.* Believing occurs in *emotion.* We don't achieve transformation by exerting effort *out there* without first addressing what's happening *in here.*

So, this book is drawing attention to what's happening *in here.* It's confronting the destructive aspects of our cultural drama that are blocking that higher path and greatest future from unfolding—not to mention, interfering with personal joy and fulfillment. And it all starts with the drama that runs rampant in our own minds.

As you'll discover, drama is an inside game. Nobody thinks drama is about them. They think drama is something that happens *out there*. That's because up until now, we've had a very narrow view and limited understanding of what drama is. But that's about to change. I think Carl Jung would agree that the drama we see in others—and even in our society—presents an opportunity for us to gain insight into *ourselves*. This book is about to call you forth, in order to *empower* you to take the only responsibility you can take, and that's over the inner machinations of your beautiful mind and the quality of energy *you* are contributing to the collective consciousness. This is what it means to *be the change*. When each individual does *that*, my-oh-my . . . what an authentically *thriving* world we will co-create.

The Chaotic World of DRAMA

Let's start where we are, with this soul-sucking monster called Drama— it's *everywhere*. It has been growing over decades, intensifying incrementally, and it's not stopping.

Our culture is massively steeped in drama. It's all around us: when we turn on the TV, tune into the radio, access the web, drive in traffic, stand in line, or open our inboxes. It blares ubiquitously through news stories, programs, and advertisements that seduce us into lower levels of consciousness—where uncertainty, anxiety, and our need for control grab hold. It's present through the insensitivity and impatience of the people we cross paths with at work, among social circles, and within our families. The drama we absorb from the collective environment bleeds into our individual thoughts, attitudes, and beliefs. If you have a human brain, without even realizing it, drama probably shows up in your car, in the shower, or while you're doing the dishes—via thoughts that swirl with worry and doubt, anxiousness and frustration.

The word "drama" is a modern-day cultural colloquialism that is generally used to describe emotional reactivity accompanied by behavioral outbursts. However, it needs to be recognized as the social survival phenomenon that it is, and broken down into its key components in a way that we can grasp and utilize toward healing and positive change. This book identifies both the inter- and *intra*-personal dynamics of drama, where it comes from, the purpose it serves, how it functions as an addiction, and what a "treatment" approach toward being enslaved by our own negative thought-substance would entail.

What most people don't realize is that drama is a wound-based affliction. It's grounded in our three core human wounds—shame, abandonment, and betrayal—and the thought patterns and beliefs that emerge from them. The degree to which we have been wounded is directly proportionate to the degree of drama we manifest—both internally and externally—in an attempt to meet our essential human needs, which you'll learn about in Chapter 4.

Internal drama manifests itself externally in a variety of expressions, such as: gossip, collusion, debt accrual, extreme diets and body obsession, abuse, rape, addiction and codependence, disease, affairs, neglect, and explosive tempers. On a global scale, we see it expressed through terrorism, war, murders and violent crime, human trafficking, drug trade, starvation and obesity epidemics, social prejudice, unemployment, poverty, economic crisis, lawsuits, corporate fraud, political scandals, and environmental desecration.

The reason drama is such a problem—a pandemic, even—is simply because we humans are modeling machines; what we witness, we learn and duplicate. Those who went before us and influenced our lives with their harmful words and hurtful behaviors were also wounded. They were not capable of teaching or offering us anything they themselves did not possess. This is not to place blame, but simply to acknowledge that we can inherit a kind of wound-based living that leaves us with drama-orienting beliefs and misaligned energy.

Modern life has us more wounded, separated, and disconnected than ever, within *ourselves* first and foremost, but also with others, with nature, and with Spirit. Our essential needs for love, connection, and belonging are silently screaming and seeking ways to be outwardly met. Although drama is not the most effective means to accomplish that, it is a familiar and (to an extent) socially accepted way. The problem is that continuing down this path of destruction is unsustainable. We are hitting a threshold, and, no matter how much we resist, life will keep urging us forward.

If we subscribe to the belief that our internal thoughts co-create our external reality, perpetuating drama will only give us more of the same on our planet and in our individual lives. *The Drama-Free Way* offers an alternative approach to the human experience: inner alignment for developing an authentically *thriving* life—a life marked by healthy connection, purpose, ease, joy, physical well-being, meaningful growth and wealth of all kinds. As we learn to identify our personal patterns of drama and gain the skills to effectively navigate the habits of our minds, fundamentally elevating into a consciousness of *thriving*, we will assuredly lead more happy and fulfilling lives. One by one, the incremental shifts in consciousness advance our collective human evolution, moving us all closer to living the truth of Who We Really Are: physical expressions of Spirit.

DRAMA Defined

People have different ideas about what drama is, so to be sure we're starting on the same page, let me give you my definition of it. Succinctly, DRAMA is a wound-based, social survival mechanism that seeks to meet our needs to be seen and heard and to feel that we matter. It is characterized by thought patterns that are:

- Disempowering
- Reactive
- Assumption-based

- Maladaptive
- Addictive

DRAMA thinking is something that has always been present in our human experience, because our wounding has always been part of the journey of expansion. In recent decades, the DRAMA paradigm has become increasingly pervasive as our use of technology has skyrocketed. Technology has us more separated from our close personal connections, focusing our attention elsewhere, while drawing us into greater levels of comparison and sense of inadequacy. *We're never enough*. We are more deeply steeped in our fears, and we feel lonelier and more isolated than ever before. So we build defenses to protect our tender hearts and psyches. With time, we start to believe that the DRAMA paradigm is "real" when, in fact, it simply floats about in the ethers as only one *potential* reality. We begin to identify ourselves as being the limited characters we've been told we are, struggling within that limited bubble to gain our sense of worthiness, value and belonging. But none of this is the truth.

True reality is found in being Who We Really Are—the exquisite Soul who's bravely embarked upon this wild human ride. And DRAMA is the *number one* thing that prevents us from living that truth.

Everything is Energy—Including Drama

"If you want to find the secrets of the Universe, think in terms of energy, frequency and vibration."

—NICOLA TESLA

Humans are fundamentally energetic beings, and we experience energy through our emotions. Just like other kinds of energy, our emotions exist on a spectrum. Light, for instance, ranges from infrared to visible to ultraviolet, and so too do our emotions range through what we experience as "highs" and "lows". When we sense high-frequency energies, we feel love, bliss, gratitude, joy, elation, and so on. When we sense low-frequency energies, we feel fear, anger, hopelessness, shame, grief, etc. The *feeling* is how we *interpret* the frequency. This is a natural part of the human experience—it's supposed the be there because it's *required* for us to grow as vibrational, spiritual beings.

But drama is a different animal. It has its own frequency bandwidth. It's a distorted version of the low vibes. In short, low energetic frequencies naturally feel bad, so we resist them. This resistance causes them to get repressed, bottled up, and become toxic *within* us. That's how they turn into drama. This repressed energy hijacks the brain and keeps us in spirals of negative thoughts that then reinforce the low vibes, and so it becomes cyclical—and, yes—addictive.

Drama energies are highly manipulative and controlling, because they mess with our free will. Drama, like any addiction, has a compulsive quality to it. It stimulates the survival parts of the brain which lead us to react out of defense and protection, rather than respond with thoughtfulness and authenticity. The more we expose ourselves to these kinds of drama energies, the more our brains become primed for them, and the more we experience them in our day-to-day lives. You'll discover more about how this works and exactly what these "drama energies" are in Chapter 3.

Vibration In, Vibration Out

"Life doesn't imitate art, it imitates bad television."

—WOODY ALLEN

Drama is a mass media staple, evidenced in advertisements, shows, movies, and headlines. Big media relies on the cheap sense of aliveness we experience through the physiological stress response when we become mentally and emotionally engrossed in their projected realities. The human brain cannot tell the difference between intently thinking about or watching something and actually *living* it. Because of our hard-wiring for survival, we easily get triggered into anxious fear, envy, worthlessness, and disdain by images and messaging that on some level threaten identity, safety, value, belonging, or even status quo.

It may seem as though exposure to drama is innocuous, and a big part of that is because we are *used* to it. While chaos, sex, and violence have long been incorporated in the thrill of entertainment, the visual graphicness and amount of exposure we experience today far exceeds anything in the past. Nowadays, the levels of stimulation required to get the same emotional "kick" are significantly more intense than they were in earlier eras of entertainment. We have an unprecedented threshold for witnessing sexual acts, abuse, violence, drug use and death. What we need to recognize is that whenever an energetic state runs through us, our systems adjust to vibrate at that level regardless of whether the stimulus is present in our literal external realities or we're just psychologically indulging in it. It doesn't recognize that we're only *mentally* engaged with a fictitious reality, so any emotional energy that gets activated within us as a result of watching a show, film or playing a video game will influence how those states take up residence in our vibrational systems and thus affect our lives.

A conversation about drama wouldn't be complete without mentioning social media. In this case, there can be a slippery slope into comparison, where we evaluate others as happier, better or more successful than we are based on pictures and posts. There's also the waft of competition at times, not to mention the pernicious "sounding off" about heated topics, blatantly mean commenting or people "airing dirty laundry". We never really get the full picture of reality, so the resourceful brain fills in the blanks with its assumptions and generalizations—leaving us oblivious to the actual truth about others as well as disconnected from *ourselves*.

Now, making the media a scapegoat for the drama in our lives is a bit excessive. It's unreasonable to hold them exclusively responsible for how we are operating inside *our own minds*. They are just doing their job—and their business has evolved to the stage we find ourselves in now *because* we indulge in it. Furthermore, there's nothing inherently wrong with entertainment or social platforms. People can have a vastly different response to the same stimuli: what's disgusting to one is amusing to another. So, of course it's okay—essential even—to enjoy music, movies, shows, and virtual interactions . . . when we're making a *conscious* choice about participating in them and not just acting out of compulsion or habit.

In our cultural landscape, it is common to hear certain people being referred to as "addicted to drama." It is the unconscious hedonistic thrill of drama that, for some more than others, is as much irresistible as it is insatiable. Chapter 5 will shed a strong light on why that is and how drama truly does function like an addiction. Although media programming feeds our drama thinking, the drama we actually experience on a personal level happens in the context of our own relationships and life circumstances—which is an external reflection of our own internal worlds.

Unless you live a completely isolated, hermetic life, you can neither avoid contact with other humans nor the greater world of messages and media. But it's up to you to decide what (and who) you expose yourself to, the ways you interpret interactions and messages, and how you shape your inner world in order to create more of what you want in your life. As we each do this, we up-level our collective human experience.

The good news is that this awakening is already underway. We are already using the power of technology and global interconnectedness to build and enhance our *higher* consciousness. People are shifting into consistently positive vibrations and greater levels of self-authority. This is a new lifestyle, based upon living in alignment with our Souls' truth. With time, as we claim our higher states of being and practice our authentic *thriving*, the DRAMA paradigm will gradually fade away.

The Call for an Inner Revolution

"If the structures of the human mind remain unchanged, we will always end up re-creating the same world, the same evils, the same dysfunction."

—ECKHART TOLLE

Nearly one hundred years ago, French philosopher Pierre Teilhard de Chardin popularized the concept of the *noosphere*. *Noos-* is derived from the Greek word for "mind." Just as we have a geosphere, biosphere, hydrosphere, atmosphere (and so on), our lovely planet also has a noosphere—the layer of existence that both contains and is constructed by human thought and the connection between minds. It is the realm of the collective consciousness. This noosphere is a living, breathing entity that expands and evolves through the addition of new human life as well as the increase in *interconnectedness*. Like any other sphere, the wellness of this space is defined by the quality of energy that goes into it: purity or pollution—and whichever is dominant is what will influence the direction of its evolution. At the moment, the toxicity of drama is the dominant defining energy, and it's time for a pivot.

As previously discussed, our consumption of media—both traditional and social—plays a huge role in our interconnectedness and the quality of thoughts that are shaping our noosphere, much of which constitute a lower frequency of energy. But the intensity of the upheaval we are experiencing now reaches far beyond the influence of the media. Given the destructive lifestyle we've developed over the last century, human life on our planet will not last long if we continue on our current course. Challenges are mounting to push us into a quantum leap that will improve our way of living and, frankly, ensure our survival. As human beings, we require challenges and adversity in order to take on the grueling work of transformation and growth. We've needed this for every revolution on the planet; life has to become limited, problematic, or painful *enough* to evoke change and forward movement. Historically, advancement in any area of life—agriculture, industry, science, technology—emerged as a result of expanding consciousness steering human awareness toward new needs and desires. Although such advances begin with a small few, when life is ready to birth the next level of our evolutionary development, one way or another the rest of us are going along for the ride.

With this next wave of evolution underway, life is now demanding we learn how to direct our mental and emotional energy—not just our physical actions—in more effective, harmonious ways. This means an *inner* revolution, empowering us to align with our Higher Selves. This next level is where we claim our power as spiritual beings in the human experience, take charge of co-creating our world and apply the skills to *consciously* live from the inside out. It's where we no longer employ internal drama to mentally fight against life's circumstances or attempt to get our needs met. Instead, we use the contrasting experiences of our lives to fine-tune our desires, cultivate new choices, and fuel our expansion.

Most people are not even aware of the degree to which their private thoughts actually effect the world they live in. Through no fault of their own, they are conditioned to operate haphazardly, driven by impulse more than focused intent. And all the stimulation we get through our environment and technology only exacerbates that turmoil. We're reaching the point where solutions for our internal chaos are vital, as the pain penetrating the human spirit increasingly seeps into our streets. It's time to address the deeper spiritual wounds that contribute to this chaotic world of drama and pioneer new approaches that gently escort us to the next level of human evolution. That's where inner alignment comes in. We need to heal. We need to retrieve our authentic selves. We need to elevate our perspectives, beliefs and lifestyles to rise into living as the truth of Who We Really Are, and gradually bring global human consciousness—our noosphere—into the space of unity and wholeness.

This is now our number-one job here on earth.

Why We Need to Live in a DRAMA-Free Way

In an environment of exceedingly amplified chaos and trauma, how do we shift our larger paradigm to move in the direction of authentic *thriving?* How do we select a future timeline that resembles some version of utopia—no matter how far off that reality may appear? What will happen to the human race if we continue along our current trajectory of disconnection, fear-based functioning, and ever-increasing tolerance for violence? While this book is about the development and healing of our inner worlds, it also assumes there is no separation from the outer world. Anything we do for ourselves we do for *all* of humanity. New levels of inner alignment will have each of us feeling more joyous and operating more authentically, raising our collective flourishing as a species. But on the path to get there, what do we do about our addiction to drama? Survival of the fittest has reached a new level, where the fittest are those who can adapt their *thoughts* and *emotions* to align with their Higher Selves, regardless of what circumstances may dictate or imply. In this human experience, how do we elevate our inner realms to align with our spiritual selves, and raise our consciousness rather than hold it hostage in the all-consuming chaotic world of drama?

We learn the skills, adopt the practices, and make the commitment to effectively live in a drama-free way. *Let's do this.*

"Life is very much like Let's Make a Deal *with your belief systems and daily choices determining whether you get Door Number One, Two, or Three! . . . What you get is what you believe you are worthy of getting. You draw that particular future that fits with your total overview of how things must be. As long as you remain stuck in the delusional thinking and addictive behavior, you will get the booby prize. If you are not happy with what you are being offered in life right now, then you can change the deal by changing your thoughts, perceptions, and beliefs."*

—DR. LYNNE NAMKA

1

The DRAMA Paradigm

"*You think that if you change things outside, you'll be okay. But nobody has ever truly become okay by changing things outside. There's always the next problem. . . . No solution can possibly exist while you're lost in the energy of a problem. . . . You will not be able to solve anything outside until you own how the situation affects you inside.*"

—MICHAEL A. SINGER

CHAPTER ONE

Separation and Chaos—The Papa and Mama of DRAMA

I sucked my thumb till I was thirteen. *Thirteen.*

I wasn't into the binky or the wubbie or any of that stuff. I just wanted my thumb. It was safer, because it was attached to me. That made it the one permanent thing in my life that I could actually count on consistently from birth. I needed it daily, moment to moment, all the time, just to know that there was something reliable I could turn to that would soothe my fears and anchor me within the chaos.

Oh, believe me, my parents tried to get me to stop. They tried wrapping my thumb with tape. They tried putting the stinky, nasty *Stopz It* polish on my nails. But in my infinite resourcefulness I just reverted to sucking on other fingers. They weren't as satisfying as my thumb, but they were just as reliable, so they still met my primary need. Now, I don't think it's *that* uncommon for little babies or toddlers to crave the security that comes from sucking or hair twirling or having a special blankie or stuffed animal. But until *thirteen*? That speaks to something bigger going on than just a scary thunderstorm or a loud barking dog or a childhood habit. Frankly, the only reason I stopped sucking my thumb *by* thirteen was because I got my braces taken off. The orthodontist made me sleep with one of those plastic retainers—you know, the one that looks like a melted watermelon Jolly Rancher stuck to the roof of your mouth—leaving no room to squeeze my thumb in for oral gratification. But can you imagine if I *hadn't* gotten that retainer? If I *hadn't* had something else to take up that space in my mouth? I could have been sucking my thumb well into adulthood! I could have had to hide this mortifying secret from college roommates. It could have infected my whole dating life. Any way you slice it, I would have been petrified for people to find out. I mean, I was already freaked out about it at thirteen, what would be different at eighteen or twenty-one or twenty-seven or thirty-five? (. . . and so the drama thinking goes . . .)

I was born into certain privilege, but it was trumped by overwhelming turmoil. My first memories are of my parents fighting, screaming at each other, even physically tussling, and me running away in tears, either to hide under a stool in the kitchen or to have my older sister take me away. I was too young to grasp the extent or the details, but I've since been told there was drug use in this household. The backdrop was of a blended family that involved my twenty-seven-year-old mother raising her infant daughter and two teenage step-kids full time, a father who was nose deep in developing his medical career, and brushstrokes of self-absorption shadowing the whole family portrait. Although the formation of this family disintegrated over several years, I truly believe that everyone was doing their best based on what they were capable of at the time.

When I was three years old my parents began the divorce process and Mom moved out with me. By seven, she remarried and began a new family. My stepdad was a large man, 6'5" and 230 pounds. He had dark hair and sharp features. To a kid—to me—he was enormous and sometimes scary-looking. Although I was, again, too young to understand the underpinnings of these adults' behaviors, I knew enough to be cautious in that household. They each had their own versions of an erratic temperament; you never knew what you were going to get. They could at times be jovial, playful, and totally caring. Others times, not so much. Jokes used to be made about the holes in the walls of our house where my stepdad punched in the sheetrock so he "wouldn't hit my mother." They used to mock and berate nearly everyone else in my life whom I loved, both friends and extended family. I myself was referred to as a "JAP" (*Jewish American Princess*—because my bio-dad was Jewish) and for years carried the nickname "Cinder-Jenni"—an appropriate title, however, given the slew of household tasks I was expected to accomplish from a very young age. I went along with all of it, to stay safe, to get approval, and to belong to the group. I learned to go along with pretty much anything just to avoid stirring the beast. Looking back now, I can see that cross-generational alcoholism and the lingering trauma of past familial tragedies played a role in their dynamics. The deceptive thing is that the interactions contained such subtle abuse. I don't reacall witnessing immediate physical assault, but there was no escaping the psychological barbarians of unpredictable volatility and chronic intimidation. As far as I could tell, my mom and stepdad were very high-functioning addicts, mostly "dry" even, meaning they did not use excessively or frequently. To their credit, they made a great effort to engage with me, care for me, teach me independence, and instill healthy values—I mean, I turned out a little bit okay—but the underlying stinking-thinking and the temperamental behaviors were also vividly present, which makes for a very confusing, untrustworthy world to a child.

In my father's household, I felt safe, for a period of time. In the early divorce years, my dad was highly attentive to me. When I look back, it's actually pretty remarkable. He was incredibly engaged in my life and committed to learning new skills for raising a little girl on his own. Some of my most cherished childhood memories are with my dad. But then he started to bring girlfriends into the picture, and things became emotionally tumultuous for me. I was a pretty easygoing kid, but nevertheless I was impacted by the relational instability and the attitudes of the various women. One of them was phony and I could tell she didn't like me. Another was begrudging and stern, leaving me nervous, on eggshells. My favorite girlfriend—the *model*—was the absolute light of my world during the preteen years when I most needed the unconditional love and acceptance she gave me. It was a huge loss for me when the adult relationship ruptured; I never even got to say goodbye. There was the Euro-cool girlfriend who I also adored. There was the interior decorator, the doctor, the economist, the farm girl, the artist—each enduring various lengths of time, from months to several years. My father's girlfriend relationships were generally long enough for me to develop my own sense of connection with these ladies, some of them mother-figures even, and then suddenly they would just be gone. A new one would show up and I had to put the pieces together myself to decipher that this was the new girlfriend—it was generally not explained to me.

In recent years, there have been "diagnoses," both formal and presumed, of borderline and narcissistic personality disorders among various family members across my households. It would certainly clarify some of the behaviors and chaos that defined my upbringing. In my current stage of life, I can embrace compassion and patience. But in my very formative and developmental years, I only knew the emotional experience of the unpredictable environments, which naturally influenced my beliefs about the world and myself in it.

There were very few things in my life that were predictable or constant. I was raised both Christian and Jewish, attending numerous churches, each a different denomination, as well as catching a few lesons in Hebrew School. I got baptized, *twice*. I have two older siblings from Dad's first marriage who sometimes I could see and sometimes not, for reasons my young mind could only grasp as them having "been naughty." At times, I was forbidden from visiting other beloved family members because the adults couldn't get along. I spent the bulk of my time at Mom's, where my precious dogs died prematurely, ran off, or were sent away, and were then replaced by a stray picked up on the side of the highway or at the pound. Even our vehicles changed at least once a year.

In all this, my child-self drew what would later become a life-defining conclusion: *I don't matter*. Without knowing any better, I assumed my feelings did not get fully factored into the equation when it came to the relationships and on-goings in my households. I intuitively felt that my needs and desires were not as important as those of the adults. Further, I inferred that people are disposable. If someone isn't perfect, you get rid of them (through stonewalling or breakups) and, when applicable, you just get a new one. Thus, the next defining seed was planted and sown: *I better damn well be perfect*, lest I be cast out myself. As a kid primed for rapid adaptation, I quickly learned to stifle my feelings, be a good girl, and just *make them all happy*, in order to secure a place within my wobbly world.

Shortly after Mom's remarriage, a series of moves around the state and country ensued over a period of seven years—and not due to job changes, but because the grass was always greener elsewhere. I was always the "new girl in school," constantly the outsider peering in. There was no place I really felt I *belonged*. I was frequently teased, made fun of, ridiculed. Bullied by the boys and taunted by the girls. I was disowned in friendships because I was "too slow" or due to mean-girl triangulation where I became ostracized. At school, I always knew where the hidden corners were or the private bathrooms so I could eat my lunch where no one would see me.

In both of my households, from the time I was eight, I was teased about my body, my shape, my size, my eating—not by siblings, though. By the *adults*. In fact, regardless of being a relatively active kid, I was put on my first diet at eleven. Like many young girls, I developed an unwarranted negative body image, along with food anxiety and a desperate desire to be beautiful. Not just pretty but, like, Cindy Crawford *gorgeous*—because I had learned that was a surefire way to get love and acceptance. But I was dorky and ugly and "fat," so no luck there.

When I was sixteen, I was no longer welcome in my mother's household. I had done a bad thing—I *lied*. In spite of my striving for perfection by being a straight-A student, excelling in a part-time job, playing sports,

7

helping at home with chores, taking care of my little brothers, living "clean" (no smoking, drinking, or drugs), and being an overall good kid, I was no longer allowed in the home after I was caught lying. It was about sneaking around to see a boy I liked, whom I was forbidden from because my parents didn't like him. In all fairness, I did spend several months orchestrating the various deceptions it took to be able to hang out with him. Like a genuine teenager, I was always where I said I would be, but conveniently he was there too. I had been a good rule-follower up until then, but my need to be accepted by a boy (and feel pretty or desirable to at least someone) became more important than my need to be a good girl for my parents. And that made me disposable. So, under the custody of my father, I ended up finishing high school living with two different families (so I would not have to change schools *again*). Ironically, at the time, I was sure that I was "the bad one" and that it was all my fault, believing the punishment of complete disposal fit the crime.

All tallied, by the time I was seventeen I had lived in fifteen different houses and attended nine different schools. I was raised most of the time with my mother, part-time with my father (and a few of those girlfriends). I lived one year each with two different families, and many childhood weekends (during the divorce years) with my grandparents.

My intention in sharing this story with you is neither to gain pity nor place blame. In fact, I have to acknowledge that without these experiences I would not have been able to develop some of my greatest gifts and refine my most useful attributes, which contribute to my success and fulfillment today. The reason why I'm sharing this story is to illustrate how what I experienced—the emotional wounding of shame, abandonment, and betrayal, along with the unpredictability, the lacking sense of belonging, the fear, and the isolation—set the stage for drama in my *mind* and subsequently in my life.

And I don't think I'm the only one who has experienced these kinds of things. I think a whole lot of us have.

The most vital human need, after our basic physical survival needs are met, is to feel valued and understood, to be seen and heard, to belong—to *matter*. The behaviors and relationship interactions that cause emotional wounding have been passed down for generations upon generations. Those who treated us learned from the ones who treated them. As a result, most of us never got to be fully seen or heard—we were never known entirely for Who We Really Are. We weren't always acknowledged as innately valuable or shown that we mattered.

I truly believe that people are doing the best they can based on their experiences, which we, from the outside, can never fully see or understand. Everyone is the protagonist in their own lives; nobody believes they are the villain. Yet, we are each the villain to someone. We all carry wounds and we have all wounded others. Not because we want to, but because of the cycle of wounding. How others treated us created a certain impact. It created our beliefs about ourselves and the world, and we then move forward to engage with both ourselves and others based on the beliefs we hold, our wounds, and the behaviors we witnessed. We chronically shame, abandon, and betray *ourselves* and others. In order to break the cycle, we need to begin to heal our own wounds from within, and let that precipitate positive changes in our lives.

Even though I gave up *the thumb* at thirteen, I eventually found other—just as ineffective—behaviors to try to get my needs for predictability, safety, value, and belonging met. Among them: overeating, gossiping, perfectionism, procrastination, lying, passive-aggressiveness, approval-seeking, and people-pleasing—just to name a few.

As a result of my wounding and my beliefs about myself and the world around me, I developed a very destructive lifestyle during the tender ages of sixteen to twenty-four. I started partying, smoking, and drinking. I stuck white shit up my nose, bonged on opium, and rolled *el cho-co-la-te* (that's hashish). I let strange men pick me up and take me with them to foreign lands—including some countries which could have been dangerous for me as a young "Western woman." I let myself be physically, verbally, and emotionally abused. I was regrettably indiscriminate. I binged. I purged. My weight yo-yo'ed, but always in an overweight range. All of which was a reflection of my extreme loneliness, the disconnection with myself—my worthlessness, my hunger to be valued, my desperation to matter.

What I assumed through the chaotic experiences of my developmental years was that "life is not safe." "Authority figures are to be feared. Power gets abused. I am inferior and other people are always right and/or better than I am." I learned to criticize harshly. I learned to hide my needs and to always put others first. I came to believe that "I'm the bad one." I learned if things go wrong or if someone isn't happy, it's *my* fault. Most of all, I learned that I don't matter. My thoughts, my ideas, my feelings, my Self: none of it matters. And to my detriment, I lived out every single one of these beliefs.

Thus, the platform for a drama-filled life.

What I have awakened to understand is that it was my drama *thinking* that generated the chaos in my young adult life. Drama is not who I was, but it was a means of getting my needs met. Manifesting drama behavior was the only way I knew to be seen or heard—the only avenue I knew to mattering, *out there*. It also fulfilled a deep need for self-preservation and fierce protection, *in here*. I wanted to feel safe. And *no one* was to be trusted. I always had to be on guard. Because of the chronic resistance and reactive cycles I was in, drama held me captive in the lower vibrational frequencies of anxiety, depression, and worthlessness. In no way did it honor my Higher Self, satisfy my Soul, or allow me to be the expression of joy, love, and harmony that is the truth of Who I Really Am.

I am hardly the only person who has had a difficult upbringing or inadequate parenting. In fact, in many ways I think I had it really easy and really good, especially compared to many people. But each of us has a personal history, and growth to be harvested from it. It is important to be aware of how that history impacts our lives today. The inner world we inhabit is a direct result of our personal experiences over our lifetime, in addition to those of our parents and the generations before them. Our thought patterns are largely inherited, through witnessing our families, from being indoctrinated into their belief systems, and learning to follow their values. The larger culture naturally plays a role in how we develop our worldview as well, but the bulk of our inner dialogue comes from our lineage.

The thought patterns are elusive at times. They are so subtle, often presenting themselves as energetic tones and moods that dominate our unconscious minds, drive our behaviors, and show up externally as the people and events we attract to us. Part of the work we humans are faced with in our current evolutionary stage is to raise our levels of consciousness and develop the skills for inner alignment. It's important to have insight into the ways our personal history—the experiences, the wounding, and the good stuff too—has sculpted our thought patterns. Being knowledgeable about our learned trends and themes will naturally enhance our conscious engagement with life, including our relationships, and will gradually lead us in the direction of healing and growing into wholeness.

And collectively, if we truly want to create the world peace and harmony we say we desire, we each have to take charge *individually* for the consciousness and energy we are contributing to the *noosphere*. Rather than looking back, placing blame, or otherwise deferring our power to effect change (to others or to circumstances we have no influence over), we have to resolve our drama on the inside first, and reach for the *thriving* consciousness that is our birthright.

My intention in writing this book is to offer a unique perspective on the drama our thoughts are creating in our lives and in the world, and to provide a manual of sorts for authentic *thriving*. Through my own experience, years of working with individual clients and groups, and consulting with others, I developed my own definition of drama and came up with the acronym to highlight the elements I think are important to understand and address. To reiterate, DRAMA is a wound-based social survival mechanism that seeks to meet our needs to be seen and heard and to feel that we matter. It is characterized by thought patterns that are:

Disempowering

Reactive

Assumption-based

Maladaptive

Addictive

These thought patterns originate from our core human wounds of shame, abandonment, and betrayal, and the beliefs that grew out of them. They pull us into the lower energetic states of worthlessness, depression, anxiety, rage, and egotism, keeping us out of alignment with our Higher Selves, negatively influencing our behaviors and interpersonal interactions.

Drama operates as a social survival method. It attempts to fulfill our essential human needs: to belong, to be valued, to feel understood, to *matter*. However, since drama originates from the lower levels of consciousness, it tends to have a poor effect, not really getting us the degree of connection and intimacy we need and desire. Drama is an assault to our collective joy. It is inherently isolating, destroying intimate relationships. It denies our values and chokes off our greater life purpose. Drama inhibits our inner alignment and gradually suffocates our spirit, preventing us from living the joy-filled, abundant lives we intrinsically deserve. It directly impedes our ability to create success, which I define as having a significant level of well-being in all areas of life that is marked by appreciation, joy, authenticity, flow, connection, and continuous growth and expansion.

As long as we continue to indulge our drama functioning, we will feel more and more dispirited. We will have ongoing depression, anxiety, and raging. Separation will dominate our relationships. We will keep ourselves small, tucked away in the dark, rather than letting the world experience our shining light and the gifts we bring. There is a better, more effective way. With years of study, work, and attention to the elements that compose this subject, I have been able to identify many of the drama patterns and themes that are pervasive in our collective consciousness. This awareness empowers new and different choices that yield more fruitful results. The goal of this book is to help you identify *your* drama thinking, so you can shift the energetic state you generate on any given subject, and live the successful, *thriving*, fun life that is ahead of you. It is also aimed at shifting the conversation about drama on a collective level, so when we see drama exhibited by others we know how to respond effectively and we understand that it's simply a call for love. Ultimately, as we each heal and evolve our consciousness, one by one, we will teach the younger generations to do the same, and eventually create a truly harmonious human experience.

The first part of this book will provide an overview of drama, discuss where it comes from, name the purpose that it serves, and look at how to approach and "treat" drama as an addiction. It will identify the fundamental drama thought-patterns and themes and how they play out to create the external experience of chaos.

The second part will look at the concept of authentic *thriving* and the healing process required in order to live more abundantly and harmoniously. It will provide the outline for developing your *thriving* lifestyle, as well as offer tools and concepts for elevating your personal consciousness. It will address the various universal laws that can be applied to living a *thriving* life, and, finally, it will propose effective ways to interface with a little something I like to call "OPD"—*other people's drama.*

The final pages of each chapter will recap the main points in Key Concepts. It will also offer an Application and Integration section for you to process the chapter content and apply the concepts to yourself in specific and personalized ways. As you go through the book I invite you to identify the thought-pattern changes you can make and actively design the upgrades that will improve all areas of your life.

The language I use is in reference to the Universe, a Higher Self, soul, and spirit. Please make the relevant adjustments in your mind to adapt my terminology to the language you use to refer to and connect with your higher power. This is your book, part of your journey, so make it work for you.

There is nothing in the outer world that does not in some way match the thought patterns, conscious or unconscious, that we first generate from within. Anything that happens *to* us is a perfect reflection of what is happening *inside* us. So to begin feeling happier and to have more of the life experiences we desire, we have to first take charge of how we *think* and how we *feel*.

Living continuously expanding, harmonious, joy-filled lives requires us to become skilled at managing our internal worlds, including the drama that we abdicate to. When we can interface with our internal drama with understanding, we can heal our wounds, honor our Higher Selves, and create the fulfilling lives we are meant to enjoy.

My father always used to tell me, "We can never be objective about ourselves." While there is likely a degree of truth in that, I can see that humans are fundamentally changing—*we're waking up*. In our current evolutionary stage, people are increasingly reflective, conscious, and self-aware, waking up to their Higher Selves and their innate power. We each have an important role to play in the expansion of the Universe and the elevation of the human experience—including *you*. When you get stuck in drama, you hold yourself back from the blessings that are available to you. You keep yourself out of the flow of life, which not only hurts you, but also deprives others of your talents and the role you are here to play. Being able to recover from drama thinking and shift into the higher levels of consciousness is *the* work now. And it is the most crucial and gratifying work you can do. Join me on this journey and watch your best life and your ultimate Self emerge. Become the Change and watch the world around you flourish!

"When I was young and free and my imagination had no limits, I dreamed of changing the world. As I grew older and wiser, I discovered the world would not change, so I shortened my sights somewhat and decided to change only my country. But it too seemed immovable. As I grew into my twilight years, in one desperate attempt, I settled for only changing my family, those closest to me. But alas, they would have none of it.

"And now as I lie on my death bed, I suddenly realize if I had only changed myself first, then by example, I would have changed my family. From their inspiration and encouragement, I would have been able to better my country, and who knows, I may even have changed the world."

—ANGLICAN BISHOP

Key Concepts

✳ DRAMA is a wound-based social survival mechanism that seeks to meet our needs to be seen and heard and to feel that we matter. It is characterized by thought patterns that are:

- Disempowering
- Reactive
- Assumption-based
- Maladaptive
- Addictive

Application and Integration

My reflections of my own personal story:

My initial thoughts about DRAMA:

CHAPTER TWO

DRAMA and Wound-Based Living

For Thanksgiving in 2012, my eighty-eight-year-old grandmother "Bepa" planned to drive herself to my house for the holiday. Sadly, the night before her trek, she made a mad dash for the ringing phone and crashed into a doorway, breaking her arm in the process. When the paramedics arrived, she was holding her arm, cradling it to calm the pain and keep it protected. As they attempted to examine her injury, she beat them back with a cane—well, practically. And the reason for that was because the *pain* of her fresh wound was too intense to let it be touched, even in order to receive care. Within a few months, however, after a surgical procedure and extensive physical therapy, her arm was completely healed. She was once again able to get dressed, shower, use her walker, hug me (most importantly), and move about as if the injury had never occurred.

Dealing with our emotional and spiritual boo-boos is not much different. When there is a fresh or an unhealed wound, perhaps one that's been festering for years, we cannot tolerate having it touched or pried into. And we will defend against anyone who approaches it, or even *appears* to come close, regardless of their intentions. We naturally make assumptions about how we *might* be hurt again, and we put up our mental dukes as a preemptive guard. Our social radar is constantly scanning for any potential threats to our sense of value or belonging, with our scanner consistently calibrated to the fight-flight-freeze setting. We gossip and collude in an attempt to get support and feel validated in our defensiveness. And thus the drama is born.

The Three Core Human Wounds

There are three fundamental ways in which we can be wounded. In *The MindBody Code*, Dr. Mario Martinez identifies a universality in what he calls "archetypal wounds" that virtually all humans experience in life. These are shame, abandonment, and betrayal. To me, these wounds are the foundation for drama. They affect us at our core, inhibiting our authentic *thriving*. We all have all three of them, though one may be more dominant, and we each have done things to cause them in others. Wretched, I know. We all think we are the innocent, good-hearted ones (because we are), but we are also modeling machines; much of what we witness, we learn and duplicate. This implies that those who went before us and influenced our lives, those who hurt us and taught us harmful behaviors, were *also* wounded. They were not capable of demonstrating or offering us anything that they themselves did not possess, like self-love, transparency, authenticity, courage, and a slew of other virtues that, had we learned *them*, would make our existence feel more whole and be more in alignment with our Higher Selves. This is not to place blame, but simply to acknowledge that there is a torch that gets passed from one generation to the next. When we continue to feed the wounded mentality and behaviors, we pass them on again.

Although these three core wounds are caused by a variety of behaviors and experiences, the dominant ones are named in the depiction on the following page. What makes these the core human wounds is that their causes impact us at the deepest level of our being. They inhibit or violate our essential needs to be seen and heard, to matter, and to be valued *just as we are*. The behaviors that cause them pose a direct threat to our sense of belonging, activating our social survival responses. They are an assault on our Souls, and they keep us from the experience of Oneness that is the truth of Who We Really Are.

Core Human Wounds

WOUND-BASED BELIEFS

"Others come first before me" *"I don't belong"* *"People can't be trusted"*

"I'm not enough" *"There's something wrong with me"* *"I don't matter"*

"I'm disposable" *"Nobody cares"* *"I'm unworthy"*

"The world isn't safe" *"I'm bad"*

THREE CORE HUMAN WOUNDS

SHAME	ABANDONMENT	BETRAYAL
"The painful feeling arising from the awareness of something dishonorable, improper, ridiculous, etc., done by oneself or another."	*"To leave completely and finally; forsake utterly; desert. To give up; discontinue; withdraw from."*	*"To be unfaithful in guarding, maintaining, or fulfilling; to disappoint the hopes or expectations of; to be disloyal to."*

CAUSES:	CAUSES:	CAUSES:
Criticism	Being left or neglected	Deception
Bullying	Parental self-absorption	Dishonesty
Sarcasm	Rejection	Violating confidence
Abuse	Being ignored or denied	Withholding
Humiliation	Inconsistency	Gossip/collusion
Contempt	Unpredictability	False accusations
Ridicule		

EMOTIONS:	EMOTIONS:	EMOTIONS:
Worthlessness	Anxiety	Defensiveness
Hopelessness	Panic	Frustration
Powerlessness	Loneliness	Rage
Helplessness	Apprehension	Combativeness
Despair	Nervousness	Self-righteousness
Desperation	Longing	Disdain

Our Wounds Shape Our Lives

"We don't see things as they are, we see them as we are."

—ANAIS NIN

The three core wounds get established and integrated into our systems during our developmental years, mostly by well-meaning (but wounded) adults, and also by siblings, cousins, classmates, and other peers. Then we continue to live out our grown-up lives based on the ways and the degree to which we are wounded, how much of our identity has been shaped around it, and the extent to which we are able to heal. We learn to speak to and treat *ourselves* according to our wounds and the beliefs they've installed, chronically shaming, abandoning, and betraying *ourselves.* We continue to behave in the ways that created, and now perpetuate, our wounding, keeping us in the cyclone of drama consciousness.

An important connection to make here is that, since we live in a co-creative Universe, our part of the creation is always consistent with our self-image and the energetic states we embody. Our life experiences will always match the vibration we emit, as generated by the consciousness that comes from our thoughts and the resulting emotional states. To put it bluntly, if your self-image is low and you treat yourself poorly, you will co-create and attract relationships and experiences that reflect this to you— but then you'll blame the person or the circumstance for how you feel, not realizing that it is the external version of what you already have going on *inside.* (Note: *Hello!* This is why self-love is *sooo* important.)

To go a step further, our woundedness bleeds into our interpersonal interactions. We cannot treat others better than we treat ourselves, especially those with whom we are most intimate. People will also naturally learn how to treat *us* based on how we speak about ourselves, how we exhibit self- appreciation or depreciation, and by how we interact with them. This is all unconsciously guided by the wounds that contribute to our self-image and our filters for understanding the world.

Continuing to operate from a wounded place consequently attracts people and experiences that will reinforce our marred (and, by the way, completely *false*) identity, leading to a vicious cycle that perpetuates the drama consciousness.

Modern-Day Wound-Based Living

"If you do not heal the sore places in your mind, you will wince every time that others rub them."

—YOGANANDA

Because as adults we are always already wounded from our childhood, as inherited from our parents and care givers, we have created a culture today of what I call "Wound-Based Living." The term "Wound-Based Living" refers to the fact that many adults are going through life operating from—thinking, feeling, and acting from—places of residual wounds, which activate the worst parts of themselves instead of the best. To understand how this plays out from a literal, practical standpoint, the tables on the following pages outline a few examples of how our wounds can potentially show up in our thoughts and our behaviors. You'll notice that our self-behaviors have a lot of similarity to our behaviors in relationships--thus, how we treat ourselves, we will also treat others.

TABLE 1

SHAME	
Self-Behaviors	**Behaviors in Relationships**
avid perfectionism	verbal or emotional bullying
harsh self-criticism	pushing others to meet our agendas
self-punishment	
self-contempt	making others wrong so we can be right
self-blame	degrading
self-abuse: verbal, emotional, or physical	criticizing
self-bullying/pushing ourselves *harder* to get it right or to do more	humiliating
	blaming
proving ourselves	contemptuousness
hiding and retreat	sarcasm
vanity/obsession with "looking good"	overt or passive/aggressive punishing
over-compensating through the demonstration of knowing it all or of having everything under control	demanding perfection/no forgiveness of error
judging ourselves as "bad" or "not enough"	holding others to impossible standards

TABLE 2

ABANDONMENT	
Self-Behaviors	**Behaviors in Relationships**
emotionally "numbing out"	avoidance
mentally "checking out"/not being present to ourselves	stonewalling
self-negating/not taking ourselves seriously	ignoring / checking out: being in the room but not present with others
neglect/lack of self-care	neglect of any kind

ABANDONMENT	
Self-Behaviors	**Behaviors in Relationships**
self-dismissal/not listening to our own needs and desires	being unpredictable or inconsistent
giving up on ourselves	dismissiveness
starting and not completing things	physically deserting, even if temporary
focusing heavily on others and the external world, to the exclusion of ourselves	not listening to others' needs or desires
withdrawal of self-support	self-absorption to the exclusion of others
avoiding our reality	approval-seeking
shushing the inner voices that are calling for help	people-pleasing

TABLE 3

BETRAYAL	
Self-Behaviors	**Behaviors in Relationships**
breaking self-promises	betraying trust
diminishing our own worth	breaking confidences
misrepresenting ourselves	disloyalty
not taking responsibility for our choices	cheating
not trusting our innate "knowings"	lying (even little white ones)
not following our intuition	saying one thing but doing another
lying to or deceiving ourselves	deceiving
inability to self-validate	misrepresenting others
not honoring our own values, morals and ethics	gossiping and colluding
looking to others or the outside world for how we "should" be	withholding or keeping secrets
	not setting healthy boundaries

The behaviors of these wounds reflect the basic beliefs that emerge from our wounding experiences:

TABLE 4

WOUND-BASED BELIEFS
I'm not enough
I don't matter
There's something wrong with me
I don't belong
I'm unworthy
I'm disposable
Nobody cares
People can't be trusted
The world isn't safe
Others come first before me
I'm bad

These beliefs are self-negating and keep us in a place of separation. They shape our self-talk as the "voices in our heads" that tell us we're not good enough, that we don't fit in, that we're better off dead, that there's no hope. They tell us to be on guard, watching out for what others are doing lest we become victim to wounding again. They tell us we have to be perfect and get it right, or else we will suffer. They keep us in a disconnected state, and ironically lead us to treat both ourselves and others in shaming, abandoning, and betraying ways. Any way you slice it, wound-based "internalogue" will lead to drama behaviors and an ineffective lifestyle.

The beliefs, self-talk, causes, and behaviors of these wounds have some overlap, and everyone has a unique experience and expression of them. It's not a cut-and-dry matter. The preceding conversation and tables are simply a way to offer comprehension to the linear mind, so it can begin to identify personal patterns in order to move in the direction of positive change.

In our modern-day lives, our wounds can be "poked into" or activated by a variety of interactions or circumstances, plummeting us into drama consciousness. A few examples include: receiving a "nasty-gram" by email or text, being misrepresented on Facebook or other widely viewed social media, a boss or coworker not taking responsibility for the negative impact of their actions, hearing a comment that suggests you've done something incorrectly or in an uncool way, not having our time or space respected, observing media messages that imply there is imperfection with our body's appearance or age, a misunderstanding with our significant other, arguing with family members and children, or losing financial status. We can also activate our *own* wounds, without even needing others to do it for us, by judging and criticizing ourselves, breaking self-promises, or responding to a stressful day with some kind of "numbing out" activity, like excessive TV or video games, drinking too much alcohol, smoking, over-eating, or relying on sleep aids to chill out. All of these will activate those old wounds as will anything else that threatens our sense of belonging and diminishes our inherent self-worth.

Never Fear! DRAMA Is Here!

Wound-Based Living leads to drama thinking and behavior. Drama is the method we developed to be seen and heard, to get our needs met, and to know we are valued and that we *matter*. Unfortunately, it's not that different from a child's temper tantrum. The goal is attention and acknowledgement—albeit negative. But then again, any attention is "good" attention, right? The reason for this psychologically is because on some level it makes us know we matter.

In its most simplistic form, drama thinking tends to focus on our need to be "right" or meritorious, and the resulting behavior functions as an attempt to gain acceptance, approval, and validation from the outside world. So drama is not just being "nuts," "acting out," "losing control," or some other form of effed-up craziness that we judge it to be. Drama is actually a modern-day social *survival* phenomenon.

Unfortunately, we end up using drama as a chintzy method for connecting with others. We gossip. We collude. We kvetch. We slander. We mock. We criticize. All in an effort to relate to each other, to be validated, to belong.

Separation DRAMA

The fundamental disempowering beliefs that emerge from our core wounds are all self-negating and life depreciating. As a result, they perpetuate drama thinking and inherently generate a prolonged misalignment with our Souls and a disconnection from others. And since we are all One, interconnected and intertwined at our core, any kind of separation will indubitably be destructive and feel painful.

It chronically and consistently feels bad to not let ourselves be Who We Really Are, to not allow our Souls to be fully expressed in this human form. And yet, dwelling on our wounds and recycling the negative self-images and world views they imbue does just that. The worthlessness, anxiety, and grievances that we yield from our fallacious beliefs directly inhibit our alignment with our Higher Selves.

We delay our own healing when we ruminate on the memories that mentally recycle the harming experience, or when we develop new thoughts (like catastrophizing) that maintain the pain within us, or when we carry out the same kinds of hurtful behaviors with ourselves and others. In fact, in some cases, we amplify the trauma so that it becomes even bigger than the initial incident.

No matter how you slice it, perpetuating the torment does not allow us to heal nor to do our part in advancing the consciousness of the planet. Our job is to move toward greater wholeness while we are here in this human form. Our job is to take what is undesirable in our experience and allow it to fuel our focus toward what we would prefer and what would *feel* better. That is, in essence, how we expand. Drama will always hold us apart, separate from our expansion, which is why it's no fun and why it fundamentally feels *bad*.

The Ulterior Motive of Negative Experiences

One thing to highlight here is that what we call negative experiences are actually an imperative part of life expanding through us. We *need* them in order to desire something new, to develop our innate gifts, to have fresh ideas, to seek solutions, and thereby create new things. Negative experiences lead us to evolve. They inspire us to grow into who we are capable of becoming. Many times, however, we inhibit our growth by dwelling too long and hard on the perceived wrong-doing and the subsequent harm that we've incurred. (Thank you, DRAMA.)

"Negative experiences" in and of themselves are not *bad*. Likewise, experiencing lower levels of consciousness is not *bad*. In fact, they can be very useful when appropriate. Where we slip into drama mode is when they are fabricated from within us, based on our wounding and disempowering beliefs, rather than grounded in an experience that's actually happening in the moment.

Recycled DRAMA

"Time heals all wounds, unless you pick at them."

—SHAUN ALEXANDER

For many years, I mentally recycled the memories and emotions of the ridicule and teasing I experienced as a kid. I recycled the experience of the day I was no longer welcome in my mother's home, getting dropped on my aunt's doorstep at midnight with a duffel bag and my boom box, and the miserable weeks and months that ensued. I recycled the loss of time with my siblings, from years of being "forbidden" from them. I recycled the death of my older sister, who was taken prematurely by leukemia. And this was all beyond the normal course of grief. I used these experiences to drum up and amplify really shitty feelings—because good or bad, amplified emotional states make us know we are *alive*. I recycled anything that emerged from my wounds, my disempowering beliefs, and my victim identity—not because I enjoyed it, but because I just didn't know any better. I didn't know how to connect with others, how to belong, or how to matter *without* it.

All of this recycling kept me from being present with myself in the moment. It kept me disempowered (because our power is always in the *now*) and reactive, constantly assuming some similar hurt would befall me, which was a maladaptive way to go about seeking social safety and belonging. Because it was all I knew, because it gave me enough sense of aliveness and connection to others, it became addictive; I didn't know how to stop or get my needs met without it.

In the movie *The Lion King*, there is a brilliant scene where an adult Simba is lamenting his past in conversation with Rafiki, the wise baboon. All of a sudden, Rafiki smacks Simba over the head with his stick. Simba cries out, "Ow! Geez! What was that for?"

To which Rafiki replies, "It doesn't matter. It's in the past!"

Simba says, "But it still hurts."

"Oh yes, the past can hurt," replies the sage, "but the way I see it, you can either run from it or *learn* from it."

I would add . . . you can either recycle it or grow *through* it.

The Cost of DRAMA

Drama thinking sustains the wounded state—and the wounded planet, I

30

might add. It is the way we continue to shame, abandon, and betray ourselves, and subsequently others, in our lives. It keeps us from engaging with life fully, from playing with wild abandon, from developing deep connections and intimacy with others. Drama thinking interferes with our ability to live out our greater life purpose. Just think of all the mental and emotional energy that gets used up on recycling hurtful memories and maintaining woundedness. It is bad enough that we have been victimized by someone in our past. What is truly tragic is when we continue to victimize ourselves repeatedly, again and again, long after our original tormenter is gone. The internal acts of recycling and re-traumatizing myself produced nothing more than the wasted use of precious physical, mental, emotional, and spiritual energy. The events were O-V-E-R. Yet, I continued to mentally and emotionally live them out every day for *years*, when I could have used that energy to create countless blessings in the world instead. That being said, there was considerable learning, growth, and expansion that I gained as a result, which has led to fulfilling my greater life purpose and my ability to write these words today. What I wish for all of us is to have a greater conscious awareness of how we want to positively, constructively direct our energy for the remainder of our *now* moments together, and to make sure we all have the skills to do just that.

Healing the Wounds, Resolving the DRAMA

"Turn your wounds into wisdom."

—OPRAH WINFREY

Looking back on Bepa's injured arm, it's clear why it could not be touched while the wound was fresh, but was fine and fully functioning once it *healed*. We need to start thinking about drama in the same way: an indication of an emotional or spiritual injury that is still tender and needs to be restored to wholeness.

31

In order to have greater social connection and interpersonal intimacy, which brings great meaning and joy to our lives, we must first take charge of healing our *own* core human wounds ourselves. We do that through a number of practices (and they *do* take practice!), such as: self-love, positive self-talk, honoring our needs and our feelings, setting healthy boundaries, keeping the promises we make to ourselves, living authentically, taking personal responsibility, acknowledging our worth, and reclaiming leadership of our own lives. Developing a *thriving* lifestyle as laid out in Part II of this book will encompass these essential elements of healing, without having to focus on the problem or the wound but rather by moving toward the person you want to be. There's nothing broken that needs to be fixed, only possibilities for growth and expansion.

Dr. Martinez names our wounds as "challenges" that we can grow through, which actually give us meaning in our lives and relationships. He identifies the healing energies for these wounds as: Honor (for shame), Commitment (for abandonment), and Loyalty (for betrayal). Anytime we consciously practice these high-powered energies with ourselves or another, we stretch into who we are capable of becoming. We align with our Higher Selves, while connecting authentically with others. I see Honoring as the most essential of these healing energies, because it encompasses the others. When we honor ourselves or another, inherent in that is loyalty and maintaining commitments. It also includes listening to, respecting, and valuing oneself or another—conveying a deep sense of *mattering*. Self-honoring further involves following our intuition, being present with ourselves, tending to our needs and desires, and accurately representing ourselves to the outer world. You will see the words "honor," "honoring," and "self-honoring" throughout these pages, which is to emphasize the tremendous healing power of this energy. If we apply nothing else, simply the observance of honoring in our lives will heal our wounds and render drama of all kinds completely null and void, restoring our Souls, cleansing the tender space of our relationships, and reclaiming our precious time and energy.

Altogether, our wounds present us with the chance to refine our capacity to live in alignment with our Higher Selves. We need them as summons, but not as lifestyles. They make brilliant lessons, but lousy guideposts. It's time to bring our wounds to resolution, to integrate the learning and discard the drama. It's time to develop the skills and practices to manage our internal states and heal our Souls so we can live the *thriving* lives we came here for.

"The soul cannot tolerate brutality. It cannot tolerate abundances of pain and irrationality. It cannot tolerate being lied to—consider that on our planet. It cannot tolerate non-forgiveness. It cannot tolerate jealousies and hatreds. These are contaminates, poisons for it. When the personality engages in these behaviors it's as if it feeds its body arsenic again and again and again. It is just like that. . . . This is the distortedness of the soul that the physical-reduced counterpart of the soul—called the personality—takes on in order to cleanse, in order to let other souls see so that it can be helped . . . so that when pain is seen it is not responded to with judgment or ugliness or avoidance, but recognized as the soul shattered. In this way, we shall say, 'In this circumstance, let us heal him, let us heal her.'
Let us not run from the unattractiveness of a shattered soul."

—GARY ZUKAV

Key Concepts

✳ Drama emerges from our three core human wounds and the disempowering beliefs we derive from them:

- Shame—"The painful feeling arising from the awareness of something dishonorable, improper, ridiculous, etc., done by oneself or another."

- Abandonment—"To leave completely; forsake utterly; desert. To give up; discontinue; withdraw from."

- Betrayal—"To be unfaithful in guarding, maintaining, or fulfilling; to disappoint the hopes or expectations of; to be disloyal to."

✳ Wound-Based Beliefs include:

- I'm not enough
- I don't matter
- There's something wrong with me
- I don't belong
- I'm disposable
- I'm unworthy
- Nobody cares
- People can't be trusted
- The world isn't safe
- Please others first
- I'm bad

✳ Wound-Based Living leads to drama thinking and behavior, which sustains the wounded state. We all have all three wounds, though one of them is usually dominant in our experience.

✳ Drama is the method we developed to be seen and heard, to get our needs met, and to know we are valued and that we *matter*. But it does *not* get the job done in a self-honoring way.

✳ Drama thinking generates a prolonged misalignment with our Souls and a disconnection from others, which always feels painful and perpetuates our overall suffering or dissatisfaction. It interferes with our ability to live out our greater life purpose.

✳ Drama is fabricated from within us, based on our wounding, disempowering beliefs, and recycled memories and emotions, rather than grounded in an experience that's actually happening in the present moment.

✳ In order to have greater social connection and interpersonal intimacy, we have to take charge of healing our *own* core human wounds first, through embracing and living the energy of Honoring—honoring ourselves and honoring others, as they innately go hand in hand.

Application and Integration

My dominant, most sensitive core wound is:

My Self-behaviors and Self-talk that activate each wound are:
SHAME:

ABANDONMENT:

BETRAYAL:

The words I use and behaviors I engage in with others that might be wounding to them:

My fundamental wound-based beliefs:

The stories I use to recycle drama in my mind:

Words of compassion I can use with myself and others when wounds are activated:

Practices I will put into place *today* to heal my own wounds and *how* I will do each:
Self-love:

Positive self-talk:

Honoring my needs and my feelings:

Keeping self-promises:

Taking personal responsibility:

Acknowledging my self-worth:

Reclaiming leadership of my life:

CHAPTER THREE

What the Heck
Is DRAMA, Anyway?

"Mind is the forerunner of all actions.
All deeds are led by mind, created by mind.
If one speaks or acts with a corrupt mind,
suffering follows,
As the wheel follows the hoof of an ox pulling a cart.

Mind is the forerunner of all actions.
All deeds are led by mind, created by mind.
If one speaks or acts with a serene mind,
happiness follows,
As surely as one's shadow."

—THE DHAMMAPADA

Consciousness creates our reality. It is co-creative in generating our external circumstances, and it also influences how we then experience those co-creations internally. Quantum physics is demonstrating more and more that our thoughts actually are *things* and that how we focus our attention actually influences the existence of the world around us. This frontier science is giving empirical support to the adage *We do not see things as they are, we see them as* we *are.* Our level of consciousness and its embodied energetic state, along with the focused attention we bring into the world around us, yields the kind of effects we produce, as well as the quality of the circumstances and people we attract.

What You See Is What You Get

There is a legend of a wise gatekeeper who sat outside his village entry. A traveler came along and asked the gatekeeper, "What type of people live here? I am looking to make a new home for myself and I wonder if this village is for me."

The gatekeeper asked in return, "What type of people did you find in the last place you lived?"

The traveler replied, "They were greedy, cruel, and closed minded."

The wise man said, "You will find the same type of people live here." So the traveler journeyed on in search of another town.

Shortly after, a second traveler appeared, also asking about the type of people who live in his town. Again, the gatekeeper asked, "What type of people did you find in the last place you lived?"

The second traveler replied, "They were generous, kind, and good hearted."

The wise gatekeeper said, "You will find the same kind of people live here."

The Energetic States of DRAMA vs. *Thriving*

"Attention may sound dull, but it is an essential aspect of consciousness. In fact, it governs what it is that we turn out to be conscious of, and therefore plays a part in the coming into being of whatever exists for us."

—IAIN MCGILCHRIST

To identify drama, one must first understand the various energetic states that it exists within, each offering a different vibrational quality. As humans, we have a full range of emotions that characterize our energetic state, influencing the level of consciousness we are embodying at any given time. Our physical energy naturally fluctuates based on whether we are hungry or fed, tired or rested, etc. When it comes to vibrational energy, we fluctuate based on our thoughts and emotions—which are determined by where we focus our attention. There is a full spectrum of natural and healthy energetic states that range from the hopelessness of shame and despair at the lowest end, to the harmony of love, peace, and joy at the highest end. You'll see this illustrated in the depiction on next page.

Contrary to what our culture suggests, the energies of sub-*thriving* are not wholly "negative." The experience of life and the growth we are here to undergo require both contraction and expansion, like a female preparing to deliver a baby. We cannot give birth to new ideas or develop better ways of doing things without the contraction that comes in response to unpleasant experiences. What this means in terms of energetic states is that we need the contrast of "feeling bad" in order to know what it is to "feel good." The lower energies of sub-*thriving* provide this for us, as they are inherently worse-feeling than the higher levels of *thriving*. Regardless of this, they are a natural—even essential—part of the spiritual journey as a human being. Most of us, when we encounter relationships or circumstances that feel "bad," would prefer something else that makes us feel "good." It is through this process that we identify new desires, which is what invites us to grow and expand, at both the spiritual and human levels. What's essential to the achievement of the growth goal is to *allow* the sub-*thriving* energies to flow through us in ways that honor our process and our experience, rather than trying to deny, repress, or judge them as being "wrong." When we do the latter, the energies flip over into the distorted realm of drama.

The lower energies of sub-*thriving* are a meaningful part of life when

Energetic States Spectrum

E
N
E
R
G
E
T
I
C

S
T
A
T
E
S

Thriving Energies

HARMONY — *The realm of peace, love, joy, serendipity; appreciation for all that is and isn't; synthesis with Divine Will*

The realm of gratitude, beauty, compassion, and deep honor for life, self, and others — REVERENCE

CURIOSITY — *The realm of logic, rationality, and objectivity; altruistically seeking solutions for the sake of the greater good*

The realm of enthusiasm, acceptance, and contribution; collaboration while taking personal responsibility — CONTENTMENT

WILLINGNESS

The courageous realm of embracing uncertainty with hope, faith, and trust

Sub-*Thriving* Energies (Allowing)	DRAMA Energies (Resistance)
PRIDE *Opinionated, competitive; energies of frustration and grievances*	**EGOTISM** *Self-absorption; energies of arrogance, insecurity, dominance, control*
ANGER *Protectiveness, irritation, impatience, displeasure*	**RAGE** *Defensiveness, forcefulness; energies of intolerance, hostility and violence*
FEAR *Fright, alarm, nervousness, doubt, uneasiness*	**ANXIETY*** *Escapism, worry / catastrophizing; Energies of paranoia, insatiability, scarcity*
APATHY *Indifference, boredom, purposelessness, sadness*	**DEPRESSION*** *Melancholy, hatred, suppressed pain, repressed self, pessimism*
HOPELESSNESS *Grief, separation, despair, shame, guilt*	**WORTHLESSNESS** *Self-brutalization, disempowerment, alienation, humiliation, lack of love*

*Terminology does not refer to clinical disorders or serious medical conditions

authentic and not fabricated, as in the case of drama. What I mean by that is, for example, when you have done something that is socially inappropriate, the feeling of shame or guilt provides a powerful guideline for ethical behavior and virtuousness. This is juxtaposed with the disempowering self-talk of drama that can result in a comparable sense of worthlessness, but it is neither effective nor a contributor to healthy functioning. Another example of the energies of sub-*thriving*: when a loved one dies, it's healthy and deeply human to experience the hopelessness and despair of grief. When someone cuts you off in traffic, you *want* to have a fright response and slam on your brakes. If your family or your physical person are threatened, you *need* to access the protective instinct of anger. The emotions found within the energies of sub-*thriving* are actually useful, when circumstantially relevant and when allowed to flow rather than resisted or repressed. They lead us to grow and expand when honored and processed appropriately. They also exhibit the useful human survival response—freeze, flight, fight—when we need it.

The energies of drama are the ineffective, distorted, wound-based versions of sub-*thriving*. Any action that emerges from the drama energies will not be effective nor will it truly serve our relationships, win us that promotion, get our significant other to do what *we* want, make our kids "behave," or meet any of the goals that we think will get us greater happiness and satisfaction in life. Drama energies always have the element of struggle and resistance to them. They feel scratchy, unstable, and agitated. There is an underlying tone to them that is false or fabricated rather than authentic and viable. Drama is a way of operating that mentally pushes against an outer force, or the *idea* of an external threat, seeking to dominate. Drama energies hold an inherent weakness, are ego-based, and focus exclusively on "my survival." Another way to think about the distinction between drama and the energies of sub-*thriving* is that drama is what comes into play when nothing is really happening outside of us (no loved-one's death, no crazy drivers, no bullies in our face) but *we still live in our minds as if it were.*

In contrast, the higher realm of *thriving* energies is fueled from within, in an authentic and self-honoring manner. *Thriving* energies are grounded in truth. They exhibit the resonant space of the spirit operating effectively on the human plane. The more advanced or higher the level of *thriving* energy, the more strength it contains and the more aligned it is with absolute truth as defined by Divinity itself. When looking at the Energetic States Spectrum, we can see a distinct crossover point in the shifting of energies occurs in the space of Willingness. At this threshold, a distinction is made between the experience of positivity versus negativity. Energies above the line gain strength exponentially, are grounded in truth, and inherently feel "good" because they are in alignment with our Souls. Energies below the line are largely ego-based, grounded in separation from Spirit, self, and others. What's important to note here is that the energetic state or level of consciousness we embody at any given time is determined by how we are directing our thoughts, and thereby generating our emotions.

The Essence of DRAMA

The drama that lives inside our minds inherently and unequivocally impacts our lives. Let's take a deeper look. DRAMA involves thought patterns that are:

- Disempowering
- Reactive
- Assumption-based
- Maladaptive
- Addictive

DRAMA IS: DISEMPOWERING

DRAMA thoughts take us out of our personal power and hold us captive in lower levels of consciousness. Disempowering thoughts are any thoughts that disconnect us from our Higher Selves, or that defer our choices and our emotional states to circumstances or other people in a self-negating way. They are thoughts that involve self-shaming, -abandonment, and -betrayal that originate from the lower energies of drama. They interfere with the relationships we have with ourselves, with others, and with the world around us. They influence us toward not believing in or trusting ourselves or others. They can be critical, bullish, minimizing, negating, or rejecting. Disempowering thoughts not only originate from the three core human wounds, but will also keep them open or activated. By their very nature, they feel bad, because they have us disconnected from the true essence of our Souls, as well as from those of the people around us.

In many cases, our disempowering thoughts can appear to be well-meaning. For example, many people think about being efficient with their time and "getting things done." Checking items off the to-do list is of the utmost importance to them. The positive intention is to produce results and to perform well, something we are trained to do from a young age. While this can be a highly effective way to operate, generating great accomplishments, it can also cross over into the zone of being disempowering when it is driven by fear or the need to prove worth. There is a point of diminishing returns on the driving energy that we employ to push ourselves into productivity. That is to say, there is a point where more is not better, it's just more. When this desire to produce is driven by the fears of falling behind, of not being good enough, or of losing control, then the fear is inadvertently running the show—instead of the *thriving* energies, like those in the realms of contentment or curiosity, for example.

I coached a client we'll call Shelly, who originally came to me to deal with her stress level. She was overworked and constantly felt like things were never getting done. She explained to me that her routine involved getting herself moving early in the morning so she could get ready before she woke her kids up and got them off for the day. She would then go to work, run around to perform her job, come home, and dive straight into her chores.

She was very specific about which tasks got done on which days. For example, the bathrooms *had* to be cleaned every Thursday. She was emphatically focused on being efficient and keeping up with her schedule so as to not fall behind or miss anything. In the initial session, I also asked Shelly about her family relationships. She described her husband and her two sons, who were around six and eight years old at the time. As she talked about her youngest son, Tommy, her eyes went dismal and her mouth turned down. She told me, "He's just one of those sad kids. I know he's gonna be a depressed adult."

Over the course of the first few sessions, we continued to examine her world and discovered that Shelly was brushing her kids aside for the sake of "getting things done." She was living according to her checklist, not according to her family. Although her intention was positive—she wanted to actually *serve* her family—it was having a negative outcome. So I challenged Shelly to simply switch the order in which she was doing things: be with your kids first, *then* do the tasks. Her immediate response was to feel frantic about things not getting done, to which I replied, "So what?" Her fear of failing, of falling short as a wife and a mother in her household duties, had become her driving focus, and she lost sight of what it was all for—her loved ones. So we introduced a new, more empowering thought into Shelly's repertoire: "I make my people more important than my tasks." As a result of this *one* new thought, Shelly started greeting her kids right away when she got home each day. She began responding to their desire to be with her. She would stop in the middle of doing laundry to sit and watch them play video games. She told me, "I don't care about the video games, but I want my son to know I care about *him*. And if it's important to him, it's important to me."

I asked her, almost sarcastically, "Well, what about the laundry? Did it get done?"

She chuckled and shrugged an "of course." Within a few short months of practicing this new thought, Shelly learned at a deep level that she can honor what's most important in her life *and* the chores still get done. As a result of this change in her, Tommy also changed. Shelly began to describe him as a happy kid, always climbing on her and wanting to connect and snuggle. This shift in him was a direct result of identifying Shelly's disempowering thoughts, her rules for getting things done, and then finding a new, more empowering thought to replace it and live out.

DRAMA IS: REACTIVE

Drama thinking has a survival fight-flight-freeze compulsion that comes from our wounds being activated or "poked into" through our own internal dialogue, triggering circumstances or interactions with others. The Reactive element is really a knee-jerk survival response. It is what happens when one of our core human wounds—shame, abandonment, or betrayal—gets bumped, prodded, or dug into by another person's words or actions, by an event, or even by our own self-talk.

In our reactive state, the brain's limbic system takes over the command center and releases adrenaline and cortisol, draining vital energy away from the cortical brain regions, where logic, empathy, and intuition live. Without access to those resources (among others), we are reduced to primitive tactics to get our needs met, while keeping ourselves hostage in the lower energetic states of drama.

The survival reaction can show up in a million ways: via meltdowns, lashing out, withdrawing, punishing, road raging, panic . . . the list can go on forever. The basic thing to know is that when we get into a reactive state, it's a sign of feeling jeopardized, threatened, or otherwise at risk of not belonging, not having our needs met, not being seen, heard, understood, or valued.

In general, my diet is pretty healthy. I'm not typically a sweets person, but every once in a while I enjoy a bite of carrot cake or a freshly baked triple-chocolate-chunk cookie. When my husband and I began living together, we noticed that anytime he walked into the kitchen while I was having an evening dessert snack, I would get anxious or upset or even start crying. I had been perfectly fine moments before, but his presence activated a fear reaction in me. He would tell me how happy he was for me that I was enjoying something I desired. Every single day since we've been together he's told me how beautiful I am or how sexy he finds me (God bless 'im). So there was nothing actually coming from *him* to warrant my backlash. What we came to discover was that I was reacting to his *role:* the man in my house, who criticizes or ridicules me whenever I eat something sweet. This was an *old* shame wound getting activated by the circumstances. I was having a survival response based on early life experiences, and the terror of being rejected or yet again abandoned was resurfacing in the present. Fortunately, my husband and I can laugh about this now. I mostly enjoy any dessert when I'm actually in the mood for it. If he notices that I'm getting nervous at all, he holds up his hand over his eyes and jokingly cries, "I'm not looking!" It always cracks me up, which alleviates my anxiety and shifts the energy within me, allowing me to see clearly and return to enjoying myself. Because my wounds around eating and body image are largely healed (there's always room to improve), I have less need to be reactive to my food-related circumstances.

DRAMA IS: ASSUMPTION-BASED

Drama comes from the stories we tell ourselves that are not grounded in actual truth, but rather are based on our wounds from the past and the lenses we look through as a result of them. Assumptions can sometimes be accurate, but drama-assumptions are the bane of authentic connection and living in alignment with our Souls. They come directly from what our painful life experiences taught us about the world. We are hardwired for survival—to protect ourselves against anything that hurts or threatens—and our life experiences teach us what it is we need to protect ourselves from, based on pain that has been inflicted on a physical, emotional, or deep spiritual level. When something even remotely looks like or resembles what we know to be hurtful, we will naturally make relevant assumptions in order to stay safe. Unfortunately, when these assumptions are projected to define another person or a situation in our minds, it prevents us from seeing the truth of Who They Really Are or the present-moment reality that holds new possibilities.

In principle, our assumptions say more about us than they do about another person. Like in the story of my husband watching me eat desserts, I made the assumption that he would tease me, reject me, or even get angry. But really, I've never actually *seen* my husband angry. I've seen him bothered or annoyed or disgusted, but never *angry*. Any teasing he has ever brought into our relationship has always been playful and kind in nature. My reaction was based on *my* assumption about "how the man I live with treats me when I eat sweets," not based on the truth of who my beloved actually *is*. I had to learn that in my misrepresentation of him I was actually *hurting* him, in addition to myself.

Our brains are meaning-making machines, so we are *supposed* to learn from our environments and experiences in order to understand and engage with the world around us in the most effective ways possible. Again, it becomes drama when it is Disempowering, Reactive, and based on Assumptions from past experiences that do not fit the current circumstance or relationship. When we do not have self-awareness or clear and effective communication with each other, we run the risk of living by the stories that emerge from our wounds rather than the current reality. That's unfair to others and to ourselves. Assumptions keep the spirit repressed and dishonor our relationships, actually perpetuating the cycles of wounding and disconnection.

It was the first year of our marriage and my husband and I were getting used to living together. I walked into the bathroom one day to take a shower when I found this slimy trail of black ooze slowly trickling its way down the back of the tub. *That's disgusting, what has he done now?* As a shaved-headed bald man, my husband uses very different personal hygiene products than I do. Upon seeing the black ooze, I figured he must've spilled something and not bothered to clean it up. I promptly left the bathroom, making sure to leave the shower curtain pulled wide open so he could see his mess and take care of it.

And then, I fumed about it. *He's so sloppy, what a klutz, how could he leave that for me to deal with, how could I marry someone so thoughtless and insensitive* . . . and so on. A couple hours later I went back to finally take my shower, but the black ooze was still there—and I *knew* he'd used the bathroom during that time. Disgusted and annoyed, I finally went ahead and cleaned it up. As I stepped into the shower, I reached for my shampoo to wash my hair, only to find the bottle was empty. I had left it open and turned upside-down on the shelf, letting the viscous substance leech out, drain through the black exfoliating bath gloves on the shelf below, and trail the now-black ooze down the back of the tub. As soon as I realized this, I started cracking up at *myself*. With my limited vision and awareness, I had built up a whole case against my husband (poor guy), about something *I* myself had done.

And voilà! The nature of assumptions. That day, I spent countless thoughts and immeasurable energy mentally chastising my husband, when, really, I could've equally directed those resources toward solving world hunger or evoking peace in the Middle East. In the end, I was the culprit! What a waste of my own precious energy. Regardless of whose "fault" it was, the extent to which I indulged the drama was life stealing, rather than life giving. Needless to say, our judgments imply that we don't see the whole picture, and that's the trap I let myself get caught in. A simple shrug of not really knowing the whole story could've alleviated hours of negativity.

Our brains are hilarious. Tricksters, really. Many times we are so *sure* of how things are, that we develop tunnel vision and cannot see outside of our self-righteousness or ego-driven internalogue. My Uncle Marshall wisely says, "I'm always sure, but not always *right*!" Our brains are very convincing of the "truth" we see based on what we know, which translates into our assumptions. Sometimes we need to keep our sense of humor and realize that *we* are the ones who are creating the experience—not "them" out there.

DRAMA IS: MALADAPTIVE

Life is a process of evolution. Since the beginning of existence the Universe has been expanding and growing. Regardless of whether you believe in the Big Bang, the Garden of Eden, or any other creation story, we know that life is constantly moving forward. It never goes backwards. And in our evolutionary process, we continuously evaluate and adapt in ways we believe will ensure our survival. The collective energy of human consciousness is the same way. We are not at the end-all-and-be-all of our expansion. In fact, we are just getting to the juicy stuff now. The stage of evolution we are in is related to our thought-energy and our consciousness. Part of that growth is about moving through our emotional and spiritual wounds in highly effective ways. Continuing to recycle them, remaining disempowered, and reacting to present circumstances as if they were the past is a maladaptive method for living life. And yet, it is a familiar survival mechanism.

By definition, something that is *mal*adaptive has the fundamental inability to alter its structure or functioning to better survive in a given environment. Social adaptation is generally a gradual and usually unconscious modification in behavior to fit one's familial and cultural surroundings. Throughout our developmental process, we came up with ways to adapt to our family and community to protect our innate sense of worthiness, and to avoid wound-generating experiences with others. It's almost as if the personality develops a shield to protect the soul deep within, which unfortunately turns maladaptive over time. With limited capacities, we relied on what we knew to get our needs met, like manipulation, withdrawal, attacking, rebelling, and the use of anger or meltdowns as a force field to protect our most essential part: our tender Souls.

Eventually, the behavioral modifications we made to fit into an old environment, which are now engrained and automatic, become outdated when we reach new circumstances and relationships that no longer warrant such defenses and justifications. When we are in any kind of survival mode, we do not have unhindered access to the higher functioning cortical areas of our brains, which provide us with linear processes, logic, questions, empathy, the desire to understand, and other functions that would represent healthy adaptation. We inadvertently and unconsciously stay stuck in our maladaptive trends. However, in the evolutionary process, we did not *yet* learn to be curious, to seek first to understand, to give the benefit of the doubt, or to meet chaos with love. That's where we are now; it's what the wounding is calling us to reach for. Instead of growth and healing, we develop drama thoughts and behavioral strategies as a means for survival, but they eventually prove to yield less-desirable results and can undoubtedly be categorized as "unskilled."

Some clear examples of Maladaptive DRAMA are:

Temper Tantrums—as a child they were highly effective; as an adult, not so much. They will still get attention, but not the positive impact your Higher Self would want.

Frozen Identity—having a self-image that is stuck in the past and is incongruent with who you've become. For example, if you've lost weight, you may still see yourself as a "fatty." If you were victimized you may still fear recurrence in spite of being capable of defending or taking care of yourself now. If you were told you were lazy or stupid, you may still believe that, even though you've realized significant accomplishments.

Poor Coping Strategies—learned from other adults who learned it from their adults. A few examples are: stonewalling to avoid difficult conversations; criticizing to feel "right," superior, or justified; and using (or abusing) external substances to flee negative emotional states.

Defense Mechanisms—these are psychological methods developed to protect the spirit within.

- Catastrophizing/Worry: A means to predict problems that could arise in various potential scenarios, but are grounded in past traumas, not current reality
- Projection/Blame: Pushing negative focus onto others or onto circumstances, in an effort to not be "the bad/wrong one"
- Rationalization: Providing reasons for one's behavior that validate choices and bolster one's sense of value in order to continue to belong and be accepted
- Denial: Lack of acknowledgment of the impact of one's choices, thinking, or behaviors

DRAMA IS: ADDICTIVE

Addiction is the result of repeatedly using external substances or influences to get the body to release its own "aliveness" chemicals—which usually carry some level of "feeling good"—and doing so with such intensity that one does not know how to stop. It is the result of becoming dependent on that external thing to generate a desirable internal state, in the absence of knowing how to do it from within.

Basically, when we are struggling in the lower drama energies, we can easily fall into the pattern of using external substances to generate a false sense of *thriving* and aliveness that elevates our energetic states *temporarily*. When the "hit" wears off, we are back to drama, but even deeper than when we started. We see this with many forms of addiction: drug and alcohol use, smoking and chewing tobacco, binge eating, sex, gambling, "numbing out" in front of the TV, even gossiping, to name a few.

That being said, drama thinking is the ultimate substance abuse and addiction. It is the misuse of *thought substance* in a manner that is destructive, and yet difficult to stop. It can come from mentally re-living our wounding experiences, or perpetuating the wounds themselves with our behavior and self-talk, and amplifying the stories that create the associated chemical state to get a bigger "pop." In many cases, we have wounding experiences neurologically connected to the feeling of love at the brain level. Things get confusing when abuse is entangled with affection, for example.

But if it's what we learned, it's just what we know.

Over time, drama becomes a neurobiochemical habit, and the lower energies of drama become our perpetual residence. We get so used to our reactions and the instant chemical release in the brain, we fall into the rut of drama being "just the way it is" or worse, our primary modus operandi to get our needs met. What's more, it stimulates a sense of "aliveness" we may not otherwise be experiencing in life.

When we are stuck in drama energies our limbic systems are on big alert. The limbic system is the home of our survival functions in the brain, namely the flight, flight, or freeze response. In order to make the body prepared for survival a series of biochemicals has to be released in the system to get us to react accordingly for preservation. This is a highly functional brain attribute for physical survival, when we need to get the hell outta Dodge or put up our dukes, like ASAP. But how often is that actually relevant in our modern-day lives? What we're more likely to run into are social threats and the potential of our pre-existing wounds getting poked into by others.

Regardless of the perceived threat, a surge of adrenaline will stimulate a sense of aliveness and actually move us up the energetic spectrum *temporarily*, but enough to feel a sense of relief and empowerment and even excitement that emulates *thriving* (but isn't really it). Over time we become addicted to that rush. And like any good addict, we will need more of the substance to get the next high. So we make up bigger stories, and find ways to generate more intense drama to get that fix. *Damn*, huh?

There is a chemical in the brain for each emotion we have. We carefully—unconsciously—hone our drama-cavorting skills to release the chemicals that corroborate our self-image, which will be directly linked to our wounding and what we learned about ourselves in the world, through shame, abandonment, and betrayal. And then we make it bigger and bigger, screaming louder and thumping harder to get our needs met. All of this comes back to the desire to be seen and heard, feel understood, and have a sense of value and belonging. Ironically, generating drama to get our needs met will fundamentally keep us from just that.

Although drama can parallel brain chemical "disorders," I think a noteworthy point to be made is that perfectly healthy brains can become *accustomed* to living in the drama energies, in the absence of a "pathology" or any "mental illness/disorder." In addition to emotional and spiritual wounding, when drama functioning is witnessed in influential adults during developmental years, a very healthy, highly capable brain can learn to operate in a drama mode, simply by absorbing it from the environment during the process of learning how to be human.

Invisible DRAMA? No Such Thing

Drama expresses itself in a variety of ways. There is loud or overt drama, which shows up as screaming, yelling, door-slamming meltdowns, etc. It is active and out in the open. Everyone knows it's going on. This is usually what people think of when they hear the word "drama." But then there is also the quiet or covert drama. It displays itself through stonewalling or the silent treatment, as avoidance, quiet huffs, sighs, or tsk-tsks. It tends to be more passive. Everyone *still* knows it's going on. No matter how the drama expresses itself, others can pick up on it, because they can *feel* the energy coming from you. The vibe you emit is always tangible, and we know it when you're operating from the drama energies.

Powerful Choices: DRAMA vs. *Thriving* . . . You Pick

Although the energetic states of drama are rampant in our culture and plague us with separation from the truth of Who We Really Are, new knowledge and awareness of the contrast between DRAMA and *thriving* energies reveals a powerful choice ready to be embraced.

Living in drama is not who you are, nor is it the only way you can operate in the world. You weren't born with drama; you *learned* it. Which means you can *un*learn it as well. The human brain continues to prove it is capable of magnificent things! That includes *your* beautiful brain as well, Darlin'.

Keep calm and read on!

"We either make ourselves miserable or we make ourselves happy. The amount of work is the same."

—CARLOS CASTANEDA

Key Concepts

＊ As humans, we have a full range of emotions that characterizes our energetic state, influencing our vibration and the level of consciousness we are embodying at any given time. The quality of our energy fluctuates based on our thoughts and emotions, which come from where we focus our attention.

＊ The lower energies of sub-*thriving* are a meaningful part of life when *authentic* and not fabricated, as in the case of drama. We need the contrast of "feeling bad" in order to know what it is to "feel good." This is an essential part of the spiritual journey as a human being, since we need the contraction that contributes to our expansion.

＊ The energies of drama are the ineffective, distorted, wound-based versions of sub-*thriving*. Drama energies always have the element of struggle and resistance to them, grounded in the falsehood and weakness of the ego.

＊ *Thriving* energies are grounded in truth and strength. They exhibit the resonant space of the spirit operating effectively on the human plane.

＊ DRAMA, succinctly, is a wound-based social survival mechanism that seeks to meet our needs to be seen and heard and to feel that we matter. It is characterized by thought patterns that are:

- Disempowering
- Reactive
- Assumption-based
- Maladaptive
- Addictive

＊ DRAMA: Disempowering thoughts are any thoughts that disconnect us from our Higher Selves, or that defer our choices and our emotional states to circumstances, or other people in a self-negating way. They are thoughts that involve self-shaming, -abandonment, and -betrayal, and that originate from the lower energies of drama.

✳ DRAMA: The reactive component of drama thinking has a survival fight-flight-freeze compulsion that comes from our wounds being activated or "poked into" through our own negative internalogue, triggering circumstances, or interactions with others.

✳ DRAMA: Drama comes from the assumptions we make that are not grounded in truth, but are based on past wounds and the way we see things as a result of them. We are hardwired for survival and our life experiences teach us what we need to protect ourselves. When something resembles what we know to be hurtful, we will naturally make relevant assumptions in order to stay safe.

✳ DRAMA: Something that is *mal*adaptive has the fundamental inability to alter its structure or functioning to better survive in a given environment. The behavioral modifications we made to fit into an *old* environment become outdated when we reach new circumstances and relationships that no longer warrant the old defenses and justifications, but we still respond with the old ways out of habit and the knee-jerk flare-up of unconscious programming.

✳ DRAMA: Drama thinking is the ultimate addiction. It is the misuse of *thought substance* in a manner that is destructive, and yet difficult to stop. It can come from mentally re-living wounding experiences, perpetuating wounds with behavior and self-talk, and amplifying stories that create the chemical and emotional states of DRAMA consciousness. Furthermore, it stimulates a sense of "aliveness" we may not otherwise be experiencing in life.

Application and Integration

What tells me—what are the indicators—that I am in the lower energetic states of:

DRAMA (resistance)?

Sub-*thriving* (allowing)?

What tells me when I am in the energetic states of *thriving*?

What's my unique version of the elements of DRAMA:

My disempowering thoughts are:

My reactiveness comes out as:

The most common assumptions I make are:

My maladaptive patterns are:

How I see drama as an addiction for me is:

CHAPTER FOUR

And Why in the World Would We *Want* DRAMA?

B elieve it or not, drama serves a purpose.

I had a client we'll call Laura, who is a mature single lady and happy to be so. She was struggling with some weight and health issues, and during one of our sessions she reported having a temper tantrum in her kitchen one day. Since she lives alone, there was no one there to witness her antics; upon realizing this she burst into laughter. Laura recognized intuitively that the purpose of the drama itself was to get noticed and to get some attention in her wounded moment. What fascinates me is how quickly she was able to rocket from her despair and frustration up to pure laughter, demonstrating the false facade drama displays for the benefit of this secondary gain. Drama is not about authentic self-expression; it's an acting out for the sake of being seen and heard, for feeling understood and valued.

Drama attempts to meet our primary (non-physical) human needs in the absence of knowing how to fulfill them in effective and self-honoring ways. Drama is the functioning that emerges from lower levels of consciousness when we seek to meet our basic needs for: certainty and security, love and connection, value and significance, variety and new experiences. The essential components of these include: being seen and heard, being understood, having a sense of belonging, feeling valued, and knowing that we matter.

Essential Human Needs: Love and Connection

"One of the oldest human needs is having someone to wonder where you are when you don't come home at night."

—MARGARET MEAD

The need for love and connection is absolutely essential to our survival and to our *thriving*. It is fundamentally about our desire to consciously experience our collective Oneness, which we tend to either inhabit in the life-giving ways of *thriving* or clumsily reach for in life-draining ways, like drama. We long to embody the truth of Who We Really Are, an extension of the greater energy that is the Source of all life. We long to be connected to something bigger, to the life force that has us *living*—more than just a body with organs pumping and pulsing—with a unique spirit that has a job to do here. Love is the energy that fuels our connection, since love constitutes the essence of Who We Really Are in our eternal nature. When we are actively giving and receiving love we are in alignment with our Higher Selves, and therefore in the natural flow of life. Because we are all one organism, floating together in the cosmos, our connection with each other on this micro, human-to-human level is essential for our embodiment of love and the fulfillment of our higher purpose.

In our relationships with other human beings, experiencing authentic connection comes through seeing and hearing one another, which leads us to each feel understood and valued. What I mean by "authentic" is that we are operating as the truth of Who We Really Are, from a *thriving* consciousness, in alignment with our Souls. When we are living from drama consciousness we are not embodying our Higher Selves, but are instead living from the ego and using drama as a means to feel connected and seek love.

HOW DRAMA MEETS THE NEED FOR:
LOVE AND CONNECTION

Relationships serve to help refine us and grow us. We love to feel the one-ness of connection, but when people aren't doing what *we* want in order for us to feel good, we plummet into the energies of drama to try to get our needs met. Drama behavior almost always has the goal of seeking attention, because in receiving any kind of focus or response, good or bad, we at least know we *matter*. As I've mentioned in previous chapters, drama can express itself in a million ways, such as: hurling slippers against the wall or smashing cookies on the floor (which I personally know nothing about), tsk-tsking, stomping around, being nasty, shouting obscenities, and so on. It can also show up quietly as passive-aggression, avoidance, procrastination, and so on. What most people don't understand is that drama behavior is really a cry out to be seen and heard and for someone *out there* to seek to under-stand and love me *in here*. Any kind of provocative behavior, one that elicits some sort of reaction, will meet the need to be seen and to have a sense of mattering. When people respond to us, we experience the connection to another human being, regardless of the *quality* of the connection. Funda-mentally, connection is the modality through which we seek to feel loved. If we can't feel loved specifically, the negative interactions of drama at least let us know that we matter enough to connect in some form, any form.

In most cases, however, we do not have the wherewithal to recognize or respond to drama in ways that fulfill the need for love. Drama is most of-ten met with disgust, contempt, anger, dismissiveness, frustration, and im-patience, which perpetuates the cycle and makes the drama-oriented parts of ourselves fight harder to feel connected to others and to be loved. When we draw on drama to feel validated, we end up digging a bigger hole to sink into, feeling worse and worse about our connections, about ourselves, and gradually generating alienation. Separation is painful, and keeps us out of the flow of abundance and joy where life can be easy, fun, and fulfilling. In contrast, connection unites us with the parts of ourselves that are seeking expression and healing, wanting to be known and accepted and loved.

ALTERNATIVE WAYS TO MEET THE NEED FOR: LOVE AND CONNECTION

The best way to experience love and connection is to first love ourselves and *listen* to ourselves. In reality, it's our job to find ways to honor ourselves and feel good, and then we can enter into healthy relationships with others. A daily practice of self-love is so much more fulfilling than turning to drama to try to get love from external sources. We truly operate from the energetic field of *thriving* consciousness when we love ourselves, are deeply connected to ourselves, and when we can see our own worth and honor our unique rhythms and impulses. When we fill ourselves up with love, we emit more love. When we emit more love, we have a positive effect on others. When we have a positive effect on others, we will receive more love in return. And so the cycle goes. What we give out returns to us. Teachings from the text in *A Course in Miracles* remind us of the timeless spiritual lesson that giving and receiving are the same thing. What that means is that when you have something to give, like love, you must start with having love first. And by that, you have already received. Furthermore, the nature of the Universe we live in has a reciprocity, or karma, to it. Every thought and intention we hold has a boomerang effect, coming back to us in a perfect energetic match to what we have put out there. This is why it is so healing and rewarding to fill ourselves up with love first and then bring that to the world around us. Practice self-love. It's not selfish or ego-centric; it's actually one of the most generous and compassionate things we can do for the world around us.

Other people cannot consistently be what we want or need them to be in order for us to feel good, to feel loved, and to be intimately connected. It's a wonderful, beautiful thing when we can get our needs met from others, and the truth is that we are more likely to invite that experience into our sphere when we can love ourselves first. When others are not available to meet our needs, we need to be able to default to our primary source of connection and oneness, which is found *within*. When our interactions with others begin to turn toward drama, it is a reminder for us to take care of ourselves, so that when we enter into interpersonal dynamics with them we can come from a place of *thriving*, to authentically express our own truth and honor the other's truth as well.

Essential Human Needs: Value and Significance

"When I am feeling small, negative feedback seems better than none. I would rather have a person hate me than overlook me. As long as I am hated I make a difference."

—HUGH PRATHER

We all have a need to feel important to others. We long to feel valued and know that we matter. We are each here on Planet Earth at this particular time for a unique reason. We each have a higher purpose to serve, a spiritual assignment as it were, that only we can fulfill. Significance implies that we are living in alignment with our unique purpose and that feels good. When we are bringing the value we innately hold, allowing it to manifest externally for others to benefit from, we are playing our part in the ecosystem of life. That's why the popular theme for countless commencement speeches is "follow your bliss." Your bliss tells you you're on the right track! Your bliss is your guidance for being in alignment with your Higher Self and the greater purpose you are meant to serve. Life is meant to be fun and easy; so doing what we do best is fun and easy, and it also tells us what we do best is what the rest of the world needs from us in order to actualize into full expression as a whole.

Unfortunately, many of us learn to live what someone *else* wants from us and for us. We talk ourselves out of our bliss by thinking we should be a certain way or do a certain thing based on what will be pleasing to someone else. We get ideas about how we *should* be from the media, from our families, friends, classmates, teachers, religious leaders, and anyone else who has influence over us while we are learning how to operate in the world. This creates a lot of confusion when it comes to understanding our unique value and the significant role we play. When we are not living in alignment with that higher purpose, our level of consciousness sinks into the drama zone, where we have to fight and struggle to survive. We seek approval from people who are inconsequential, we compare and compete in order to prove our worth, we watch what others are doing to figure out how to "get it right," and we bully our Souls into stress and struggle, believing that's the way to achieve success.

In contrast, when we are in alignment and fulfilling our purpose, we let our inner desires, impulses, and insights guide how we go about our business and take effortless action. We step out boldly and show the world how *we* do—we give them the gift of experiencing us in our Souls' full expression. We naturally inhabit a degree of *thriving* consciousness and allow that vibe to positively impact with the world around us. Not to mention, we have a lot more fun!

HOW DRAMA MEETS THE NEED FOR: VALUE AND SIGNIFICANCE

In the case of meeting our needs for Value and Significance, drama behavior is the survival militia coming to the rescue of the repressed soul. When we cannot live out our spirit's higher purpose, we naturally feel depressed, frustrated, anxious, and even worthless. Drama will naturally ensue as a means to feel some sense of mattering, some sense of making a difference. Living in alignment with one's purpose has a sense of accomplishment and satisfaction to it, knowing that we are bringing value and making life on Planet Earth a little better in our own unique way. Being disconnected from that is almost more painful than death, especially the longer the period of disconnection continues. To compensate, we find other ways to "make a difference"—for better or for worse.

ALTERNATIVE WAYS TO MEET THE NEED FOR:
VALUE AND SIGNIFICANCE

For some, value and significance comes through their job or career. But that's not always the case for everybody. When we are feeling like our ability to fulfill our purpose is lacking in our work, we can still find it in other places in life: family, friends, spiritual organizations, community service, hobbies, connecting with nature and animals, or physical activity.

Bringing value and feeling significance is really about how we show up wherever we are and with whomever we encounter. We can always find pockets of fulfillment by making a positive difference with simple acts that allow the light of our Higher Selves to shine through us, like buying someone a cup of coffee or offering a listening ear or smiling at strangers who cross our paths. When there are gaps in life where we are not experiencing the fulfillment of our greater purpose on a larger scale, we can still feel useful and make our unique contributions through how we direct our thoughts and emotional energy, and how we impact others. In fact, we are constantly being called to do so in a variety of ways, which may not look like what you think it *should* look like.

I have a male family member who has been unemployed for a stretch of time. While others are criticizing him for not "providing" or for relying on his wife to work, I see this as an opportunity for him to fulfill part of his role in the greater family experience and align with his life purpose. As a result of his not hitting a nine-to-fiver, the rest of us are enjoying the digital memoirs he is making available to us by spending his time scanning thousands of old family photos, converting slides, and making unique DVDs and books that capture our family history. I see his not having a day job as being absolutely perfect and completely in Divine order. He is bringing tremendous value by showing up with his passion and sharing it with the rest of us.

Part of the trick to meeting the need for value and significance is learning to trust that life has put us exactly where we are needed at any given time. Then, within those circumstances, we can "follow our bliss," letting our passions and our feelings guide us to what we are meant to do with what we are given. Hold tight! Tools for that are coming in the following chapters.

Essential Human Needs: Variety and New Experiences

"Variety's the spice of life, That gives it all its flavor."

—WILLIAM COWPER

Whether you know it or not, your brain needs variety and new experiences in order to build and grow and make new neural connections. We need novelty—new vantage points and new thoughts—to maintain a healthy internal biochemical system. Our Souls need fun and play to expand. Naturally, these work in tandem with one another. By seeing and doing things in new and different ways, we develop parts of ourselves and our brains that we don't habitually use. This is a part of our personal expression, particularly when the variety involves developing our talents and using our gifts in expansive ways. New experiences offer us the opportunities for moments of illumination and insights, seeing old things through new lenses so we can experience relief, peace, pleasure, and aliveness. They also provide opportunities to connect with others in unique ways via shared interests and joie de vivre.

When we begin to get into a rut of being under-stimulated with new stuff or burnt out on the same old stuff—work, routines, patterns, habits— we are prone to drama. We have shorter fuses, limited attention spans, and less tolerance for others' foibles and eccentricities. We are less creative and more easily frustrated. In short, we are much more reactive simply because we need some renewal. We need to get back into our sense of aliveness, creativity, and exploration of life. Children know how to live this way. They know that each day is a new day and there is something new to discover. We adults think we know what to expect, because we stop following our feelings and using our imaginations, and instead we allow our current external reality to dictate what we do and how we think within our daily human operations.

HOW DRAMA MEETS THE NEED FOR: VARIETY AND NEW EXPERIENCES

Without imagination, joy, and curiosity, we default to drama to experience a sense of aliveness. Drama fabricates excitement through anxiety and purpose through control. Drama consciousness drives behaviors that serve to generate the enthusiasm that we get with new experiences. It attempts to give us variety by getting us worked up over different topics (what the neighbors are doing or what that politician said). Although we tend to get stressed in the same ways repeatedly, we find different sources to blame it on or project it upon. In our drama consciousness, we get the cheap thrill of an adrenaline rush when we indulge in behaviors that activate our core wounds. We will then attract the same kind of wounding we are accustomed to, though it comes via different sources (for example, you thought it was a different significant other, but the same drama showed up in *all* your marriages), giving us variety through alternate means (or people). What we truly need instead is to access the elements of *thriving* that we want to experience within ourselves, but that are underdeveloped or otherwise presently inaccessible. When we are authentically connected to our Higher Selves, we experience the aliveness of our Souls engaged in action in our lives. Drama is a disconnected, ego-driven state that seeks without, as opposed to generating from within.

ALTERNATIVE WAYS TO MEET THE NEED FOR: VARIETY AND NEW EXPERIENCES

When we need a little divergence from the mundane, it's helpful to reference a list of options to get the novelty need met. I frequently have my clients generate a "menu" of things they find fun or that give them pleasure that they can select from when they get stuck in a rut. In those moments the brain needs a little help, and having a list already available provides just that. For brainstorming that list of options, ask friends or colleagues what they do for fun. Surf the Internet to get ideas of something that would be new and different to try. Pick areas of life where you are willing to take a risk of trying something new. Plan a vacation. Drive a different route to work. Pick a new food at lunch. Start wearing a color or style that's different for you. If you're bored in your job, start doing secret acts of kindness for your co-workers. Keep the list going for *you*. The key is to inject a little *authentic* aliveness and excitement into your life, so you can do with less anxiety and boredom. Give it a try!

Essential Human Needs: Certainty and Security

"Human beings the world over need freedom and security that they may be able to realize their full potential."

—AUNG SAN SUU KYI

Certainty is the absence of doubt and the presence of faith. Security is the absence of fear and the presence of trust. In a sense, certainty and security empower the fulfillment of each of the aforementioned needs. Our Souls rely on these elements to effectively live a human life and serve the purpose we were born for. Doubt and fear are the big kahunas of drama, inciting outbursts and desertions of all sorts. They deter the fulfillment of purpose, they interfere with the experience of love, they steal the authenticity available in connection with others, and they keep us running the hamster wheel instead of getting on that flight to Tahiti. When we feel a sense of certainty—of absolute knowing—we are more at peace. When we feel secure and safe, we can relax into ourselves and into our relationships, and we can take risks and explore life more deeply.

HOW DRAMA MEETS THE NEED FOR: CERTAINTY AND SECURITY

Many times, drama is looking for reassurance. It is testing the boundaries and thresholds to see where it is safe and at what point the bottom drops out. In effect, it is intentionally activating fear and doubt to ironically avoid having them crop up unexpectedly. We tell ourselves cockamamie stories all the time to try to anticipate wounding, making wild assumptions in order to insulate and presumably avoid getting hurt. We look for differences to see where we might be excluded. We evaluate how perfect we were or how "right" we got it to assure our acceptance in the group, whether it is in our personal or professional lives.

ALTERNATIVE WAYS TO MEET THE NEED FOR: CERTAINTY AND SECURITY

When we can develop ways of feeling certain and secure within ourselves first, our worlds expand. Relying less on what others are doing or not doing and more on our own inclinations, choices, and abilities to generate the feelings we desire opens up possibilities and allows us freedom. What you'll learn in the following chapters is how to begin to do this for yourself first within, and allow the external evidence to follow. When we practice feeling certain and know where to access a sense of security, then we are truly free—free to love, to connect with deep intimacy, to live out our purpose with passion and fervor, and to enrich ourselves and embrace experiences of all kinds.

A Sense of Belonging

"A deep sense of love and belonging is an irreducible need of all people. We are biologically, cognitively, physically, and spiritually wired to love, to be loved, and to belong. When those needs are not met, we don't function as we are meant to. We break. We fall apart. We numb. We ache. We hurt others. We get sick."

—BRENÉ BROWN

What drama is really calling for is affirmation of our belonging, knowing we are secure, loved, valued, connected. Like it or not, we are tribal creatures and we rely on our belonging to the group for survival. When this appears to be threatened, we will kick into preservation mode and the drama will ensue. Most of the time when we are frightened or generating drama, the "reasons" are irrational. Our mental capacities can know this and even see things with logic, and yet our reactions may still be based on the emotional chaos within.

When my husband and I first met, I was not interested in dating anyone with kids (which meant him). I didn't have my own, didn't want my own, and certainly didn't want to raise anyone else's. My experience of being part of a stepfamily as a child was not good. I was the outsider and part-timer in each of my households and the oddball among extended family, being the only one from divorced parents. I never really had a complete sense of belonging; it was always fragmented. I knew people loved me—my parents, grandparents, aunts, uncles, cousins, dad's girlfriends, friends I lived with—but I also believed that if anyone was disposable within each of those groups, it was *me*.

Needless to say, I was not about to marry myself into a similar situation. I had already dated someone with kids, and in that experience I found that children rule and biology trumps all. I spent two years on the back burner, begging and pulling teeth to try to be included like a team member, which is not a sustainable or healthy way to live in a partnership

72

or marriage. Admittedly, however, I probably unconsciously co-created that relationship as a manifestation of my belief system, attracting exactly what I was emitting: disposability and feeling like a second-class citizen. By golly, the Law of Attraction delivered. Since I had already been to that dog-and-pony show, I decided I was never again going to date anyone with kids. I was clear inside myself about the kind of love and companionship I desired. I was to be valued as an equal partner and unequivocally included, feeling to my core that I belong.

Enter Terrence Collins (or so we'll call him in these pages). We had a lovely, surprisingly long, eight-hour first date. Concluding that evening, he secured another soiree with the offer to make me dinner next time. It wasn't until that second date that I found out he has two daughters, and not until our third date that he also has a son. I would've politely declined further explorations, but his vibe around fatherhood felt different to me. In getting to know this guy, he stated upfront that his first priority is his partner. He loves his children, supports them, spends time with them, and is invested in their healthy development. But he also appeared to recognize that children need adults who love each other and work *together* for the kids' well-being, which eventually leads to them growing up and moving on to have their own healthy family lives. Partners are left with each other at the end of the day. Given that this was what I understood to be his way of thinking and an expression of his value system, I continued to date him. I could see a possibility of having a positive partnership and family experience, so I married the dude. It also helped that his kids lived a few states away, so I was not involved with raising them beyond supporting my husband in visiting them and enjoying getting to know them during holidays and summer vacations.

My step-kids are really great people. They are so gentle and kind, loving and lovable; it's almost ridiculous how easy it is to be with them. Their immediate acceptance of me still blows my mind and warms my heart. Yet, there has always been this quiet nagging inside me, reminding me that I am the outsider; I don't *really belong*. So when my husband approached me in the summer of 2013 about having his youngest daughter, the then-fifteen-year-old we'll call Kari, come live with us full time in 2014 for her last two years of high school—in our one-thousand-square-feet, two-bedroom apartment—I got very nervous. The drama hijacked my thought-train like nobody's business, and throughout the decision-making process I was flooded with all sorts of survival-based, irrational thoughts: *I don't know how to be a parent. What if I screw it up? She has her own mom; she's gonna hate me. We don't have enough space in our little apartment. What if Terrence and I can't get along as co-parents? If this doesn't work,* I'll *have to move out. If I invest myself and start to really bond with this kid and then things go bad, I will lose everyone. They will get to keep each other, but I will be alone and heartbroken.*

And so the drama goes, running around in cahoots with the trickster brain. Nothing was actually happening, but in an attempt to protect my tender spirit, my brain was throwing out all possible scenarios to avoid wounding and pain. Like a jokester. The most comical moment, I have to say, was when I got worked up about not belonging based on my human brain identifying literal physical differences between me and my family. You see, my husband and the kids are all Caribbean-blooded and have gorgeous mocha-toned skin, which does not match my Euro-Scandinavian coloring. Seriously, in meltdown mode one night, my brain actually went there— looking for, digging up, searching, and scouring for any potential barriers to belonging. I needed to scope it all out to preemptively protect myself from rejection and loss. In my less-than-enlightened moment, whimpering in the living room (with a *Sesame Street* melody droning through my mind to the words, "Four of these things are not like the other; one of them doesn't belooong . . ."), I was trying to articulate to my husband how different I am and how I really don't belong, which was not making any sense to him.

So to clarify, to really get him to understand, tears rolling, I cried out, "But I'm . . . I'm . . . I'm white!"

My husband gasped, and jumped backward, an expression of shock and horror washing over his face.

"You are?!"

With that, all drama was dispelled—I mean it literally: the spell was broken. I was able to get out of my survival brain and into laughter and recognition of the comedy of my kooky story and goofy state. I got a good chunk of the irrational fear out of my system and from that point on was able to have more effective conversations about Kari moving in with us and set positive intentions for becoming a full-time step-mommy.

As I write these words, now five months into the role, I am growing with the ups and downs of change, with at least some reduction in the petrification that previously gripped me about being disposable. The truth is that there are certain gifts available in this opportunity, even if I can't see them all yet. My husband and I are discovering new things about each other that will take us into new expressions of our relationship, whatever they may be. Kari and I get to do cool girlie things together. I get to experience "parenthood" and be part of the development of a beautiful young woman. The overall experience is a sort of "*thriving* boot camp," calling me daily to manage my thoughts and energy with explicit focus and conscious intention at a whole new level. Most of all, I am being invited to embrace the life-altering realization that no one else can speak my voice or choose my belonging for me; that's my job.

We humans have to look for and define our own way of belonging and getting our needs met in relation to what shows up in our life experience. It's nice if a strong sense of belonging is instilled in us during childhood, but I think most of us have to create it for ourselves. We have to claim it for ourselves. Belonging has a number of elements to it: the first and foremost being self-acceptance and self-love. When we are at home inside ourselves, when we feel our own belonging within, then having other people included in that just becomes a bonus.

Marianne Williamson said, "What is not love is but a *call* for love." In its simplest form, that's really what drama is all about; that's the function it has in our society and in the world.

Drama is simply a call for love. A way to get our needs met, to be seen, to be heard, to feel valued, to know we matter. And yet it is an ineffective way for meeting these healthy needs. It pushes others away and destroys connections, creating outcomes opposite of what we intend and desire.

When we can learn to live and embrace a DRAMA-free world, then we can stop the desperate scramble for surviving and start authentically *thriving!*

"If we have no peace, it is because we have forgotten that we belong to each other."

—MOTHER TERESA

Key Concepts

＊ Drama is the functioning that emerges from the lower energetic states when we seek to meet our basic needs for: love and connection, value and significance, variety and new experiences, certainty and security. The essential components of these include: being seen and heard, being understood, having a sense of belonging, feeling valued, and knowing that we matter.

- Love and Connection: Love is the energy that fuels our connection, since love constitutes the essence of Who We Really Are in our eternal nature. Drama behavior almost always has the goal of creating a sense of connection through attention-seeking, because in receiving any kind of focus or response, good or bad, we at least know we *matter*. The best way to meet the need for love and connection is to first love and honor *ourselves*. As we tend to our needs and desires, taking charge of our own feeling good, we can then enter into healthier relationships with others.

- Value and Significance: We each have a higher purpose to serve, that we are equipped to fulfill through our innate talents and passions. Significance tells us we are living out that unique purpose. Prolonged disconnection from our purpose will lead to drama as a means to feel some sense of mattering. Bringing value and feeling significance is about how we show up in life, making a positive difference with simple acts that allow the light of our Higher Selves to shine through us.

- Variety and New Experiences: The brain needs novelty in order to build and grow and make new neural connections. Our Souls need fun and play to expand. Falling into a rut of being either under-stimulated or burnt out primes us for drama. Without the adventure of creativity and curiosity, we default to drama to experience the sense of aliveness we would otherwise yield from exploring the full spectrum of life. We can intentionally generate aliveness and excitement through actively switching things up and seeking to discover new things.

- Certainty and Security: Doubt and fear incite drama. Certainty and security provide foundations for *thriving*, empowering the fulfillment of all other needs and desires. Certainty instills a sense of peace. Security gives us freedom in our relationships and safety in the world. Drama seeks reassurance through testing the boundaries and thresholds of safety. Developing ways of feeling certain and secure within ourselves first allows us to live fully and *thrive*.

✻ A sense of belonging is key to our survival as tribal creatures. Drama seeks affirmation of our belonging that we are secure, loved, valued, connected. It is a call for love. As individuals, it's up to us to *choose* to belong exactly where we are and with whomever shows up in our life experience, or make the changes required to get our needs met in self-honoring ways.

Application and Integration

The ways I use drama to meet my need for . . .
Love and Connection:

Value and Significance:

Variety and New Experiences:

Certainty and Security:

Alternative ways I will put into place and apply today to meet each of my needs in a *thriving* way . . .

Love and Connection:

Value and Significance:

Variety and New Experiences:

Certainty and Security:

CHAPTER FIVE

Enslavement—The Addiction to Our Own Minds

"All our emotional attitudes—ones we may believe are caused by something outside of us—are not only the result of how we perceive reality based on how we are wired, but also of how much we are addicted to how we want to feel."

—DR. JOE DISPENZA, D.C.

In the Netherlands, the word for addiction is "verslaving." It literally translates to "enslavement." Anyone who has tried to quit smoking, stop overeating, break bad habits, give up Coca-Cola or sugar or Starbucks mochaccinos, or get off any pleasurable hooking substance, knows that "enslavement" is a pretty accurate description of the addictive experience.

Similarly, anyone who has ever tried the kind of meditation where you're supposed to "clear your mind" and "stop your thoughts" knows how addictive (hard to stop) our thoughts can be. In a way, we are slaves to them. That is, until we become aware of this fact and begin the revolution to take over, become present, and start directing our thoughts instead of them directing us. This is the essence of "inner alignment."

When we can manage our thoughts, we can attune our emotional state and our vibration to align with the things we authentically desire, like meaningful connection and intimacy, better circumstances, improved lifestyle, and success in our endeavors. But this takes some awareness of the biomechanics of our thoughts and emotional states, as well as some specific tools to begin making transformative changes at a deep level.

The Brain Chemical Basics of DRAMA

Chemicals run us. Most people aren't aware of the bazillion (a rough estimate) biochemicals—hormones, peptides, neurotransmitters—that are coursing through their system each day. But there they are, generating the intercellular communication our bodies need to function internally and engage with the outer world. Every time we have a thought, the brain produces an associated chemical that generates an emotional state and penetrates our entire system with information. Since thoughts are vibrational in nature, by the Law of Attraction, they will continue to attract similar thoughts. Once a neural net is "turned on" it will generate more of the same kinds of thoughts that reinforce that specific emotional state. According to Dr. Joe Dispenza, the peptides and hormones that correspond to each emotion then flood the body and, based on their chemical makeup, will "plug into" related cells and influence how those cells develop and express themselves. Over time, if we practice a certain emotional state day after day, the cells of the body that are influenced by that emotional "peptide cocktail" become accustomed to the presence of its particular biochemical wash and establish it as "normal" for the body. In other words, the body gets used to our emotions. The cells of the body then "require" that particular emotional state to maintain homeostasis. What's more, as the cells divide and carry on the need for the "peptide cocktails," the body will naturally need more of the addictive substance to be satisfied, which requires us to create bigger and badder dramas in our thoughts or our lives.

What happens in our developmental stages is that our external experiences generate emotional responses within us, which fall somewhere along the spectrum of pain and pleasure as well as correspond to our core wounds, and we become accustomed to those emotional states. Over time we begin to associate specific people, places, vocal tones, facial expressions, events, and thoughts with particular states. This programs our neural nets for specific emotion-related peptides to be released so we can maintain the chemical balance we have grown accustomed to. We become addicted to the chemical rush stimulated by our own thoughts, our environment, and interactions with others.

When our habitual emotions are not being activated by our environment, we will fabricate them internally just so the cells can get their biochemical "fix." In essence, drama becomes a chemical driver. Our bodies get used to the levels of chemicals we are generating and that saturate our neurology, which means that any shift or imbalance will lead the body to seek homeostasis, bringing the chemical state back into balance based on what's familiar. Because of this, we will drum up drama unnecessarily. We will also unconsciously seek to maintain a continuity of biochemicals at the cellular level by attracting similar relationships and circumstances into our lives, perpetuating the cycles of drama we "enjoy." In effect, we become addicted to the chemical states we identify with and come to know as our unique Self.

Dealing with emotions, and just being a human in general, is a complicated business. When any of our wounds are activated or poked into, we not only experience the chemical rush of adrenaline as our limbic systems prepare us for fight, flight, or freeze, but we also experience the effects of the associated emotional peptide at a cellular level in the body. This can be stimulated by how we are thinking about ourselves, the assumptions we are making about another person or circumstances, or it can come from a real-time experience with something in the outer world. We will draw from memories to assure our survival and react to anything that appears threatening or wounding. In the same vein, when we experience the kinds of behaviors from others that create our core human wounds, the brain stores those feeling states in our neurological system through our memories, which is how we can later regenerate the same emotions when something appears to resemble the original wounding event(s). Because this rush gives us a dramatic sense of aliveness we will continue to perpetuate our wounds and recreate similar dramas, on increasingly bigger scales, to get that "high" again.

When we live with the same emotions day after day and fail to develop new responses, we must be addicted to the chemical states created, which become familiar, integrate into our identity, and seal the addiction, making the same compulsive assumptions and reactions very hard to stop. Thoughts can *feel* very real, which is why drama is so gripping and compelling. This is what makes inner alignment essential to our *thriving*. When we fire off even one solitary thought from an energetic state of drama, more of the same kinds of thoughts will come. And the same goes for a thought that originates from *thriving* consciousness; it will attract more thoughts that match that energetic level. So the good news is when we interrupt old patterns and consciously generate positive emotional states, we can become habituated to joy, peace, gratitude, and inspiration, making *thriving* consciousness the new normal. Let's finish exploring the concept of drama addiction and then we'll get to the juicy stuff: how to live your *thriving* life!

The Addiction Path

The image on the next page illustrates how drama flows through us. You can see that a neutral event, any kind of stimulus, can show up in our experience, and when it activates our wounds or perks up our assumptions it can launch the biochemical cascade that generates the associated feeling state and energetic vibration. From here, drama behavior ensues as an "acting out" in order to generate a release of the intense emotion. This is the part of drama most of us think of as "drama"—the externalization that we witness. This always has some sort of impact on others, which at times can yield the

DRAMA Paradigm: The Addiction Path

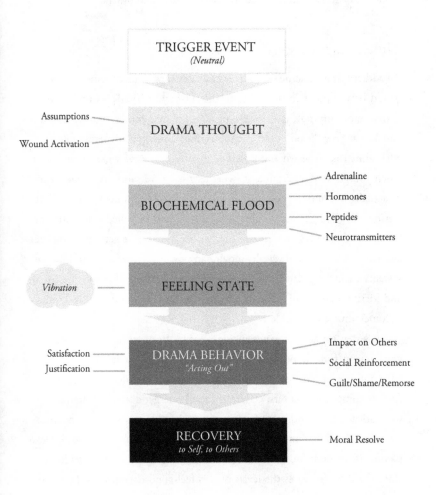

social reinforcement of being seen and heard, but it can also activate shame, guilt, or remorse for the behavior once the chemical flood has subsided. On the flip side, there can be satisfaction or justification that the drama behavior was warranted for a good reason, which of course only perpetuates the drama. Eventually, there is a "recovery" where we return to higher levels of functioning and regain the ability to operate with compassion, contentment, and curiosity, in connection with ourselves and others.

The "Pleasure" of DRAMA

All addictions have some sort of pleasure or reward to them, otherwise what would be the point in indulging in the substance? The "pleasure" of drama, very bluntly put, is the sense of *aliveness* that comes with it. C'mon, you know how "good" (a.k.a. empowering, animated, dynamic, etc.) an adrenaline rush feels when it floods your system. It gives you a certain kick when you get into an argument (whether the conversation is in your head or actually live and in person). The surging sense of running late in a panic during rush hour lights you up (in fact, it should be called *rush* hour not because everyone is in a hurry, but rather because they're getting off on the adrenaline buzz from physically moving in slow motion when their internal systems are in warp drive). The feeling of being submerged in worthlessness and victimhood, or of having to fight to prove that your way is "right," becomes almost irresistible.

When we are not experiencing pleasure from authentic sources like engaging in fun, doing things that feel fulfilling, or living in alignment with our greater purpose, we will drum up drama in order to feel *alive*. To further complicate matters, certain (not all) energetic states of drama that we fabricate, like egotism and arrogance for instance, can be accompanied by a release of dopamine, the neurotransmitter for pleasure and *reward*. Dopamine is the same biochemical that makes drugs like cocaine so addictive, since the drug increases the levels of this feel-good chemical in the brain, creating a sort of euphoria. As it turns out, drama can sometimes work in a similar way. This is why people say they "thrive off of drama," but this is not authentic *thriving*. It is a false sense of aliveness that is ego-based, born from a place of fear, separation, and woundedness, rather than the aliveness we experience when we are aligned with our Higher Selves and going with the flow of life. Drama is a hedonistic pleasure, while *thriving* comes from seeking greater meaning and authentic purpose.

Additional "rewards" for indulging drama include being "seen" and "heard" and feeling like we "matter." Drama behavior is generally *not* making a positive impact on the world, but it assures some sort of response or connection to another person. Our need for social acknowledgment trumps all. We'll get it any way we can. Outbursts and tantrums will accomplish this, in spite of being ineffective methods. Part of the trouble is that drama is so familiar and easy to access, a default program most people unconsciously run under the guise that *"it'll just have to do until some day when my world is perfect and I can be all zen and enlightened."* This, of course, is backwards. We cannot reach a place of peace and joy, nor can we embrace meaningful relationships, while continuing to seek satisfaction of our needs and desires through drama means.

Withdrawal

"If someone is determined to not risk pain, then such a person must do without many things: having children, getting married, the ecstasy of sex, the hope of ambition, friendship—all that makes life alive, meaningful, and significant. Move out or grow in any direction and pain as well as joy will be your reward. A full life will be full of pain. But the only alternative is to not live fully or not to live at all."

—M. SCOTT PECK

As with any addiction, there is the withdrawal that comes from changes to the chemical balance the system is used to. In order to transform, we must be willing to depart from the old familiar ways and enter into new experiences with a willingness to tolerate the pain and discomfort of change. Departing the comfort zone of our emotional past and entering into a new future of our own creating is uncomfortable and risky business. We have to risk not getting our needs met. We have to risk changes to our relationships and our work. Some "growing pains" can be expected. In fact, letting go of who you know yourself to be and allowing a new, higher version of You to come into existence involves some birthing pains. You will want to go back to the old ways. You will have the urge to employ the same old behaviors. The voice in your head will tell you how stupid this is, how you'll never make it, how it's just better to do what you know. You can just plan on all that. It's just a part of withdrawal and your system trying to get you back into homeostasis. That's *all* it is. And you can tolerate it! You can overcome it! You are hardly the first person to deal with addiction, so just know that this is part of the process and you *can*, you *will*, become the new person who lives from *thriving* consciousness, who truly enjoys life and enhances it for those around them. By setting clear intentions and making a fierce commitment to redefining ourselves and our lives, we *can* transform. It's just a new biochemical abode that needs a little settling into. Soon enough it will become the new normal and we will have evolved.

Waking Up

"Consciousness is a full-time job."

—CAROLINE MYSS

The worst part of drama, like any other addiction, is *not* the experience of being in it. It's when you *wake up* from it and realize that, no, it's not the outside world that is "doing this to you"—it's *you* doing it to yourself. The reason this is the worst part is because it's so much easier to project and place blame than it is to face the music and take personal responsibility. It's so much easier to find a scapegoat in the people and circumstances that compose our lives, asserting that they are "making things happen" outside of our power. It's more comfortable to think that *they* are the ones who have to change in order for us to feel better, not us. From the addictions perspective, however, we call this denial.

Your brain, your thoughts, your emotions, your life, and your experience are *your* domain. Really, no one can run them for you. And would you even want them to? On some level, the answer is yes, because we tend to want to denounce our authentic power and make ourselves smaller than we are in order to "belong" and to fit the prescribed world we were born into. We defer our power, our choices, to not "outshine" others. And drama functions to perpetuate this suppression of the Higher Self.

The Truth of who You are, however, wants you to be the most authentic, loving, empowered, creative, fully expressed, and actualized version of yourself in the highest possible way. That's what the discord in your life is calling you to, begging you to hit your tolerance threshold where you can no longer deny your Higher Self. But instead of following the passion, taking the path of joy, and actually *thriving*, we go down the familiar road of drama instead. It's time to say ENOUGH!

The Addiction "Recovery" Plan: Concepts for Authentic *Thriving*

"We may think there is willpower involved, but more likely . . . change is due to want power. Wanting the new addiction more than the old one. Wanting the new me in preference to the person I am now."

—GEORGE A. SHEEHAN

Dealing with the addictive component of drama is most comparable to compulsive eating. We have to eat; you can't just stop cold turkey. In a similar vein, we have to *think*. Most of us don't really have a choice. Thoughts just appear. We don't have to consciously summon them or drum them up. When we wake in the morning, they are already rockin' and rollin' their way across the screen of our mind. What do we do about the drama thoughts? Fret not, friends. We have tools for that, which you'll find in Part II. But before that, here is an overview of certain concepts we can apply:

- Take 100 Percent Responsibility
- Identify Your DRAMA Triggers
- Find Alternative Thoughts for Each DRAMA Trigger
- Get Support
- HALT
- Develop State-Breakers
- Relapse Prevention

TAKE 100 PERCENT RESPONSIBILITY

Conscious, authentic *thriving* begins by taking 100 percent responsibility for your world and your life experience. That means how you're thinking about yourself and everything around you, the emotions you are generating, and the behaviors you are choosing. I was so annoyed when I first started to adopt this concept, 'cause I soooo wanted it to be *them* who had to change and I wanted the problem to be *out there*. Now I know that taking personal responsibility for *everything* in my universe is the only way for me to live with abundance and in alignment with my Higher Self—but making that internal shift took some time. Remember to be patient with your beautiful self. Like the famous phrase from AA says, we're always going for *progress, not perfection*.

IDENTIFY YOUR DRAMA TRIGGERS

Most of us know the scenarios and people that can arouse drama in us. If you're not sure, just start paying attention to when you get upset or start feeling "bad" and notice what the common denominators are. Write out a list of your triggers with the associated dominant drama thoughts so you can be awake and aware of them next time they come up. In some cases it could be specific people or places that trigger you, but it helps to think in terms of themes, such as "authority figures" instead of "my boss, Nancy," for example. To help you get started, common triggers can include:

Expectations differing from our experience—When we create a certain picture in our minds of how things will be *beforehand*, and then get into a situation that does not match that picture, it can have a sort of startle effect on us. The sense of disconnection, instability, or frustration resulting from our inaccurate prediction can poke into our wounds, throttling us into the limbic reactive state.

Knee-jerk assumptions and stories—Our brains can only process so much information on a conscious level. Many times we will automatically filter for protection; we sort and organize external input through our wound-based lenses as it comes in. We will instinctively attune what we literally see and hear in the moment to match what we "know" about anything similar from the past. When our frequency is set to vibrate at a lower level—as seen in the energetic states of drama consciousness—our physical senses will automatically hone in on whatever information we need to stay safe, and our brains will react from there. When we assume treason, we will find evidence of betrayal. When we assume love, we will see the affirmation of that as well. Our assumptions and stories can fluctuate from moment to moment, depending on the associations we have with various relationship roles, certain environments, and other contextual attachments.

Dogmatic beliefs—When we get too fixated on being "right," vehemently defending our beliefs, we set up a blockade with anyone who does not agree with us. In our desire for safety, acceptance, and validation, we can easily be triggered into a survival mode, fighting to "prove ourselves." In reality, there is no singular "right" way to do anything in life, or at least there are very few. Really. But we get very convinced that ours is the best, most appropriate, and correct way to think about or do something. Others doing it "wrong" can disproportionately push our buttons and launch us into drama.

Rigidity and Chaos—Drama consciousness is activated by either being too strict about things or getting too overwhelmed by them—via our inner dynamics or our external circumstances. When we try to force ourselves into certain actions or states—pushing and driving in the absence of inspired flow—we activate an internal rebellion that inhibits effective action. This rigid stance interferes with our ability to authentically connect with others, and only leaves us feeling frustrated. When we have rigid rules for how things "should" be imposed upon ourselves or others, we launch into drama and are left feeling the need to fight for "our way." Likewise, when we feel the chaos of worthlessness, depression, or anxiety, we will experience the "freeze" reaction through shutting down, or we will "flee" through avoiding or numbing out by way of food, alcohol, sleeping pills, or indulging in other escapist activities that give us a temporary sense of relief.

FIND ALTERNATIVE THOUGHTS
FOR EACH DRAMA TRIGGER

Once you list out your triggers and their dominant drama thoughts, come up with one or two *new* thoughts that you can begin to use instead. Keep it simple, fun, easy, and memorable; stick to one line you can bring to mind when you get hooked by drama. It might help to brainstorm with a friend. Sometimes getting silly or extravagant helps you shift your emotional state more easily than something "practical" or "realistic." The goal is simply to have a new, better-feeling response. We don't have to reach world peace with a one-liner, but just shift our vibration one thought at a time, which incrementally nudges us in that direction anyway.

GET SUPPORT

Undoing any addiction takes a metropolis (forget the village). You will need your positive peeps to help you when you get triggered, or even better, *before* you go into one of your trigger-potential scenarios. Let your support team know what you want from them, and how you will best feel supported. Help them help you. Chapter 11 will help you define what will be most supportive for you so you know what to ask for, in addition to knowing how to resist taking on OPD: Other People's Drama.

HALT

This term is known well in the substance-addictions world as Hungry, Angry, Lonely, Tired, which are all common triggers to relapse. In dealing with drama thinking, I have a variation of this. We tend to be more susceptible to drama when we experience too much or an imbalance of the following:

H: Hunger or Hormones
A: Alcohol (or other drugs)
L: Loneliness (or boredom)
T: Tiredness

If you are, as my Aunt Vicky calls it, "going bad" and slipping down the tubes of drama thinking, HALT and do a quick scan to see if one of these things might be the culprit. If you can pinpoint the source of the drama as one of these, suddenly you can access a new solution (like having a snack or taking a nap) *before* you go into full tantrum mode.

DEVELOP STATE-BREAKERS

State-breakers are just what they sound like: tools and strategies to interrupt the chemical flow and emotional state you are in the midst of generating. Breaking that pattern and taking your neurology in a new direction will gradually begin to break the old neuropathways and biochemical habits so you can establish new responses and a new normal that feels better and is more empowering. We'll go into this more in subsequent chapters, but for now you can start by using the 5 D's. (And no, one of them is not Dramamine—though we love MollyAnn Wymer's ingenuity!) When you feel yourself going down the rabbit hole of drama thinking, try one of these strategies (or a combination) to shift and go down a new path:

> **Delay**—Wait and let the drama urges pass. This could take from ninety seconds up to several minutes. Just wait before you react or launch a verbal spew that will circulate out there in the vibrational ethers and come back to you as Drama Karma. Simply *wait*.
>
> **Distract**—Get busy and focus your mind on something else. It is essential to interrupt the thought pattern and completely shift your biochemical state. This will help break the drama thought path, making it easier to shift emotional states and see the trigger scenario more objectively. You can then respond in a way you will actually feel good about after the fact. Distraction can come through a variety of means, such as: thinking of something pleasurable like a vacation you're planning, reading a magazine, watching an inspiring TED Talk, doing a crossword puzzle, laughing out loud, or finally having a copy of your completed book in your hands (yes, that's one of my go-to thoughts at the moment). In the story of my

former client Laura (who had the unwitnessed temper tantrum in the kitchen), she was able to immediately shift her internal state with laughter, the ultimate state-breaker, releasing "happy chemicals" into her system. This allowed her to instantaneously recover from the drama episode and refocus her energy on something that felt better.

Deep Breathe—In through the mouth . . . slowly . . . all the way in . . . and now, out through the nose. Repeat. Repeat again. Get some oxygen into your beautiful brain! It'll calm the chemical surge and help you come back to your center.

Depart—Sometimes leaving the physical space of a situation really is best, until you can recover and get into alignment with your Higher Self, whereby you can have a healthy interaction and make new, better-feeling choices.

Dance!—Literally—or figuratively. But either way, get your body moving. And if you move your body enough, it will help you release feel-good brain chemicals—like the endorphins of a "runner's high"—to offset the drama rush. Use music to help you shift; it'll activate another part of your brain. Either way you are interrupting the old pattern and creating a new way to respond. Plus, dancing or otherwise moving the body is just fun. We all need a lot more *fun*!

RELAPSE PREVENTION

The final component to a good "recovery" plan is relapse prevention. This involves some simple forethought about your drama triggers that you can address *before* you enter a situation you know has the potential to activate your wounds. Preventing drama relapse can involve structuring your environment to enhance your positive thinking, like putting Post-it notes as reminders for new thoughts or alternative responses. It can also involve identifying your healthy boundaries and knowing how you will honor them *prior* to interactions with people you know can push your buttons. It can be something as simple as keeping a snack bag nearby so you don't get too hungry in between meals. It's anything that will have you prepared in advance to offset the drama before it starts.

Going from the DRAMA Paradigm to the *Thriving* Paradigm Over Time

Most addiction models depict a cycle that needs to be broken in order to overcome the enslavement. Although we could frame it that way, I prefer to think of drama as being linear—increasing or decreasing depending on whether we are consciously interacting with it or not. It is not cyclical, but growing stronger or weaker based on our choices. The value in this perspective is that it means we're in charge of our future outcomes, not *stuck* in a loop we can't get out of. Cycles can feel disempowering. They seem never-ending and appear hard to break out of. They almost operate as permission to keep going, to repeat the same old meshugas, to not change, improve, or grow. In contrast, a linear process is the movement through various "now" moments, and any *now* moment is an opportunity for something new, an opportunity to change, to advance toward more authentic *thriving* living. It offers us continuous opportunities to practice recovery, patience, tolerating, and self-honoring.

The Paradigm Timeline on the next page illustrates how drama can evolve into *thriving* over time. What used to be a trigger to react can transform into a stimulus to simply respond, when we learn to consistently operate in the higher levels of consciousness by following what feels better and better, based on the circumstances we find ourselves in. As we apply the methods, lifestyle practices, and inner alignment tools in this book, we will gradually flow in this direction toward habitual *thriving!*

The Paradigm Timeline:
The Evolution from DRAMA to *Thriving*

DRAMA Paradigm ➤ *THRIVING* Paradigm

Trigger	Trigger	Trigger	Trigger
DRAMA Thought	DRAMA Thought	DRAMA Thought	
Biochemical Flood	Biochemical Flood	Observation	
Feeling State	Feeling State	Curiosity	
DRAMA Behavior *Guilt/Shame/Remorse*	*THRIVING TOOL Relief and Feeling Improvement*	*THRIVING TOOL*	*THRIVING* THOUGHT
Recovery *Moral Resolve*	Recovery	Recovery	RESPONSE

TIME

Love Yourself to Freedom

*"All the suffering, stress, and addiction comes from not realizing you already **are** what you are looking for."*

—JON KABAT-ZINN

Fundamentally, addiction behavior is grounded in and emphatically reinforces self-rejection. When we operate from our wounds we tend to exhibit drama behavior, which leaves us feeling badly. When we get "high" off of making ourselves "bad" or "wrong," the drama and resulting behaviors (overeating, gambling, promiscuity, picking fights, etc.) continue to serve a purpose. Once the drama indulgence from these habits stops, the behavior is then no longer reinforced. As we gradually heal our wounds and start getting high off of joy and self-appreciation *instead*, the drama thinking and behaviors no longer meet our needs, because the needs have changed. We don't need victimhood to define how we belong, where we fit in, or as a method to be seen and heard. We can now stand in the higher energies that are the Truth of Who We Really Are. A pathway for something new, an authentic aliveness, is now opened up and becomes available as a way of operating that is more powerful, joyous, and peaceful.

So part of the solution to the drama addiction is a practice of self-love. Louise Hay introduced us to the idea, and millions have discovered the power of this incredible force. The self-love that I'm highlighting here is of the unconditional and eternal variety; it is not the self-love of vanity or self-absorption. It is more than a passing sentiment, but a compassionate, supportive, accepting, and kind way of *BE*ing. It allows for letting go and being present in the moment, without judgment, without neediness. It is boundless and timeless. *A Course in Miracles* teaches that only love is real—it is the only part of our existence that is actually True.

A mega part of self-love is self-honoring—both in thinking and behavior. It's about not making ourselves wrong or bad anymore. It's about listening deeply and attentively to actually hear the whisperings of what our Souls want to say. Self-honoring includes listening to our intuition, following our inner guidance, and consciously valuing ourselves. Self-honoring is about being with *what is* in a state of appreciation and openness. It focuses on our strengths, lets go of worrying about our weaknesses, and knows that *both* are meaningful parts of the perfect creation we already happen to be.

The reason why self-love is essential to our release of the drama addiction is that it heals at a profound spiritual, mental, emotional, and physical level. It begins to create new neural nets that we can inhabit; it generates a healthier, more effective "peptide cocktail" for us to flood our cells with, giving us freedom of choice in how we respond to ourselves and our lives. Self-love also gives us vibrational alignment with the Source from which we come, as well as access to the wisdom of our Higher Selves. When we focus our energy on self-love we will naturally become more attractive to the positive people and experiences we desire, making our life experience better and better. Having a daily practice of self-love is a transformative experience. We can make love, gratitude, and joy the new "addiction." Then, when we look for the evidence of what we are practicing, all the blessings life holds for us will gradually appear in our new reality and little miracles will unfold themselves in exponential proportions.

It's Your Life, Your Brain, Your World

"When I have creative insight, there is a high. I think back in the day, I made music as much as I did because it made me feel so good. I think you could argue that there is a creative addiction—but, you know, the healthy kind."

—LAURYN HILL

In closing this chapter, keep in mind that you are not a slave. Your brain and your thoughts are here to serve *you* and your greater purpose in this world. As you begin to break the drama habit and live more frequently and consistently in alignment with your Higher Self, you will find your life unfolds fluidly, in the best possible ways, with a whole lot more peace, happiness, and authentic *thriving*. The following chapters will give you even more insights and tools to make the journey rewarding, effective, and *fun*.

Key Concepts

✳ Drama is the addiction that results from our bodies getting used to our habitual wound-based thoughts and emotions and the biochemical rush that accompanies them. We will continuously think thoughts and seek out people and experiences that activate those emotional states in order to maintain physiological homeostasis, while perpetuating our limiting beliefs about ourselves and the world.

✳ The addictive "pleasure" of drama includes being "seen" and "heard" and feeling like you "matter." It is also the sense of *aliveness* that comes with the biochemical rush.

✳ Thoughts are vibrational in nature. The quality of our thoughts—true or false, strong or weak, Spirit- or ego-based—will influence our energetic state, emitting a certain vibrational frequency. The Law of Attraction will continue to attract similar thoughts by way of them being a vibrational match. Once a neural net is "turned on" it will generate more of the same kinds of thoughts, reinforcing that specific emotional state—be it DRA-MA or *thriving*.

✳ Giving up the drama of our emotional past is uncomfortable and risky business. We risk not getting our needs met, along with change to our relationships, lifestyle, work. Letting go of who you know yourself to be and allowing a new, higher version of You to come into existence involves the journey of rebirth; just expect there will be "growing pains."

✳ Your brain, your thoughts, your emotions, your life, and your experience are *your* responsibility. Your spirit wants you to be the most authentic, loving, empowered, creative, fully expressed, and actualized version of your human self in the highest possible way. Only you can do this work; no one else can get in there and think the thoughts or make the emotions *for* you.

✳ Part of the solution to the drama addiction is adopting a practice—both in thinking and behavior—of self-love, which is synonymous with self-honoring. This means being kind and listening to ourselves, following our feelings, trusting our intuition, and speaking our truth.

✳ To "treat" the addiction, we need to:

- Take 100 Percent Responsibility
- Identify Your DRAMA Triggers
- Find Alternative Thoughts for Each DRAMA Trigger
- Get Support
- HALT
- Develop State-Breakers
- Prevent Relapse

Application and Integration

The DRAMA "Treatment Plan"

Taking 100 Percent Responsibility

Make the declaration that you are ready to reclaim your power and stop deferring it to others or to the DRAMA. Then practice saying it to yourself daily (in the mirror is best).

Today, I, _____, claim 100 percent responsibility for my life, my thoughts, my choices, my emotions, my energetic states, and my Self.

Write your own declaration in your own words here:

DRAMA Triggers and Alternatives

MY UNIQUE DRAMA TRIGGERS INCLUDE:	ALTERNATIVE THOUGHTS/RESPONSES FOR THIS TRIGGER:
(Example) Running late for a meeting	Everything unfolds in perfect timing
Getting together with my sister	I will be loving and kind no matter what

Get Support

MY SUPPORT PEOPLE ARE:	WHAT MAKES HIM/HER A GOOD SUPPORT FOR ME IS:
Suzie	She is really laid back and listens well
Paul	He always makes me laugh

HALT

I find what makes me most susceptible to DRAMA is:

Hunger/Hormones

Alcohol

Loneliness/Boredom

Tiredness

My solutions to offset drama triggered by HALT *before* it starts include: (Examples)

Keep snacks in my purse/desk drawer/car glove compartment

Call a friend

Power nap

_____

_____

_____

_____

Develop State-Breakers

Strategies that will help me use the 5 D's:

DELAY

DISTRACT

DELAY

DEPART

DANCE

Prevent Relapse
What I can plan in advance to prevent a DRAMA episode from occurring in response to my common triggers:

CHAPTER SIX

Help! I'm Stuck on the DRAMA Station and Can't Switch Channels

"If danger arises in the present moment, there may be an emotion.
There may even be pain. But that's a challenge, not a problem.
For a problem to exist, you need time and repetitive mind activity."

—ECKHART TOLLE

I ruminate. A lot. I can catch my mind a million times each day thinking about the past. Well, technically, that isn't really thinking—it's remembering. But I do it. I imagine alternate scenarios of what could've been or what I might've done knowing what I know now. I rerun conversations; I review and edit my former choices. Come to think of it, I kind of replay my life like a *Choose Your Own Adventure* novel, wondering how the story would've played out differently had I picked "attend the tea party" on page 37, rather than "enter the dragon's lair" on page 96.

Why would I recycle my old experiences mentally and then hope to have different results in the future? It doesn't work that way. Which is why I have to catch my mind and redirect it—constantly—to focus on something more kind, useful, and fulfilling. It's not just while ruminating about the past that I have to do this. It's also when I'm focusing on present-day issues or worrying about the future that I find myself slipping into the patterns of drama thinking. *Sigh.* This is why consciousness is a full-time job.

When it comes to drama thinking, there are a variety of ways it can show up, through various themes, thought patterns, roles, and traps. It is very sneaky at times, appearing to be entertaining or practical. It is cunning enough that it seems to make sense to the linear, logical mind, yet somehow it still just doesn't feel right. Drama thinking will always have some degree of "feeling bad" imbedded in it. But, in a way, that's its job—to make us aware of unmet needs and desires in our lives. If we stop and listen, it is pointing us toward our essential human needs so that we pay attention to them and find effective ways to get them met. If we ignore our needs or try to push through or, worse, buy into the drama, we will continue to perpetuate the same reality over and over and over and over and . . .

Drama thinking leads to drama behavior. Period. (Well, unless it's interrupted and refocused with the state-breakers mentioned in Chapter 5 as part of undoing the addiction—but more to come on that.)

When in full force, with complete lack of awareness, and even during the initial stages of change, the drama of our minds seeps into our language, choices, and actions, and it influences our personal vibration and thereby the sphere of what we attract into our lives. Identifying the general themes and patterns of drama thinking can help us recognize when we've been suckered into going below the line into the lower energetic states. It'll also help us find ways to recover to *thriving* consciousness. Let's take a look.

The DRAMA Thought-Smorgasbord: Step Right Up, Folks! Pick Your DRAMA, Any DRAMA!

"Bondage is—subjection to external influences and internal negative thoughts and attitudes."

—W. CLEMENT STONE

To get us started, here's a quick glance at the general themes or patterns of drama thinking that we'll go through:

TABLE 5

COMMON DRAMA THOUGHT PATTERNS AND THEMES
Objectifying
Superiority and Inferiority
Entitlement
Vanity/Insecurity
Quid Pro Quo
Scarcity
Criticism
Rigidity and Chaos
The Drama Triangle Roles of Victim, Hero (Rescuer), and Villain (Persecutor)

In *The Anatomy of Peace*, the Arbinger Institute authors identify four different thought patterns that I would say inevitably lead to drama behaviors. They involve thinking in terms of being "better than" or "less than" others, of being "deserving," and of having "the need to be seen as" being a certain way. All of these thought patterns stem from a place of woundedness and the need to feel valued. In addition, the authors describe the concept of "objectifying" other people, whereby we render them void of the emotions, needs, and values that make them human, creating a painful state of separation. In the context of drama, when our needs are threatened or going unmet, we will tend to turn other people into "objects" as part of our self-preservation. We fixate exclusively on our own needs and desires and dismiss those of others, especially if they seem to compete or interfere with ours being satisfied.

These patterns are all grounded in the lower levels of drama consciousness and inevitably keep us out of authentic connection with ourselves and with others. Here's a closer look at each theme or pattern:

OBJECTIFYING

When we objectify others, we are not seeing or acknowledging them as human beings, but treating them literally as if they were an object, a *thing*. We will mentally detach ourselves from the humanity of another if our needs are seemingly threatened or if we get caught up in wanting to have "our way." We will then take on the rigid stance of fighting for ourselves first, conveniently ignoring the fact that the other person has valid feelings and values, needs and desires, just like we do. A simple example is when you're in a rush and you just want everyone to get out of your way, assuming your time is more important than theirs. We objectify our family members, our friends, our bosses, employees, and coworkers, treating them with contempt when they are not doing what pleases us. We also objectify on a greater cultural scale with politicians, celebrities, athletes, and models, for example, judging and gossiping as if they were a thing to have at our disposal, rather than a thinking, feeling, living human who is trying to get through life just like the rest of us.

SUPERIORITY AND INFERIORITY

Seeing ourselves as "better than" or superior to others keeps us from seeing the other person's value and what they have to offer. We want to make them "wrong" so we can be "right." It is a dominating stance that is also objectifying, turning people into peons, who are worth less than we are, and ultimately seeing them as disposable.

On the flip side, seeing ourselves as "less than" or inferior to others keeps us from seeing *our own* value and contributing what we have to offer. We put others on a pedestal and downplay our unique contribution and gifts. It is a submissive stance that seeks approval and defers our power and choice to others, rather than claiming our authentic worth and accurately representing our Higher Selves.

Fundamentally, superiority and inferiority are comparison-based thought patterns. When we are comparing ourselves to others in a way that makes us feel badly, we can never win. We only activate anxiety, worthlessness, and arrogance. Like Suzanne Evans says, "Comparison is self-abuse." It's an assault on our Souls, a degradation of our humanity and a subversion of our relationships. When we compare, we are in a state of separation and looking outside to determine our inner worth; this is the epitome of drama.

ENTITLEMENT

Entitled thinking says we have a "right" to something, which will inherently activate a fight-based energy to make sure we "get ours." Falling into thought patterns of being entitled or deserving, we will see ourselves as superior to others, or as being taken for granted, leaving us feeling self-righteous or unappreciated. Again, it will objectify others, creating separation and fueling the stance that we should get privileges or special treatment over others, since we are more valuable or the exception to the rule. When we don't get what we feel we deserve, we will become resentful and untrusting.

VANITY/INSECURITY

Vanity, the "need to be seen as," is another doozy, where we obsess on performance and looks, rather than allow our authenticity to shine through. Our vanity comes from a dominating sense of insecurity and our need to belong and get approval, but it also immediately hinders our authentic connection and keeps us from fulfilling our unique role. When we need to be seen a certain way, we negate vast parts of ourselves that could make meaningful contributions or otherwise have a positive effect. Brene Brown, in her books and popular TED Talks, teaches us about embracing vulnerability in order to foster authentic connection and derive meaning from our relationships. The "need to be seen as" is the *opposite* of this. It keeps our Higher Selves hidden behind the masks we think we need to display to gain acceptance.

QUID PRO QUO

Quid pro quo thinking has two sides to it. It is a way of contingent giving that later demands reciprocity based on the justification "you owe me," rather than giving from pure generosity or genuine care. The flip side is "beholden-ness," thinking we will owe someone for what they give us. This leads us to resist receiving from the fear of becoming trapped. We grow apprehensive of the unknown costs in the form of demands that will display themselves down the road, not knowing whether we will be able to afford it, mentally, emotionally, spiritually, even physically. Contingent giving is an objectifying stance that has us disconnected from others, and seeing ourselves as meritorious. Beholden-ness leads to behaviors that separate us from *ourselves*, as we feel the need to appease someone else because we "owe" them, and if we don't live up to it we will be abandoned or otherwise rejected. We are then giving unwillingly in order to preserve the relationship, stay safe, and guard our sense of belonging. Both sides of the quid pro quo dynamic inhibit authentic relationship as they prevent both freely giving and freely receiving. They generate a cycle of resentment (I did this thing I didn't want to do *for you*) and guilt (you did that thing you didn't want *for me*). This kind of conditional living aborts freedom and thwarts meaningful connection, leading us to seek drama as a means to get our needs met.

SCARCITY

Most drama thinking is scarcity-based. It operates off the belief that there is not enough to go around, and that if we don't "get ours" our needs will forever go unmet and our lives will be threatened. We're always afraid we're going to "run out"—of money, of time, of opportunities, of chances, of love and affection, of whatever would most threaten our particular needs for survival, based on how we view ourselves and maintain our identities. Scarcity, being grounded in the drama consciousness of anxiety and panic, is the foundation for worry and greed, keeping us out of the flow of abundance and blind to all that is inherently available to us.

CRITICISM

Criticism is a way of negatively judging or evaluating ourselves or others as being "wrong." To make the distinction, the word "judgment" tends to get a bad rap because it commonly gets collapsed with "criticism." A judgment is simply an evaluation, a measuring, a differentiation made based on our experiences—a mechanism we need for connection and survival. We humans are always evaluating and checking things out, but when it turns harsh or starts bullying, it's become criticism. Criticism defines things as unacceptable; it "wrongifies" them. Being wrongified will instantly activate our wounds and thrust us into survival mode. When our own drama thinking criticizes ourselves or others, we are again in a state of separation and unable to function authentically from an empowered place.

RIGIDITY AND CHAOS

Rigidity and Chaos are opposite sides of the same coin. Rigidity imposes rules and structures in an attempt to mitigate Chaos. Chaos runs wild to break free from the confines of Rigidity. When we are overstressed, overwhelmed, or triggered into anxiety or worthlessness, we enter into a chaotic state, where we have a hard time focusing, we can't make decisions clearly, and we are flooded with emotions we don't know how to put words to. Then Rigidity comes in to reestablish order, but that usually comes with a kind of forcefulness—driving, bullying, objectifying, and setting a whole bunch of goofy rules that are not really effective. Take the case of wanting to lose weight, for example. When we feel out of control with food (Chaos), we implement a diet plan with very strict rules (Rigidity) that are almost impossible to follow, which makes us throw our hands up in the air and head straight for the nearest Ben and Jerry's—which brings us back Chaos, and then the cycle starts itself all over again. When we are in drama consciousness, we will tend to bounce back and forth between these two stances to try to regain a sense of balance, but we end up spiraling even deeper into the lower energetic states.

THE DRAMA TRIANGLE: VICTIM, HERO (RESCUER), AND VILLAIN (PERSECUTOR)

In 1968, Dr. Stephan Karpman, M.D. brought the world the "Drama Triangle," derived from ubiquitous and perpetual fairy tale themes. He identified the three main roles we step into and put others in when we create relationship drama: the Victim, the Hero (Rescuer), and the Villain (Persecutor). These archetypes offer a unique view of the drama thinking we embody in our interpersonal "transactions" and even in our own internal dialogue.

> **The Victim**—embodies a "poor me," inferior, and helpless or powerless mentality. The Victim needs perpetual rescuing and saving, and relies on others (their designated Hero) to do so. The Victim allows him or herself to be overrun by fear. This fear creates a sort of paralysis through an inability to take action. It compromises decision-making, inhibits effective problem-solving, interferes with a healthy sense of Self, and seeks approval exclusively from the outside.
>
> **The Villain**—is the one doing the persecuting. The Villain mentality is dominated by entitlement, criticizing, bullying, and "shoulding" on others. The Villain works to keep the Victim oppressed, and is fueled by rage, arrogance, and paranoia. What usually goes

unseen is that the Villain is generally operating from some level of shame and self-protection, rather than a mean-hearted desire. The Villain never thinks they are in the wrong; they are just doing what's needed for self-preservation or even to defend another.

The Hero—is the trickiest of these roles, since the Hero appears to be the "good guy." But the drama Hero is not like a firefighter who literally rescues someone from a burning building. The drama Hero tends to have ulterior motives (which are largely unconscious) and is not interested in helping from a purely altruistic stance. The Hero "needs to be seen as" the powerful one, the kind one, the good one, because fundamentally the hero needs to be needed. The Hero therefore indulges and reinforces the Victim's helplessness, from which the Hero selfishly benefits by being needed and having someone dependent on them. This fuels the Hero's self-esteem and sense of belonging, but in unhealthy ways. The Hero tends toward a pattern of superiority, which really emerges from insecurity rather than bravery or unadulterated goodwill.

Interestingly enough, we are all prone to falling into these roles, and revolving around them in our interpersonal relationships, generating drama to no end.

Gain Insight into Where You're At

"There is nothing so terrible as activity without insight."

—JOHANN WOLFGANG VON GOETHE

Sometimes we can get triggered into drama thinking so fast it could blow the panties off a seven-layer-bundled-up Minnesotan in January. We just blare on inside ourselves, with our themes and patterns, in a drama rampage. We remain ignorant to it, unaware of our mental state, believing *that's* what reality is, until it seeps through into our behaviors and we realize that we not only feel shitty, but we're also acting like a royal schmuck-hole.

There are certain feelings and behaviors that can point you to whether you are having drama thinking about a person or a situation. Since these feelings and behaviors are often automatic, they can actually be the first clue that we are having drama at all. Not to worry! This is just what it is to be human and have a brain. Brains get triggered to fire off drama thinking. They just *do*. It's our job to catch it *before* we generate a massive biochemical cascade and the associated emotional state that is hard to recover from, not to mention before we speak out loud or act in ways that impact others and spread the drama. The feeling states and behaviors in the table below offer some examples to clue you in that you are having drama thinking, so you can trace back to determine what thought patterns you're stuck in, and then choose something new to put in their place. When you notice you are feeling or behaving in one of these ways, you can now identify and change the thought pattern causing it.

TABLE 6

FEELINGS RELATED TO DRAMA THINKING	
Worthlessness	Arrogance
Powerlessness	Disgust
Rage	Contempt
Resentment	Impatience
Anxiety	Insecurity
Uncertainty	Pessimism
Distrust	Doubt
Hatred	Envy

TABLE 7

BEHAVIORS RELATED TO DRAMA THINKING

Colluding	Abusiveness/Yelling
Procrastination	People-pleasing
Perfectionism	Approval-seeking
Bullying	Punishing
Passive-aggressiveness	Hoarding
Avoidance/Stonewalling	Sarcasm
Blaming	Glorifying
Complaining	Defensiveness
Gossiping	Contemptuousness

It's Time to Pick a New Thought Pathway (Oh, Yes You Can!)

"When negative thoughts come—and they will; they come to all of us—it's not enough to just not dwell on it. . . . You've got to replace it with a positive thought."

—JOEL OSTEEN

Like in any addiction, you can't just take away the abused substance and call it good. As we'll see in Chapter 10, the Vacuum Law of the Universe just won't allow it. You have to replace it with a healthier alternative, otherwise you're left like a rat in a dead end: no place to go but back into the maze. Any time we leave an empty space, it will automatically fill itself in with the old ways, defaulting back to what's known. So here are some alternative thought patterns that can help shift out of drama and into *thriving*:

TABLE 8

THRIVING THOUGHT PATTERNS AND THEMES

Personify Others

We Can Trust

It's Not Personal

No One Right Way

Values Matter

Be Curious

Create Structure

Acceptance

Give the Benefit of the Doubt

Be Abundance-Oriented

Transparency and Authenticity

Take Personal Responsibility

Attitude of Gratitude

Illumination of Appreciation

PERSONIFY OTHERS

As the opposite of objectifying, *personifying* others helps us connect to their inherent value and worth. It recognizes that other people are human too, with unique values and needs just as valid as our own. It also takes the stance that people are more valuable than things, more important than tasks, and more expansive than what we see on the surface.

To personify others we need to look for the ways we can see the humanness in them. We need to consider how they might feel about things. We need to seek to understand their value system, what's meaningful to them and why that might be. We can imagine their families and loved ones, their laughter, their tears, and we can connect to their humanity in our minds.

A teacher of mine once said, "If we could see the wounds of our enemies, it would break our hearts." When we acknowledge the realness and the tenderness in others, we automatically and instantaneously *thrive* in our internal worlds, which in turn shape our external lives.

WE CAN TRUST

Trusting life is about knowing that there is a perfect timing and a Divine order to all things. It's the thought pattern that reassures us and reminds us that "it's all good"—really. You think you're running late, but actually the other person is too. You're mad that you're hitting all the red lights, but because of that you're averting an accident. You think something bad that happened shouldn't have, but without it the growth could not have been possible. Although there appears to be chaos consuming us, there is an order and a sense to it on a larger scale. It's not necessarily our job to figure it out, but simply to *trust* it and continue on our path.

Trusting others is about having confidence in their Souls and believing they have good intentions. It's also trusting that people are competent and capable. In the Co-Active Coaching model, which is the school I'm trained in, there is a foundational concept that states: "People are Naturally Creative, Resourceful, and Whole." What this means is we don't need to fix anyone, because they're not broken. This is the stance that everyone else (not just us) is precisely who, how, and where they are meant to be—and *not* be. When we don't have to "fix" anyone, we are free to honor them and ourselves, allowing for truly authentic connection.

Start looking for ways you already trust. We all have our wounds, which means we also have our doubts and skepticisms, but there is still a degree to which you already *do* trust life and the people in your world. It may be as simple as beginning with trusting other drivers. I mean, if you get into a car and go out on the streets, you must trust—on *some* level—that other drivers will stay in their lanes and stop at red lights. You can also trust that people will be exactly as *they* are (not how you think they *should* be) which is probably what they've been doing all along. In trusting life you can know that the sun will rise each day and the seasons will change. That's trust! So start with the easy ones and build from there.

IT'S NOT PERSONAL

It's not about you. It's about them. I know it *looks* like it's about you, but that's only because our human brains are self-referential. That's a fancy way of saying we make everything about ourselves. We're simply wired to sort and filter information and experiences based on how it pertains to us. What's more, we want things to be about us because it makes us feel that we matter. The ego digs that level of self-importance. But again, that's from a drama consciousness. Not taking things personally is a way of staying present with ourselves and not getting caught up in OPD—other people's drama. It's also a way to stay out of the line of blame, either self-blame or taking on blame launched by others.

NO ONE RIGHT WAY

Being of the persuasion that there is no one right way to do or be or have anything in this world is an enormously life-honoring stance. When we believe that there is no one right way, it immediately obliterates the option of there being any "wrong" way, which expels criticism before it can enter the room. It makes me okay and you okay. Recognizing that there is no one right way means being fully accepting of all ways, and honoring all people as equally worthy and valuable.

When we notice that we've been criticizing people or "shoulding" on them, it's our cue to think in terms of "no one right way." In our household, between my husband, my stepdaughter, and I, we all have our unique ideas about how things should be organized, cooked, stored, cleaned, etc. I can get really caught up in how things are *supposed* to be, which only causes me angst and gets me looping in my drama thinking. When I can remember that there really is no one right way to do *anything* in life, it gives me a sense of relief and calm (however small), and invites me to respect my family and even learn from their ways. Maybe mine isn't even the *best* way, and thinking in terms of *no one right way* allows me the possibility of finding something better. Having a world full of all different kinds of ways is what makes us effective as a species and gives life a greater range of variety and sense of fulfillment. Imagine *that*.

VALUES MATTER

Our values express our Souls in the human experience. We're born with the essence of them in our spiritual blueprint, as opposed to adopting them during our human development like morals or ethics. They are the things we hold to be *most* important to our sense of fulfillment. Without them, we cannot live effectively in a *thriving* capacity. When our values are violated or "stepped on"—by us or someone else or a certain life experience—we will feel upset, depleted, dispirited. When our values are being honored, we feel alive, joyous, at peace, inspired. Some examples of common values—which can mean different things to different people—are freedom, integrity, joy, humor, fun, connection, peace, love, and loyalty, just to name a few.

In our thinking about ourselves, life, and others, we need to take values into consideration. Many times in our states of drama we have two opposing values that we are trying to meet at the same time, competing with one another and creating a nasty game of tug-o-war within us. For example, we may want to honor our values of both "connection" and "independence" at the same time, and struggle to find a way to express both simultaneously. Acknowledging this, knowing that values matter, helps us become aware of what's happening, which leads to solutions for us to get *both* values honored. That feels good!

When we bump up against opposing values in others, values different than our own, we can also feel the friction of discord. At that point, we need to get curious and look for what the other person's values are and seek to understand how they might want to honor them. We tend to get caught in wanting other people to live by *our* values; but that's *our* job, not theirs. Other people get to have and honor their own values, just like we get to have and honor ours.

Thinking in terms of honoring our unique values is a way of staying connected with our Higher Selves and getting our needs met, which frees up our relationships and gives us more flexibility to be with whatever is showing up in the circumstances of our lives. We can even apply our values to seemingly undesirable situations to make them feel better to us. For instance, I have a value I call "new experiences" that I can access and apply to things that might seem unpleasant—like jury duty. When I think in terms of my value I come up with thoughts like, "I've never done jury duty! I wonder what I'll learn and who I'll meet along the way," which brings me into alignment with my Higher Self. In this way, we can apply our values to all things in life to be DRAMA-free and embody a *thriving* consciousness.

BE CURIOUS

Curiosity may have killed the cat, but it *thrived* the human. Being curious opens up the mind to new types of awarenesses. When we are criticizing and making assumptions, we implicitly do not see the whole picture or understand the full story. Being curious gives us the relief of discovering new insights and it gently counteracts our limited views. While our judgments may determine that someone is "wrong" or making "poor" choices, our curiosity will lead us to think: "I don't know what's really happening for them," or "I wonder what their life experience has been that led them to this opinion or behavior." We can remind ourselves that we don't have the full view of things, and that—by the way—we are not the all-knowing God; it's not our job to know the answers or to solve it or fix it or even figure it out.

We just need to stay present and get curious.

Curiosity will also relieve rigidity by looking at the big picture of things. Rigidity is very narrow focused and curiosity is a brain-opener. Asking questions generates a new state and helps us get out of the spiraling of drama thinking and into more effective levels of consciousness where we not only feel better, but we can also access new possibilities, follow unforeseen paths, and find novel solutions.

CREATE STRUCTURE

When we get overwhelmed by the chaos that life inevitably brings, it's time to shift gears and get organized. An important part of creating effective structure is having a general outline or formation while still maintaining flexibility in order to avoid bouncing into the realm of rigidity. Writing a list, making a plan, setting an intention, analyzing the issue, and creating structure to move forward will alleviate the chaos and empower a *thriving* consciousness. Being overwhelmed is paralyzing; not a whole lot gets done, and if it does, it's not at the optimal level. When we can think in organized, logical, and analytical terms, we can get into useful action and create positive movement.

ACCEPTANCE

A mentality and thought pattern of acceptance is the source of freedom and peace. It's the bridge to being with "what is" without having to make it be different. Acceptance stops the arguing and invites a sense of calm. It's the emotional "chill" station we can turn our dial to. When we argue with life, when we try to control it, we feel pain. When we accept *what is* and allow life to just do its *thang*, we feel peace. The mind is a cunning place, so it's easy to believe our arguments are real and true, which just keeps us in the drama of the fight. Yielding, surrendering, and *accepting* lightens our load and frees up our energy to devote ourselves to more important and effective things, like living out our purpose or simply doing something fun.

Byron Katie, in her wonderful book *Loving What Is,* teaches us that when we begin to question our thinking about things, when we get curious and take personal responsibility for our experiences, we can come to live with great peace in the flow of life. I highly recommend her method called "The Work" (cause it's really *work*) to develop a practice of inquiry into the veracity of our thoughts and gain skills to shift into acceptance. We'll look at more tools for this in Part II of this book as well.

GIVE THE BENEFIT OF THE DOUBT

Giving others the benefit of the doubt is a thought pattern of openness, generosity, and trust. We never really know what's happening inside someone else or what their intentions are, separate from what they display or how they *seem*. We don't really know what drives their decisions or what led them to particular outcomes. Giving the benefit of the doubt allows us to accept and embrace the humanness in others, expecting that their spirit is good and knowing that the human part is just goofy sometimes.

Giving *ourselves* the benefit of the doubt is an equally important thought scheme to embrace. We are just too dang hard on ourselves. It is a way of encouraging and believing in ourselves, which are true elements of self-love. We can remind ourselves that we didn't *mean* to screw it up; we're just mere mortals. We can know our intentions and desires come from a good-hearted place, despite how well we performed or what we produced.

BE ABUNDANCE-ORIENTED

In the natural world, of which we humans are a part, there is an abundance of *everything*. This is the antidote to scarcity drama. There is more than enough to go around. Knowing this influences how we look at the world, and it reminds us that we are safe. We can trust life. One way to think about this is to look literally at nature and see the abundance of leaves on trees, of blades of grass, grains of sand, flakes of snow, droplets of rain, rays of sun. The Universe holds more than enough of *everything* we desire—food, time, love, money, security, fun, work, new experiences—to satisfy us completely. We just need to remember that and consciously connect to the evidence we already have of abundance on the planet.

When I first started my coaching business, while I was still in training, I began by charging a moderate, mid-point sort of rate. Then, once I was certified, I raised it to match what's more standard in the field. The new amount felt so high to me; I didn't think anyone would want to pay it and I got into scarcity-thinking about there not being "enough clients." My husband reminded me of the abundance in the world when he said, "There are more people in this country who can afford your rates than you have time to coach." This refocus on plenty immediately snapped me out of my scarcity mentality and into what is *more* true—there are infinite opportunities and countless people to serve.

TRANSPARENCY AND AUTHENTICITY

Being transparent and authentic about who we are, about our ideas and values, is risky business. It's also the most effective way to live. Imagine not having to hide anymore, but just getting to be *You,* and bringing the world all your gifts and talents as well as your foibles and shortcomings. This takes a willingness to be vulnerable, which takes mega-courage. The truth is, it's how we become more relatable; it's how we connect more deeply with ourselves and others. When we can be honest about ourselves and real with others, letting them actually *see* us, it not only creates a powerful space for intimacy to grow, it's also an invitation to freedom for them as well.

To be really transparent and authentic we have to claim our strengths and own our weaknesses, inside ourselves before all else. We have to evaluate our likes and dislikes and come to know and live by our values. And then we have to trust ourselves and others enough to be willing to bring it all into the relationship. But there's something very gratifying about showing all our cards: it brings relief from having to keep up a poker face to play the game. It opens up space for our Souls to truly *thrive* in our relationships and our work. The world needs us, in all of our uniqueness, to fulfill our role and play our natural part in the greater circle of life. Let's not deprive them by holding it all in!

TAKE PERSONAL RESPONSIBILITY

The first time I heard the concept that our lives are 100 percent our responsibility, I got excited! And then, after a quick second, I got *mad*. I liked the idea of being in control of my world—but I wanted it to include other people. I wanted them to change *for me*. If they would only do what *I* wanted them to do, be the way *I* wanted them to be, *then* I could be happy. But that's not what taking personal responsibility is about (darn it all).

Taking 100 percent personal responsibility for our worlds means knowing that we're creating *the whole thing*. There is nothing outside of our experience that we have not co-created, with the Universe or with other people. And everything we experience meets our needs and desires. *We* did it—we made it, we accepted it, we tolerated it, we invented it, we orchestrated it. When we take responsibility, it means we can actually create something new and different too. We are not victims to the world around us—we are collaborators.

When something undesirable happens in life, the personal-responsibility question to ask is, "What is it in *me* that created this experience?" There is some kind of thought pattern or habitual feeling you have that has generated the energetic match to that experience. Many times for the "bad" stuff we say, "But I would *never* create that! I didn't want it." On some level, you did—and this could be your unconscious "comfort" or familiarity with certain feeling states (remember this from the last chapter?) that need to be activated in order for your physical-emotional system to maintain your unique biochemical homeostasis—even if those aren't the feeling states you think you want.

The good news is that the more we take personal responsibility for our lives, the more authentically empowered we become, and the more we can evaluate what we are encountering from the perspective of being able to influence it. The next question is, "What does this experience lead me to desire?" Think in terms of: What desire or need has to be met? And what will it *feel* like to have that desire or need fulfilled? Discovering alternate ways to meet our needs and generate new feeling states *on purpose* will lead us to create new, more desirable experiences and different, more pleasing realities.

ATTITUDE OF GRATITUDE

Gratitude is a powerful thought pattern that helps us refocus on abundance and on what we have that is already great. It shifts our attention from the negative within our experience to the positive stuff that we already enjoy. Being grateful actually helps us get our heads out of our cute, sassy bottoms and see the beauty in life. Like Abraham says, we can get on a *rampage of gratitude* by focusing on all the things we like and that feel good. We can highlight simple things like our abilities to see, hear, walk, sing, chew, sleep, breathe. The Law of Relativity, which we'll visit further in Chapter 10, reminds us that all things in life are relative and that there is always a "worse than" out there, which can be a powerful access point for finding our own gratitudes.

ILLUMINATION OF APPRECIATION

While gratitude highlights what we perceive to be positive or what already feels good, appreciation is looking for ways to feel good about *anything*. Appreciation takes whatever is happening, good or bad, and uncovers the *value* inherent in it. In essence, appreciation illuminates the silver lining. Most of us, when we experience something we would call "bad," get fixated on the problem of it. Whereas when we can find what there is to *appreciate* about it, we will more quickly feel better about it, which has us more primed to find a solution than when we are kvetching and focused on the negative.

One point to clarify here is that feeling "better" does not necessarily mean feeling "joyous" or "peaceful." It simply means having some relief from the intensity of your negative viewpoint and the resulting emotions. Feeling "better" can be a subtle shift, which is all you need to continue moving in a direction of improvement. One subtle shift after another and you are climbing the ladder of consciousness to go from drama into *thriving*.

To start finding ways to *appreciate* whatever you're in the middle of, begin asking yourself these questions: "What can I appreciate about this?" "What value is available to me in this?" "What are the opportunities I can see in this?" Many times I discover that my appreciation largely has to do with growing and learning about myself, developing my gifts and talents, enhancing certain virtues, and coming to know myself more and more. For example, when I feel "disrespected" by someone, I can appreciate about *myself* that my standard for both respecting others and being respected in my relationships is increasing to higher and higher levels—which was not always the case.

As another example, I got injured in the early part of 2014 and went from training daily for a body transformation challenge to not even being able to walk a block to the store and not being able to carry as much as a handbag. What I found to *appreciate* in this circumstance was: I had a lot less laundry to do without all my workout clothes in the hamper; my schedule had less demands on it without squeezing in time at the gym; I learned that I can rely on healthy eating to maintain my weight in the absence of exercise; I met new people to connect with and enjoy in the process of seeking help with my recovery; and I got to splurge on a new, organic bed and plush pillows!

The "bad" things that happen in life always offer an opportunity for us to more clearly define what we desire, how we want to live, and how to go even more deeply into discovering the essence of Who We Really Are. The more we connect to ourselves, the more we *thrive*.

Tuning to a New Station

"Positive thinking will let you do everything better than negative thinking."

—ZIG ZIGLAR

Getting stuck in the tract of drama thinking is normal. We all do it. That's not the issue. The issue is whether we recover to a *thriving* consciousness before we speak or act, and how quickly that recovery happens. How big is that gap? How much time do we actually spend in the drama zone? Set an intention—right now—to shrink the lag time and shorten that gap. You can recover to your Higher Self with increasing speed and grace. It just takes some conscious focus and a little practice. Oh, and some more tools, which we're coming to. The excellent news is that we *can* change; we *can* tune in to a new station. Decide what that station will be; you have some choices now.

Positive thinking, from a *thriving* consciousness, will let you achieve all manner of feats and live with greater joy, wealth, and ease than your drama mind thinks is possible. It is the means by which your Soul expresses itself in your human form, which is the pinnacle essence of our purpose here on Earth.

Now that you have some insight into what drama is all about, where it comes from, the purpose it serves, how it operates as an addiction, and the themes and patterns that comprise it, it's time to shift into the next level of your personal evolution: Your *Thriving* Life.

Let's go!

"The truth is that you are responsible for what you think, because it is only at this level that you can exercise choice. What you do comes from what you think."

—FRANCES VAUGHAN AND ROGER WALSH

Key Concepts

✳ DRAMA thinking can be simplified into common themes and patterns in order to easily identify where we get triggered and stuck. These include:

- Objectifying—making other people "things" devoid of feeling or values like ours.

- Superiority—Seeing ourselves as better than others.

- Inferiority—Seeing ourselves as worse than others.

- Entitlement—Feeling deserving and that one has a unique "right" to certain things more than other people do. Feeling that people owe us for something we did or gave.

- Vanity/Insecurity—Self-absorption and obsessing about the ways we need to be perceived by others.

- Quid Pro Quo—This is a combination of contingent giving that says "You owe me," and beholden-ness, believing we will owe someone for what they give us.

- Scarcity—The chronic fear of loss or of not having enough.

- Criticism—Negative judgment of self or others as being "wrong" or "bad" in some shape or form.

- Rigidity—The inability to be flexible or to see the big picture accompanied by stringent adherence to rules of any kind, whether effective or not.

- Chaos—Being consumed or overwhelmed by an inability to function or think clearly.

- The DRAMA Triangle Roles of:
    - Victim—Perpetual disempowerment and need for rescuing.

- Hero (Rescuer)—The desire to "save" others fueled by a need to be needed rather than authentic altruism.

- Villain (Persecutor)—The perceived need to defend oneself or another expressed through criticism, contempt, or bullying.

✳ Alternative *thriving* thought patterns include:

- Personify Others—See other people as humans with valid needs and feelings just like you.

- We Can Trust—All things unfold in perfect timing and Divine order, which means it's all good; we don't have to worry so much or fix anything.

- It's Not Personal—Nothing anyone else says or does is about us since they are viewing things through the lens of their own experiences.

- No One Right Way—There are a multitude of ways to see or approach or do most things in life, each holding their own unique value or meaning.

- Values Matter—We each have a unique set of values that are essential to our personal sense of fulfillment and spiritual expression. Honoring our values is our job, not the job of others. Others have their own values to live by that we can appreciate as part of their unique contribution.

- Be Curious—Being curious gives us the relief of looking for insights. It counteracts our limited views and helps to relieve rigidity.

- Create Structure—Making plans or otherwise generating a linear approach to seeing things helps to alleviate chaos.

- Acceptance—Being with "what is" without trying to make it be different invites peace and calm.

- Give the Benefit of the Doubt—Giving the benefit of the doubt invites openness, generosity, and trust toward ourselves and others; people really are doing the best they can with what they've been given.

- Be Abundance-Oriented—There is more than enough of everything to go around in this infinite Universe that has the capacity to meet all our needs and desires.

- Transparency and Authenticity—Keeping it real invites intimacy and facilitates freedom in relationships.

- Take Personal Responsibility—We co-create all things in our lives, and everything we experience meets our needs and desires, conscious or unconscious.

- Attitude of Gratitude—Takes our attention from the negative within our experience to the positive stuff that we already enjoy.

- Illumination of Appreciation—Helps us find value in *what is*, the good and the bad.

✴ Drama thinking is just there. It's part of what brains do. Our goal is to recover to a *thriving* consciousness *before* we speak or act. We can set an intention of shrinking the lag time. With conscious practice and application of new thought patterns, you can recover to your Higher Self with increasing speed and grace.

Application and Integration

Using the tables included in this chapter and referenced below as relevant, identify the following:

DRAMA thought patterns and themes I most easily get stuck in:
(Table 5, Page 109)

DRAMA Feelings I most commonly experience:
(Table 6, Page 116)

DRAMA Behaviors I most frequently engage:
(Table 7, Page 117)

Alternative *thriving* thought patterns and approaches I think will be useful for me:
(Table 8, Page 118)

Ways I will consciously apply these new thought patterns:

PART II

Your *Thriving* Life

"One of the most constant and powerful things I have experienced is the desire to be more than I am at the moment—an unwillingness to let my mind remain in the pettiness where it idles—a desire to increase the boundaries of myself—a desire to feel more, learn more, express more—a desire to grow, improve, purify, expand. This energy within me is seeking more than the mate or the profession or the religion, more even than the pleasure or power or meaning. It is seeking more of me; or, better, it is releasing more of me."

—HUGH PRATHER

CHAPTER SEVEN

Welcome to the
Thriving Paradigm

*"Authentic thriving is living in alignment with one's Higher Self and keeping
pace on the physical plane with the expansion of the Soul."*

—JENNIFER ALLY

Thought-energy creates our lives, and yet how good are we at embodying the energetic levels that manifest the stuff we desire? I mean, we have these pesky brains to deal with and emotions to manage, which isn't always the easiest thing to do. As humans, we can expect that we will get triggered into the drama dynamic simply because it is one of the most basic and well-ingrained programs our brains can run. The good news is we don't have to stay there or act from there.

As the antithesis of drama, *thriving* is keeping pace on the physical plane with one's spiritual expansion, a way of living that naturally and easily yields happiness and joyous life experiences. *Thriving* is experiencing deep fulfillment in all areas of life, while navigating human challenges with self-honoring choices, conscious attentiveness, presence, deliberate joy, and profound gratitude. This is the "expansion of the soul." Here's how it works.

When life's challenges come up and there are things we're unsatisfied with or stuff we don't want, it's actually a positive thing! (Yeah, imagine *that.*) It's a sign that our Soul is expanding into greater possibilities and opportunities. Once we have a desire, the answer or fulfillment of it is created out there in the ethers, first in the amorphous form of our *idea* of the solution. When we discover something we *don't* like, it automatically generates a new concept that we *do* like in the form of our desire, which may even be unconscious at first. The beauty of this process and how it works in our system is that we don't even have to consciously identify the desire; our subconscious minds will do that work for us and the Universe will "hear" it too (just like God hears your prayers even if you don't say them out loud). Since anything we conceive we can achieve, allowing ourselves to move toward the desire on the human plane is keeping pace with soul's expansion.

Most people get stuck, however, on the literal happenings in their current circumstances—the things they don't want—and, blinded by the drama of their dissatisfaction with "what is," they miss the fact that simply having the desire for something different means that something different *is possible.* Once that difference is identified, we either allow the fulfillment of the desire by focusing on it, letting it feel good and believing it's possible, or we maintain a state of resistance by focusing on the negativity of "what is" in the energy of pessimism and doubt, which blocks the new good stuff from coming into our experience by perpetuating the lower energetic levels of drama. *Thriving* is the result of being in the soft state of allowing our desires to come to us by holding the energy of what we want in *belief* and allowing the physical world to catch up—which is the means by which the human life grows along with the soul.

Want to know the secret to how we allow the good stuff in? I'll tell you. By seeking relief and feeling "good," whatever good means in a given moment. Seriously, that's all it takes. Simple. Yet, with these mettlesome brains and our programmed drama, it's not always easy to navigate our feelings or to shift into "feeling good" at will. We have a hard time feeling good in the midst of circumstances that we dislike or that activate our pain. So we need to develop a lifestyle that supports our *thriving*—neurologically, mentally, emotionally—and empowers us to feel good most of the time. To do this, we have to actively shift out of the drama and recover to our Higher Selves, which inhabit the higher energetic levels of *thriving*.

When we revisit the Energetic States of *Thriving* on page 42, we can see that there is a full range of energetic states and emotional capacities that are part of the human experience. The essence of *thriving* is allowing each of these states to process through us when appropriate. True, the lower levels of sub-*thriving* are not necessarily a place of empowerment or pleasure, but we can still engage alignment with our Higher Selves by identifying when these states are warranted because of a current life experience and then *honor* the feelings that come along with them. The goal is to recover to the higher levels, but sometimes we need to baby-step our way in that direction. For example, if you can get from hopelessness up to apathy or fear, you're going the right way! Even though you don't want to remain there, it feels "good" because each ascending level has more energy and provides a sense of relief. We make these baby steps through the process of *allowing*, which is letting the energy flow in order to be processed and integrated in healthy ways, fueling a state of alignment. This is truly what it is to navigate both the human experience and our spiritual beingness simultaneously.

When we bump up against things that have the potential to trigger our wounds, but aren't necessarily immediate threats or emotions that merit "processing," we need to identify the drama for what it is and get the hell out of it, like *yestahday*. This section of the book is designed for you to learn the steps for moving through the levels of sub-*thriving* and drama, develop skills to consistently feel good, and discover how to live *your* life of *thriving* so you can fulfill your greater purpose and have a whole bunch of fun along the way.

GRATE-full Living

In order to live continuously expanding, harmonious, joy-filled lives with ease and flow, we have to become skilled at managing our internal worlds of thoughts, emotions, and motivations. We have already seen how our wounds fuel our drama states, creating an addiction to the cheap thrill we get from fear, discord, and the like. Now what do we do with all this? How do we actually start the shift out of drama into living predominantly in a state of *thriving*? We develop a lifestyle that incorporates a Daily Alignment Practice, and we apply strategies to recover to our Higher Selves quickly and effectively. Moving from drama into *thriving* can be achieved by taking specific steps that comprise what I call GRATE-full Living. This is more than just feeling grateful; it's actually an acronym for a series of stages we pass through to grow and evolve.

One day in the fall of 2013, I was out for a run when the concept of GRATE-full Living came to me. At that time I already knew about the scheme of drama as I am conceptualizing it here, but I hadn't yet identified what to do about it, how to "solve the problem." As I rode my legs along the northeast side of the Mississippi River, overlooking downtown Minneapolis, I was mulling over this question. My mind went through the various stages that made sense to me for how to get out of drama, when about halfway through the five-mile course, I recapped the ideas back to myself and exclaimed aloud, "GRATE-full!" I discovered that the process I had just identified naturally created the acronym, which (if you hadn't noticed) I always find to be a groovy, helpful reminder tool. I got so excited about this revelation, and then, just as quickly, I heard a voice inside me say, "Good. Now just enjoy the rest of your run." What had been highly focused thinking just faded away; I felt something in me relax and I plugged into the present moment to do precisely that—delight purely in the trot of the day.

I'm sure I've had a number of inspired moments in my life, but this is one that really stands out for me. The reason why I'm sharing this story is to offer an example of how life naturally guides us and answers our questions when we are in alignment with our Higher Selves. When we are in a state of joy or calm, untainted by the scratchiness or static of drama thinking, life just flows through us via our thought processes and ideas, intuitions and urges. This is a benefit of living in a *thriving* consciousness. Not only does it feel good, but it also allows us to serve and fulfill our greater purpose—which is really fun! And life is supposed to be *FUN*. Don't buy it if anyone tells you otherwise.

The "GRATE-full" Living flow is comprised of these elements:

- Grieve or Get Out

- Recover

- Align

- Take Action

- Evolve

GRIEVE OR GET OUT

Grieve or Get Out is the initial stage of shifting from below the line and recovering to *thriving*. We need to identify whether there is a negative emotion to honor or whether we are just making up drama fiction in our head that we need to get out of.

Grieve is a word choice that represents the processing of what we would call a "negative" emotion. Distinguishing the true emotion that is activated by our wounds being bumped into or by facing challenges allows us to actually *feel* and process the experience and effectively move through it. *When we name it, we tame it.* This is actually one of the most powerful ways to traverse the drama. Consciously identifying a negative emotion will in and of itself dial down the intensity and generate relief, allowing us to be intentional about how we release the energy, directing it in nontoxic ways. When we avoid the emotion through denial or numbing or arguing, it lingers and seeps into our mental, emotional, and spiritual fabric. This is when the "acting out" of drama ensues, creating damage to ourselves or the people around us.

When negative states arise, there is usually something going on at a deeper level than what the drama chatter allows us to recognize. The drama is a desperate attempt to be in control, but if the underlying energetic state is in the realm of sub-*thriving* there is something deeper that needs to be honored if we want to effectively move through the experience and return to *thriving*. In fact, the energetic states of sub-*thriving* are an essential part of our growth into greater expressions of *thriving*. We *need* them to expand. Emotional wounding of any kind requires literal, physical healing, just like a broken leg. When we experience a hurtful event, micro-damage occurs in the brain that requires the standard process of repair through clearing out damaged tissue and replacing it with growth factors that facilitate the development of new, healthier, and more effective neural connections. During this breakdown and rebuild process, the affected area of the brain will become inflamed and tender, just like any other injury. Pain will ensue as a protective mechanism *to allow the healing process to run its course*. We will be hypersensitive to "touch" on that area, and we even need to shut our systems down in order to conserve energy that's necessary for the wound healing. When we allow this process by taking it easy on ourselves, tending to the pain and feeling the emotions at a deep, honoring level, the old neural connections that may no longer be useful can get the upgrade they need to improve our functioning as we move forward. This is the essence of what's called "the breakdown before the breakthrough." However, if we try to brush past it and avoid or numb the feeling, we directly disrupt the healing and the growth available to us.

Allowing the emotions is like doing the physical care and getting the rest needed to heal a broken leg. By applying patience and attentiveness, the ingenious nature of our bodies will take care of the healing process for us. Resisting the emotions is like trying to run on that broken leg, toughing it out, and pretending it's just fine. It'll not only keep us from healing, but is likely to re-injure us, exacerbating the damage and pain of the original wound. This is what happens in the energetic states of drama. Wound healing is denied. There is breakdown, but no chance for the breakthrough that would take us to the next level of our personal evolution. The GRATE-full step of **grieve** is how we *allow* the feeling of the pain, which means we are releasing toxicity and developing the new resources we need to grow into Higher versions of ourselves.

For Bepa's eighty-ninth birthday, our family—her kids—planned a big birthday party for her. Invites went out, a DVD of her life story was made, food was ordered, balloons and special T-shirts were procured and distributed. The whole bit. I told a Family Member (who we'll call **FM**) that I would bring the cake, happy to contribute because I knew a bakery that made heavenly carrot cake, which is Bepa's favorite. Within minutes I received the first of a very mean series of text messages asserting something about how I was trying to control everything. I don't recall verbatim what all the messages said, but I can tell you they were blaming, accusing, and instantly upsetting—and all over the fact that I wanted to bring a cake. Although I knew it was not really personal, and even though I was able to see the woundedness of the other person and access compassion for FM, I still felt very hurt myself. Now, to give you the picture of this relationship, FM was a favorite family member of mine who I always completely loved and adored (still do) throughout my whole childhood, who also cared for me in times when I needed it. So the text-accusations, the rejection and the not-being-understood or seen for the truth of who I am was particularly painful. Over the following days I found myself getting into a lot of drama thinking about it. I would have full-blown arguments with FM, and then finish brushing my teeth. I would be the Hero and rush in to "save" FM from what I perceived to be depression, and then I'd realize I passed my highway exit. After several of these conversations *in my head*, I realized I was not really allowing myself to feel the true emotion. My drama was distracting me from honoring the deep sadness that I *really* felt about the whole thing. It wasn't about a cake or the texts or what FM was doing; it was a sadness, an actual grief in this case, about losing the relationship we once had. It was about my powerlessness and hopelessness in the scenario, because nothing I could say or do would really make a difference. I could stand in love and compassion all I wanted, but I couldn't *make* FM accept it from me. Once I had the light bulb moment about this, I began to sob. I dove straight into the pain, instead of dancing around it, and in doing so I allowed the emotion to move, process, and become something new. I didn't exactly time it, but I would guess that the crying lasted about ninety seconds or so. Really, it wasn't that long. Now, this is not a reflection of the depth of my sorrow, but rather an indicator of how quickly we can recover once we stop the mental arguing and just honor the feeling. In letting go of my arguments and honoring myself, I opened up a soft space *inside me* to allow a new interaction with FM. When I saw FM at the birthday party, I was not carrying resentment or pain about the situation, which I believe is what allowed FM to offer me an apology, in FM's own way, which I didn't really need but was nice to receive.

When we find ourselves in the insecurity, anxiety, or defensiveness of a situation, we need to hit the pause button and ask ourselves, "What's this drama really about?" (or some variation of this question) and see what the brain comes up with for an answer. Once the root emotion is identified, we can honor the feeling of whatever is going on. The founders of the Co-Active Coaching Model led a workshop in Minneapolis a few years ago, where they introduced me to the concept that "(E)motion" is just "Energy in Motion." I like this way of thinking about our feelings as just energy. That's all they are. They represent a part of ourselves that wants to be honored. Too often we shy away or avoid them altogether, but that only makes matters worse. When we can **grieve** and process them, releasing the negative energy in healthy ways, we open the door to recovering to the *thriving* consciousness of our Higher Selves.

Now, sometimes we get caught in our drama thinking when nothing is really happening, but we are mentally recycling memories or fabricating stories that we need to hurry up and just **get out** of. There is no emotion to process, 'cause it's all cockamamie bullshit. We start making up crap because of something that triggered our wounds, but there's nothing *actually* going on in the moment.

Not long after my stepdaughter Kari moved in with us in August 2014, she told me her mom wanted to have my email address, since Kari would be with us full time, which certainly made sense to me. Terrence and I had been married for over three years already and in that time I'd only ever seen him talk to Kari's mom on the phone *once*, so it was definitely a first for me to interact with her. I believe it's in the best interest of the kids when *all* their parents can have healthy, drama-free interactions, so I sent her mom an email to establish contact.

In that same conversation, Kari and I were discussing the schedule for the school year and vacations. I was asking her what she thought she would want to do for the holidays and she told me her aunt, my husband Terrence's sister on the East Coast, invited Kari, her sister, *and their mom* to Thanksgiving. This news caught me by surprise, since we had also been invited to Terrence's sister's for Thanksgiving—and I did not anticipate sharing that with his ex-wife, whom I'd never met or interacted with. Given some unique family circumstances during that time, it was a perfectly appropriate invitation on my sister-in-law's part, but regardless of my brain knowing that, it still activated my abandonment wound, in particular. I told Kari that sounded lovely for her, which I authentically meant and believed it would be. Then I excused myself to go out for a bike ride.

You know what happened next. Yup. Drama. Hit me like a *BAM*. I was halfway through the ride when I realized I was building a case for my worthlessness and disposability—*I'm not as important 'cause I'm not the real mother of the children.* I don't need to elaborate on that one any more, but there was a whole soliloquy with this theme; I can dunk myself right into a vat of "inferiority" in a heartbeat. When I woke up and realized I was wasting a perfectly good bike ride on an absolutely gorgeous autumn afternoon, I knew I had to break the state and **get out** of the drama—because nothing was actually happening! I was making it all up in my head.

I pulled out one of my tools and asked myself, "What if the kids' mom is one of the nicest people I could ever meet? What if she could become a friend, but I let myself miss it by cooking up drama that I don't even know is true?" In asking the questions, I created a new image of her (a total stranger) in my mind, while aligning with my Higher Self, which dispelled the drama and got me back into the present moment to finish my ride, enjoying my healthy body, the nature in my surroundings, and the beauty of the day. Since I did not indulge the drama and was able to recover to that soft space *inside me,* I literally allowed a new external experience to unfold. When I got home I had received an incredibly kind and warm email from Kari's mom, stating that she heard great things about me from her kids and that she believed Kari was in good hands with Terrence and me. Amazing.

Now, you can see that this case is very different than my scenario with FM. In that story, there really was something "happening" in text exchanges that warranted an emotional processing. In the drama of the *potential* Thanksgiving plans (which, comically, never ended up transpiring) there was nothing happening "to me," no actual occurrence that required me to **grieve** or process any emotions; it was a clear case of **get out** of the drama. In the past, when I was more drama-prone and in an active **grieve** stage of life in general, I would've really dug into it and gone to drama-hog heaven, to the point of crying, raging, and pleading with the outer world to acknowledge me and reaffirm my worth. Knowing what I know now, and having the skills to recover, I can make the distinctions. You can start this process too. As soon as you recognize you're in a negative mental pattern, recycling old issues or caught in a story, hit the pause button and ask yourself, "What's this drama really about?" See if there is an emotion to process or if you'd be better off to just **get out** of it altogether, to **recover** right away.

RECOVER

Recovering is about getting grounded in the present moment and returning to our center, which buoys us up to the threshold of *thriving* consciousness. Willingness is a solid crossover point to work with because it is reasonably tangible. The only thing required is being open to seeing things differently. From there you can more effectively evaluate what the drama says about what's needed and desired. This will be your guide for whatever changes need to be made or actions need to be taken.

In my story about FM, once I processed the sadness in the **grieve** step, I was able to **recover** to my center and access a place of acceptance about the whole thing. As a result, I let go of needing anything from FM. I could reflect consciously and be choiceful about what would be both self-honoring and respectful of the relationship.

In the would-be Thanksgiving story, there was no authentic emotion to process or **grieve**, so I had to be intentional about using a specific tool to **recover** and not miss out on my present-moment experience. In that case, I was knee-deep in the quicksand of drama thinking and just had to hurry up and **get out**.

In a recent coaching session with a client this topic came up about when to **grieve** and then **recover**, and when to just **get out,** skip the drama, and go straight to **recover**. My client, in her infinite wisdom, stated, "I think that one I feel in my heart, and the other is just in my head." When there is something of the heart, something deeply moved or touched, the emotion *must* be honored and processed in order for it to shift and resolve. On the contrary, when the feeling is being stirred by mental chatter, it's a solid sign that we're being seduced by drama, in which case we have to **get out** and **recover**, like ASAP.

It is essential to **recover** and get into alignment with your Higher Self *before* taking action. Any action taken from a state of drama or even sub-*thriving* will not be as effective or fulfilling as action taken from the energies of *thriving*. This can be applied to all things in life, whether it is working on a project, engaging with family, connecting with friends, giving a presentation, participating in a sports match, whatever. **Recover** from the below the line states *first*. Your brain will work better, it'll be easier, and you'll have more fun. If you're already in the middle of doing something and find that you're starting to dip below the line, hit the pause button, step away, and do what it takes to get back into *thriving*. It might be using one of the techniques in this book, or it could be something completely different that you figure out by answering the question, "What do I feel like right *now* that will help me **recover** to feeling good?"

ALIGN

Next we **align,** which means we authentically connect to our Higher Selves marked by any kind of feel-good state, such as: calm, contentment, curiosity, joy, appreciation, love, harmony, etc. This is more than just coming back into balance when we **recover**; it's a step further into genuinely feeling good and moving into the higher realms of *thriving* consciousness: Contentment, Curiosity, Reverence, Harmony. My colleague-friend Nova Wightman, whom I would call an "alignment specialist"—she's truly an expert on the matter and a master of the process—says her checkpoints for whether she's in alignment are if she feels: "good, calm, and clear." She said if all three are *not* present for her then she's not fully aligned. I would build on that idea to highlight that if one or two of the three are present, in that moment she is still in **recover** mode, in the process of moving back into alignment. "Feeling good" can range in attributes from being quietly content all the way up to feeling ecstatic, excited, or exhilarated. For me, alignment has a quality of being grounded "in my body" in the present moment, along with a sense of peace and joy.

The energy of alignment will give you access to guidance from your Higher Self—received as intuitive urges or inspired ideas—and provide the most powerful platform for taking highly effective action and being in authentic connection with others. I would say that after my **grieve** and **recov-**

er moments with FM, I was able to **align** so that once we saw each other at the party I could show up in a really loving way, regardless of how FM was behaving, which of course allowed for the apology from them and a more calm stance within me.

TAKE ACTION

Once we **align** we will inherently be inspired toward some sort of action. The action that is fueled by the alignment with our Higher Self will yield highly effective outcomes, and it will *feel* effortless, which is part of the fun. This is what it is to *thrive*; it is the action that we take from the place of alignment that allows our human experience to keep pace with our Soul's expansion. The action could be related to family, friends, work, physical health, travel, hobbies, managing physical environments—a variety of things. When we **take action** based on the guidance we receive—which we determine by identifying what would feel good or be self-honoring in any given moment—we can't help but live out our life purpose, even when taking small incremental steps. When we are aligned we are in the higher levels of *thriving* consciousness, so any action we feel an urge or a calling to do will be fulfilling. In this state, the action itself is easy and fun; it flows naturally and inevitably creates desirable outcomes, which can show up in a number of different forms. Being in alignment can also call us to *no* action, which—when it feels good and self-honoring—can be just as fruitful simply because we maintain a high vibration when we follow what*ever* feels good. It's the quality of the energy we bring to what we do that counts when it comes to creating the lives we desire. Sometimes less is more; slow is fast. The key is to follow the flow of whatever our energy is leading us to do in each moment by way of how we feel and to **take action** from the *thriving* energies as much and as often as we can.

EVOLVE

When we **evolve**, we grow with the new experience that results from **taking action**. We have now reached a new "next level" of our expansion and development, which is what life is all about. We are growing into who we are capable of becoming, and we establish a new normal. **Evolve** has its own "challenge," for lack of a better term, which is to settle into the new normal and let it become comfortable. I have a client who has just recently made the big leap out of an old, long-term level of existing and operating, and into a more self-honoring, life-affirming way of being. She keeps saying, "It's so weird. I mean, it's *good*, but it just feels strange." We do have to let the new level of *be*ing settle in, like letting the cake cool before adding the layers of frosting. After a while, from this new normal there will be another level to come, which we'll be invited into through more life experiences. We will always discover new stuff that poses a potential for drama or that takes us back into sub-*thriving*. Life will automatically lead us again to **grieve** or **get out**, **recover**, **align, take action,** and then on to more realizations and new desires. This is life's way of facilitating the deep growth that we are here for, leading us to **evolve** to the next new level, which will only be better and better. **Evolve** is always an upgrade, and then you get used to it, and you go through the process to **evolve** again.

In 2013, my husband and I sold our house. It was a house I had bought around the time we met, and it eventually proved not to be an "us" home. After a few years it made sense to sell it and go to something new. Part of the impetus for this was the lack of an attached two-car garage that the Minnesota winters warrant, and also not wanting the upkeep that a property requires. My husband is not one of those who enjoys house projects, and there are certain things I'm just not skilled at doing. So we moved into an apartment. Now, when we found this place, I fell in L-O-V-E. We live on the top floor of a brand-new ten-story building, facing southeast, with a wraparound balcony and lots of sunlight streaming in. Our view is amazing, overlooking a park and the downtown Minneapolis skyline. It feels like living in the penthouse—totally luxurious.

Coming into this apartment emerged from **taking action** from an **align**ed space that felt exciting and compelling, which made finding the new digs flow naturally. Now, in **evolve**, we have gotten used to the view, the lifestyle, the pleasure of underground heated parking, the on-call maintenance folks, and the basic perks we enjoy here. As we get used to it, we also become aware of things that we *don't* like about it, so new preferences or desires crop up. It's like this in life: we follow our bliss into new experiences and discoveries, and once we settle into each higher level of *be*ing we are naturally called to **evolve** to the next level beyond that. Said differently, as we experience the contrast of what we don't like versus what we would prefer, we are given the opportunity to expand into the new next level of *be*ing, which allows the fulfillment of our desires. This is why there are always new things to be aware of that would make living feel better, so we stretch to reach for them. In that process we **evolve.**

Time, the Endless Idiot

In applying the GRATE-full Living process to move through drama, don't worry yourself with the question, "How long is it gonna take?" This process is the essence of life itself, G-R-A-T-E, G-R-A-T-E, G-R-A-T-E . . . life is full of it; you will do this over and over again, many times. The steps that make up GRATE-full Living will inherently vary in their duration, depending on their stimulus and what other factors are involved. A step can define a life phase, where the primary purpose and processing needed during a period of weeks or months is precisely what's necessary to learn and grow at that level. Within a life phase, we can still fluctuate and move through the steps for shorter durations, as illustrated in the image on the next page.

Something to note is that this process is not always linear over the course of a lifetime; we can experience a period that's characterized predominantly

GRATE-Full Living Timeline

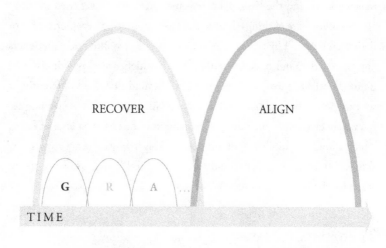

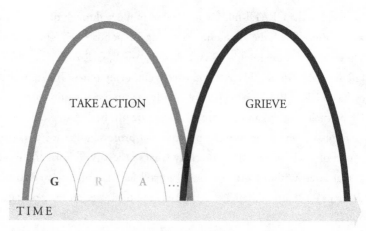

by **taking action** and then have an experience like the loss of a loved one, for example, that launches us into a period of **grieve** where we have to continuously process emotional states as they fluctuate and writhe about in our systems. This is not a bad thing, and it doesn't mean we are going backwards (we couldn't even if we wanted to), but there is growth and expansion to be harvested in that particular way at that particular time. We can still move through the GRATE-full Living micro-steps, even though the wider range of time in **grieve** is marked by the processing of the emotions of loss and separation.

Regardless of the step we are in, we always just are where we are. As we **grieve–recover–align–take action–evolve** on a daily, moment-to-moment basis, we develop at deeper and more expansive levels, growing and keeping pace with the expansion of our souls.

Everybody Gets to *Thrive*!

Living in the *thriving* paradigm, with authentic joy, is our birthright. We all have the capacity for it and access to it. *Thriving*, however, requires courage—the courage to heal and return to wholeness, the willingness to change, the bravery to evolve into a new level of *be*ing, shedding an old identity and taking on a new one, which is the scariest part of all. It means letting go of our habituated drama states, our convenient roles, and the familiar ways we use to get our needs met. It involves practicing new skills and ways of thinking about ourselves, our work, our communities, and our planet. It may not be something that everyone is ready for or even desires, but for those of us who are, we need to lead the way, pave the path of what's possible for our world as a whole. It is the most fulfilling, gratifying way to live.

Drama gives us a cheap thrill and just begs for more of what we don't want. Learning to *thrive* DRAMA-free will be one of the most important and impactful investments you can make in your life and personal development. *Thriving* gives us an authentic power, through joy, love, peace, and the consciousness of the higher energetic states. It brings us into the truth of Who We Really Are and allows us to experience the authentic thrill and excitement that life is really designed to be for us. Join me on this journey! It's so much fun! Let's look now at the elements of the DRAMA-Free Life-style, so you can get rockin' and rollin' on your way to living in alignment with your Soul and enjoying a fun, easy, and wealthful life!

*"We should deemphasize our quest for happiness that is dependent on external circumstances, and instead redirect our commitments to an **internal joy** that cannot be plucked from our grasp by the vicissitudes of life."*

—DR. MARIO MARTINEZ

Key Concepts

✳ Thoughts shape our emotions and our energetic states, creating our life experiences.

✳ *Thriving* is experiencing deep fulfillment in all areas of life, while navigating human challenges with self-honoring choices, conscious attentiveness, presence, deliberate joy, and profound gratitude. This is keeping pace on the physical plane with the "expansion of the soul."

✳ There is a full range of emotional states and energetic capacities that are part of the human experience. The essence of *thriving* is allowing each of these states—including the lower levels of sub-*thriving*, such as grief, fear, or anger—to process through us when appropriate.

✳ When life circumstances trigger our wounds but aren't necessarily immediate threats or emotions that merit "processing," we need to identify the drama for what it is and find healthy ways to resolve it and recover to the higher energetic states of *thriving*.

✳ GRATE-full Living is a series of steps we take to process emotions, grow, and maintain alignment with our Higher Selves. It is an acronym for:

- Grieve or Get Out—Grieve represents the conscious processing of what we would call a "negative" emotion. It involves identifying and actually *feel*ing the true emotion, then directing the release of the energy through self-honoring, kind means of expression. Get Out is the alternative when there is no true emotional experience to process, but the drama is stirred up from disempowering stories and ruminations that are not relevant to current circumstances.

- Recover—Recover is the step of getting grounded in the present moment and returning to your center, feeling a sense of relief, coming back into the levels of *thriving* consciousness. The crossover energy is Willingness, which empowers the shift to the higher energetic states of *thriving.*

- Align—This is the step where we authentically and deeply connect to our Higher Selves in a *thriving* consciousness. It is generally found in the energetic states of Contentment, Curiosity, Reverence, and Harmony.

- Take Action—Getting into meaningful and inspired action (which could be *in*action) from the place of alignment, allowing our human experience to keep pace with our Soul's expansion.

- Evolve—Growing with the new experience that aligned action takes us into, reaching a new "next level" of expansion and development, growing into who we are capable of becoming, and establishing a new normal.

✳ The steps that make up GRATE-full Living vary in their duration, depending on the various factors involved. A step can define a life phase, where the particular stage provides what's necessary to learn and grow at that level. Within a life phase, we can still fluctuate and move through the steps for shorter durations.

Application and Integration

For me, *thriving* is like:

For me, sub-*thriving* shows up in these ways:

How I can identify when I need to **get out** of DRAMA versus **grieve** in sub-*thriving* to honor and process the emotion:

Ways I can apply the steps of GRATE-full Living are:
Grieve or Get Out

Recover

Align

Take Action

Evolve

CHAPTER EIGHT

The DRAMA-Free Lifestyle

"We are what we repeatedly do. Excellence, then, is not an act but a habit."

—ARISTOTLE

Living a human life is an elaborate business. Yet it's really designed to be quite simple. Our job is to follow what *feels good*. Period. The key to a *thriving* life is to manage our internal states so we feel good most of the time, and when we don't, to know how to recover to feeling good when we feel bad. When we feel good, it's a sign that we are in alignment with our Higher Selves, in the strength and truth of *thriving* consciousness. When we feel bad, it's a sign that we are out of alignment and need to recover. "Feeling good" can take on many meanings, as it will vary depending on what we are facing at any given moment. Feeling good is not just found in joy or elation or pleasure. It can also be in the conscious release of sub-*thriving* energy found in screaming, punching a pillow, or crying. That kind of choiceful relief will allow the emotions to move and thereby facilitate the recovery to better-feeling states. We just need to take one step at a time in the direction of feeling good; it does not have to be done in one fell swoop or momentous leap. Baby-step it, baby.

Every time we experience variation in life—as change, divergence, or simply stuff we don't like—we have the opportunity to resist it *or* to expand and grow with it. Living the expansion is generally a lot more fun and rewarding, but to do so we need to learn to manage our thoughts and our energetic states. The reason for this is because our energetic state determines the quality of our vibration, which in turn influences the kinds of experiences we attract. To effectively fulfill our desires, we must first emit the vibrational match that puts us on the same wavelength with them; feeling good will tell us we are a match. Then Law of Attraction will just do its thing to bring us solutions. When we fixate on the unwanted, generating the states of drama, we just get more of the unwanted. Again, Law of Attraction doing its thing. Whatever energy is dominant in our vibration will draw to us people and experiences that match it.

Ergo, to live a fruitful, productive, and fun life, we need to create a lifestyle that facilitates our alignment with our Higher Selves on a daily basis. Unfortunately, most of us did not learn how to live this way while growing up, so we need to retrain our brains, revising the ineffective thought habits of our drama themes and patterns. There are certain specific practices we can adopt to prime the brain for living more above the line and recovering more quickly when we get triggered into drama. In case you were wondering, this is not a one-time schtick, folks. Like, we wouldn't brush our teeth once and call it good for the month or the year. We know we have to clean them *daily* or we will build tartar and get cavities, not to mention stinky breath (eww). Similarly, we don't expect our physique to transform in one session with a personal trainer or even one month at the gym. To have a healthy, fit body we have to move it and exercise it on a consistent, long-term, ongoing basis. To enjoy personal physical hygiene we have to shower, floss, brush teeth, and so on, *daily*.

So it is with our emotional and spiritual selves: they need hygiene too. *Daily*.

Enter: The Daily Alignment Practice

"Like any natural force, gravity pull can work with us or against us . . . we can use the gravity pull of habit to create the cohesiveness and order necessary to establish effectiveness in our lives."

—STEPHEN COVEY

We need certain types of care each and every day in order to operate at maximum potential. Physically, we need fuel, rest, and activity. We need stimulation and novelty mentally, love and peace emotionally, and connection and purpose spiritually. These are continuous needs that require tending to, and when we don't tend to them, we suffer and cannot fly at full throttle. Most of us do a kickass job at taking care of one or two of these areas, but can fall into the pattern of neglecting the others. Perhaps we never learned to think about how to care for our whole system, comprised of these four essential components, or maybe we just didn't know what to do to maximize them. When it comes to having a full, *thriving* human experience, there are certain practices we can adopt to be sure we have all bases covered. I do these myself each day and I require my clients commit to at least forty consecutive days of these practices as well, aiming to evolve them into habits that just become a part of life, like brushing their teeth or taking a bath.

Living a DRAMA-free lifestyle becomes easy when you cultivate a conscious Daily Alignment Practice. This is a compilation of practices for brain, heart, body, and spiritual self-care, including:

- Meditation
- Journaling Gratitudes and Appreciations
- Acknowledging "Miracles, Magic, and Manifestations"
- Asking Constructive Questions
- Spending Time in Nature
- Body Movement

- Diet of Whole and Brain-Power Foods
- Connecting to Universal Energy through a Personal Invocation

MEDITATION

Meditation serves several purposes. It's a means of feeding one's spirit. It provides some relief from the barrage of drama thoughts, the drive to solve problems, the busyness of the checklist, and the consumption of the task-oriented world. It gives us some rest and reprieve. It allows us to just sit back for a moment and reset. It's a way of tuning in and listening to one's spirit. It can also be a way to set the tone for the day and come into alignment with our Higher Self before going into the onslaught of modern life.

There are a lot of methods for meditation out there, with mindfulness meditation being among the most popular right now. Personally, I run the gamut in my approaches. I've done the kind of meditation where I stare at a specific picture or fix my gaze on a candle flame. I've meditated with my eyes closed and "watched" my thoughts—well, until I jumped into the whirlpool with them and caught myself swimming around (or drowning) and had to crawl out again and just "watch." Sometimes I bring daydreaming into my meditation, or a question I want to have answered. I have an internal team of personal "allies," which are character representations of different thought patterns or virtues that serve my connection with my Higher Self. I will frequently engage with them while I am in meditation. Other times I focus on my physical body in the present moment and intentionally generate feeling states that represent where I want to go, like feeling "rich" or "compassionate" or having a solid sense of certainty. I generally complete my meditations with an invitation to my Angels and Guides to travel with me throughout my day or as I go into my dream state at night and give me all that I need to feel good, self-honor, and serve or connect with others in the most meaningful ways. I also ask for good parking spots and the best tables in restaurants. (Hey, I'm already in there connecting with them, so I might as well put in my order.)

Like with most everything else in life, there is no one right way to meditate. The ultimate goal is to come into alignment with your Higher Self and to give the drama brain a rest. It's also to unplug from all the stimulation of interaction with others, performance demands, and the incessant implanting of ideas from others' brains and belief systems on how we "should" be. Meditation allows us the space for communion with the Divine that resides within us. That Divine essence can manifest in the imagination in myriad ways, so it's important to remain open to how the communications can come through. Spirit frequently works through the right hemisphere of the brain, which specializes in imagery, music, color, metaphor, and most emotions. Then the left hemisphere uses logic and language to help us decode it so we can get human-level application. This is how the Divine can work with our human hardware system, and it's where Higher wisdom comes from. Meditation empowers this connection and communication, so we can "hear" the message and "get" it and then know what to do with it. It helps our hemispheres work together more cohesively, and empowers our Higher Selves to guide us and lead us in the direction of our purpose, which will always feel joyous and good to us in a self-honoring way.

JOURNALING GRATITUDES AND APPRECIATIONS

The written component of the Daily Alignment Practice involves a focus on what we're grateful for and/or what we can find to appreciate, which are two distinct things. The focus on gratitudes involves finding things that you already feel good about, things in your world that you are thankful for. Appreciations can also fit into this category, but they go a step further to take your mind into the discovery of the silver lining. Appreciations connect us consciously with the *value* inherent in anything. Usually the things we are grateful for are things that make us feel good or that we like, that give us fun or pleasure. We are rarely grateful for the breakup or getting fired or having a disturbing diagnosis. But the Law of Polarity promises a gift in all "bad" things or undesirable circumstances. The gift in the breakup was the freedom to discover more of your Self. The gift in getting fired was the chance to invest your time and energy in a new, more promising endeavor. The gift in the diagnosis is the ability to inspire others and connect more profoundly with the experience of life. These "gifts" are accessed or identified when we can find what to appreciate.

I recommend my clients simply start with the phrase, "What I can appreciate about _____ is _____." If that's too big a leap, just start with the question, "What can I appreciate about this person/circumstance?" Then just sit with it. Your brain will probably scream, "Nothing!" But that's what brains do. So just wait a little longer. Keep asking the question. Eventually you will find something, however small. When you do, hold it for at least sixty-eight seconds. This will empower you to ride that thought-wave to the next better-feeling thought that will help you move through **grieve** and get you flowing in the direction of **recover**, then **align**, **thrive**, and gradually into **evolve**.

We make this a daily habit to help train the brain to automatically identify what we're grateful for and to easily find the value in the less-desirable occurrences of life. Putting it all onto paper helps to solidify the new neural connections that will lead us to reach and maintain alignment with our Higher Selves. Eventually, with daily practice, we won't be triggered by the same ol' "bad" stuff, because we will immediately know there's a gift waiting. Imagine what life would be like if the "bad" stuff actually made you feel excited for the new "good" stuff that's coming!

ACKNOWLEDGING "MIRACLES, MAGIC, AND MANIFESTATIONS"

Here is where we get to the fun stuff: the recognition of the Universe's fulfillment of our desires. When we are working within the energies of *thriving*, our wishes are in fact *already* fulfilled. It's our job to recognize them and acknowledge them. They are the evidence that we are creating the life we want and that our focused attention on feeling good and GRATE-full living are delivering us yummy, juicy fruits.

Acknowledging the little miracles, magic, and manifestations is really identifying the "coincidences" in life and the unexpected gifts we receive. If what we focus on expands, then seeing the evidence of our inner work in the outer world just brings us more of it. It also helps our logical brains see how randomly and non-linearly the world of energy works. It reinforces the concept that "the how is not up to us." Our job is to live life, feel good, and then receive what we desire. When we give some spaciousness to the process (*ahem*, that means *not* trying to control it), we *will* receive, even if it isn't exactly in the form or the manner we thought we would.

In the fall of 2014, I was invited to a fashion show put on by a friend of a friend. That evening I was driving in from out of town and did not have time to stop home to change. So like any good party girl, I brought my sassy black dress and my little clicky heels along and I changed in the car. What I forgot was lotion for my pasty-dry legs. Yech. I just hoped no one would glance south before I could get to my girls, one of whom I was sure would have lotion to share. When I got into the restaurant where we met for pre-show drinks and apps, no one—not one of the six other women there—had lotion. Seriously? But, okay, whatevs. I just let it go and then hoped for dark lighting at the event. When the time rolled around to move on to the show, we walked down the street to the venue and checked in with our tickets at the entrance. Since I had pre-purchased online in advance, I was escorted over to a side room to pick up my *unexpected* gift of a swag bag. Too cool for school! But you want to know what was even cooler? The swag bag had just what I needed, wanted, was asking for—body butter cream. *Bam!* Thank you, Universe!

That's a great example of a "miracle, magic, manifestation." It was something I wanted. It was not delivered by a source I expected it to come from. I did not stress, fret, or kvetch about it. It *still* came, in perfect timing and Divine order. As a bonus, it was *mine*, not just a borrowed dollop, but my own pretty jar of Gold Body Butter. I was grateful for it, certainly. I appreciated the receiving of it. But it was the *surprise*, the not expecting or knowing how it would come, that distinguishes it from being a "gratitude" or an "appreciation."

ASKING CONSTRUCTIVE QUESTIONS

If there is this all-powerful Universe, and we are co-creators within it, extensions of it, how do we get this stuff we want? Well, we *ask* for it. Constructive Questions are the way we "put in our order" with the Universe, collaborating and co-creating with a specific positive focus on what we want to receive or experience. We just ask and then—here's the key—*don't* try to answer them. Just leave them alone. Ask and walk away. Pose and let it go. It's the job of the Universe to figure out "how," not yours. Your meddling mind will only muck things up. Ask and then stay open to receiving by keeping yourself in a good-feeling zone, emitting the vibrational match to your answer or solution.

As seen in the fashion show story, while in the midst of my super-chick-phone-booth moment (which means changing from my daytime visit-Grandma-gear into my hot-sassy-party-girl attire in the car), I was asking, "Where will I find the lotion I need for these all-out legs?" I had no clue where it would come from. I left the HOW up to the Universe. By asking I made it known out loud that it was something I desired. I also programmed my subconscious mind to look for resources in my environment that would fulfill my desire. This is a non-earthshaking example, but the Constructive Questions can be applied to any kind of "problem solving" or "solution seeking" you can imagine.

Recently, my favorite physician's assistant left the clinic I go to, much to my dismay. I *loved* her. CQ (Constructive Question): *Where will I find a new primary care practitioner who I will love as much or more than my last PA?* Within a few weeks I randomly walked into a nearby clinic and my question was answered.

I have a client who is hitting the wall on a certain topic. CQ: *What's the best exercise I can do with this client to get them where they need to go?* In our next session I'm inspired to take them through a specific guided imagery that does the trick.

Constructive Questions can be applied to any and all things. Try playing with them *without* answering them; allow your mind to stay open and alert for the answers while following your instinctive nudges. Then, when you get your answers, be sure to acknowledge yourself and the Universe in your co-creation through the "miracles, magic, manifestations" written expression.

Constructive Questions are also the means by which we can shift our energies when we get stuck in drama thinking. Like the story from the last chapter, about the day I was riding my bike and immersing myself in negative rumination about my stepdaughter and her mom. I used some Constructive Questions to help change my focus and alter my thinking, which freed me up to feel better and come back into alignment with my Higher Self. When we get consumed in the disempowering thought patterns of our assumptions and reactive ruminations, we have to shift gears. They are just thoughts. It's tricky, because the mind is a very illusory place, so they appear to be real. When you do a present-moment check, however, you will probably find that whatever you are fixated on is not actually happening. It's all in your imagination. Now, if you try to just tell your brain what to do, it's likely to rebel, to push back with a resounding *eff you*, or to bombard you with all the ways its story is valid. But if you ask a *question*, there's nothing to fight against. When you give your brain a question, it has the chance to take you down another neural pathway than the one you were just riding. It will, at a minimum, interrupt your ranting thought flow and offer you the opportunity to find something new, which will feel better. Ultimately, that will serve *you*.

What makes a question constructive is how it's formulated. The basic way to determine whether a question is "constructive" and will take you in the direction of *thriving* is whether it elevates or drops your energy. We generally learn to ask the energy-dropping (or *de*structive) questions, like, "Why does this always happen to me?" or "What will go wrong next?" These are very victim-oriented, by the way, and continue to hold us in the fields of drama consciousness. Here are a couple simple guidelines for how *not* to craft a Constructive Question. You generally *don't* want it to be a yes-or-no question, and you *don't* want it to focus on the negative. Some examples of what *not* to ask would be, "Should I leave my relationship or not?" or "Why can't I ever get a break?" The first question does not invite clarity since it is focused on the confusion, and the second just puts emphasis on what you don't want. The more constructive versions of these would be, "How clear can I be about the best direction my relationship can take to serve the highest good of all involved?" and "What are the great things coming to me now in my current situation?"

To make a question constructive—supportive, useful, valuable, and collaborative—you want it to be open ended, positively oriented, and good-feeling. It's something you *want* to know the answer to. In formulating it, you want to give a lot of spaciousness for the Universe to give you the *best* possible answer, especially the ones you would never in a million years come up with on your own. You also want to just feel good in asking the question. "How hard can I laugh?" This question creates a certain image in your mind and a feeling in your gut—a good one. "How easy can I let this be?" This question brings a sense of relief, and in relief there is already an ease, which allows things to flow organically.

SPENDING TIME IN NATURE

Time in nature, even if you live in a city, is essential to a *thriving* life. The reason for this is because the energetic field of nature holds an inherent ease and flow and alignment with the Universe. I mean, there's no confusion in nature. There's no comparison, no envy. Everyone knows exactly Who They Really Are and what they're meant to be doing. We don't see the deciduous tree lamenting that it doesn't have pine cones. The shoreline doesn't begrudge the sea for crashing against it, nor for being "too calm" (read: *boring*). The animal kingdom is not "in the grind"—it is in the flow. Nature is a powerful access point for coming into alignment with the truth of Who We Really Are, independent of our roles, our demands, our "shoulds," and our limiting human-minded beliefs. Nature reminds us of abundance, of beauty, of peace, of joy, of fun, and play. These are the real-life essentials—not the latest gadget or the faster car or the news flash or the bigger-bigger-best-best. Time in nature connects us with what's most relevant to our *thriving*, our evolution, and our abundance, even if we are not consciously aware of it. Go to a park. Walk barefoot on the grass. Tromp through the snow. Let the rain fall on your face. Thank the leaves on the trees for their infiniteness. Gaze at the stars in awe. Tell the flowers or the birds or the spiders they are each your favorites. Align your brain-mind with the spirit of who you Are and let nature make the process a little easier.

BODY MOVEMENT AND A DIET OF WHOLE AND BRAIN-POWER FOODS

Living a DRAMA-free, *thriving* life means priming your physiology to operate at a higher level. This requires some level of care for the physical body. After all, that's your Soul-suit (kinda like a spacesuit); it's the only way your Soul has to get around the planet and have fun while here in its human experience. Having a body that feels good, that you like living in, is important. Not to mention, when you are making a change as powerful as letting go of the drama and moving into authentic living from your Soul, your anatomy needs a little help along the way.

Exercise or any kind of body movement will help to oxygenate your brain. The brain needs oxygen to generate new connections and build new neural pathways, to support new thoughts, new emotional states, and a new point of vibration. Your muscles need to be strong, your cardiovascular system needs to be efficient, and your flexibility, well, that just makes everything else more fun, so you might as well stretch.

Having a diet of whole foods and brain-power foods will also empower your ability to manage your thoughts, which in turn generate your emotional state and your vibration. If you eat too much sugar you crash, and when you crash you get cranky, and when you get cranky you can't focus on peaceful interactions or seek effective solutions to the problems in your workplace or even be kind to yourself. If you starve yourself during the day, your brain doesn't have the fuel it needs to function at its highest potential, and then you likely binge at night and your GI tract suffers.

I'm not a dietician or a nutritionist, and there are plenty of resources out there if you want to learn more about how diet impacts your brain functioning and your physical potential overall. I can tell you a few basics: your brain needs glucose (whole grains and high-quality complex carbohydrates), protein (from meat, fish, poultry, egg, or plant sources), and healthy fats (from nuts, avocado, olive products, coconut oil, etc.) as building-blocks, fuel for functioning, to support learning and memory, to enhance how rapidly neurons transmit information, and a variety of other essential operations. The brain also needs plenty of hydration, so drink your water.

Now, all this doesn't mean you can never eat a Dorito or treat yourself to a mammoth slice of New York–style cheesecake again; what it means is that the primary intention behind your eating is to maintain a high-functioning, well-balanced system to keep your energy optimized. Pick healthy options on a regular basis—salads, organics, non-GMOs, hormone-free meats, happy cheeses, and all that jazz. If you buy packaged food, just check the label to see that there are as few ingredients as possible—the less additives and preservatives, the better.

The whole physical body experience is about fun and play, connection and intimacy, pleasure and well-being, so you can do what you came here to do, so you can live your purpose and feel good while doing so. That's why we make caring for it a daily habit.

CONNECTING TO UNIVERSAL ENERGY THROUGH A PERSONAL INVOCATION

Finally, we come to the Personal Invocation portion of our programming. An Invocation can have a variety of names and themes. You may have heard them called incantations, affirmations, or positive self-talk. The power in creating a Personal Invocation that connects to Universal Energy is very specific to remind both your conscious and unconscious minds of the inherent power you hold. It's designed to have you amplify your good feelings, become conscious of the abundance available to you, be certain of your well-being while trusting in the flow of life and feeling confident in your Self. I tell my clients it's kinda like an affirmation on steroids. Bigger, more impactful, more powerful, more *effective*. Your Personal Invocation, when practiced daily, has the potential to instantaneously catapult you into *thriving* consciousness when you run into drama.

The Personal Invocation habit has three parts to it: the words, a physical body movement, and an emotional state. The words do not have to be lengthy, but they do need to be power-packed. You want your Invocation to be worded in the present tense, as if the declaration you are making is already true. You want it to have "I AM" statements and positive-feeling words. You may also want to include some sort of language that ties you to whatever you consider to be your higher power: God, the Universe, Mother Nature, or whatever resonates for you. The physical body movement is intended to create what is called an "anchor." Basically, our muscle contractions activate emotional memory, so when we need to draw up some positive emotional juices, we can reverse-engineer it by activating the muscle movement, like clapping or snapping, for example. When reciting your Invocation, you will want to do this out loud, looking in the mirror, while utilizing your vocal inflection to amplify the positive emotional state. The whole looking-in-the-mirror thing is simply to attach these powerful statements and feelings to your personal image. So much of our identity, how we view ourselves, has to do with our appearance. Linking our visual image into this whole formula is a highly effective channel for activating *thriving* consciousness. Oh, and our names too. Plug in your name at the beginning of your Invocation to really own it.

Here are a few examples of powerful lines you can use and adapt to resonate for you. The initial sentence is a bit reminiscent of Mad Libs—pick your adjectives and your nouns to describe your most powerful and aligned Self. Who are you when you are feeling the most *you*, the best you, like you are on top of the world? You'll notice that the word *now* is plugged into a number of these lines, which is simply to emphasize the present-tense element of the Invocation.

"I, (so-and-so), AM a gentle-kind-loving-peaceful-serene-playful-influential-reverent-wise-strong-powerful-(pick your adjective) Soul-Spirit-Being-Creator-(pick your noun)." Play with it to fit your style and what feels good to you. "I AM a beautiful spiritual being."—"I AM a powerful creator."—"I AM a wise old Soul."—"I AM a strong and compassionate leader."—"I AM a force of love and unconditional acceptance." Feel the exquisiteness of Who You Really Are!

"I manifest magic and miracles all the time, every day!"

"Infinite wealth of all kinds flows through me in oceans of abundance."

"I trust that life unfolds itself in perfect timing and Divine order."

"I have complete confidence in my abilities and absolute conviction in my Self."

"The joy and certainty I feel *now* empowers me to make a powerful positive impact on my personal world and the world at large."

"I gratefully receive all that I need and desire easily and effortlessly *now*."

"I am humbly, joyously, ecstatically fulfilling my greater purpose *now.*"

"I am a master at manifesting all that I wish to be, do, and have."

"I joyously live in the flow of life *now.*"

You can see this Personal Invocation thing is BIG. It's meant to be big, to feel big, to stretch your self-view beyond the limited human you think you are and reconnect you to the Divine within you, actually tying the two together, both consciously and unconsciously. Way, *way* too cool for school.

One more thing to mention about the Personal Invocation is that this is not prideful self-glorification. It is not a means of narcissistic self-absorption. Instead, it is a personal empowerment tool, intended to feel good and to serve the world around you by way of *claiming* and becoming the best *you* you can be.

General Practices for *Thriving*!

"We first make our habits, and then our habits make us."

—JOHN DRYDEN

The Daily Alignment Practices for cultivating a *thriving* life are an excellent start to living with greater ease, joy, and wealth of all kinds, for sure. There are also some additional practices that will support your transformation and your ability to sustain a *thriving* consciousness, sans drama. Here are a few extra puzzle pieces.

KEEP YOUR MEDIA CONSUMPTION IN CHECK

A drama-free lifestyle involves conscious choice regarding engaging with the media: what to watch on TV, how to spend time online, which music to tune in to, being selective with gaming, etc. Notice how you feel when you are exposed to various forms of sensory stimulation. Not everyone has the same tolerance for various visual or auditory influences. Be aware of what your tolerances include. There are all manner of topics under the sun out there in media contexts, including: violence, rape scenes, sexual objectification, abduction, trafficking, drug use, unfaithfulness, war, dirty politics, you name it. The question is, how is what you're exposing yourself to impacting your mind and your spirit? How is it influencing your vibrational state?

Whenever an energetic state runs through you, you automatically adjust to vibrate at that level. Your system doesn't recognize that you're blubbering away because of *fiction* . . . because a faux couple broke up or because your fave character got killed off. Your system only registers the emotional state you are generating in the moment, and that translates into the vibration you are sending out to the Universe. Uh-huh. And the Universe responds with like experiences in your *real* life (not on the next episode). Double uh-huh. Now, if you're into horror series or murder mysteries, that doesn't necessarily mean someone is going to literally show up dead on your doorstep or that ghosts are in your attic. It's more like whatever *your* personal ways of living with the lower energetic states are, they will be amplified or otherwise remain activated in your vibration and thus in your life experience.

I understand there is an entertainment factor we receive from the media that countless people enjoy, myself included. What I'm suggesting is that we each keep it in check for ourselves, based on our unique engagement with it. Start to notice if watching sports gets you pumped up in a mode that's ready to riot? Or can you enjoy a good game simply as entertainment? Do you find yourself getting emotional night after night from binge-watching a Netflix original series (insert any relevant show for you)? Do you catastrophize rape and murder in your own life after watching a detective thriller with gruesome forensic procedurals? What about all the pharmaceutical commercials or newscasts about the latest pandemic—do you paranoiacally scan yourself for symptoms? What happens to your self-talk just after watching a lingerie commercial or the latest rejuvenating skin cream ad?

In contrast, how do you feel after watching an inspirational story or uplifting movie? What about listening to heavy metal compared to India Arie or James Taylor? Is what you're experiencing fear-based or frustration-oriented? Or is it empowering, inspirational, relaxing? Just *notice* the difference.

I'm throwing out these examples just to pique your brain a little bit; you can adapt the selection to explore your own listening and viewing habits. I don't know enough about the current gaming scene to give any good examples (I'm admittedly fixed in the eras of Pac-Man, Atari, and the original Nintendo), but I've seen enough commercials about them that I have concern for the spiritual development and healthy human engagement of many of our youth.

The media is everywhere, and we can't avoid it, really. I heard Caroline Myss say that, archetypally, the media (advertisers in particular) are "spellcasters." Their job is to influence us to develop actual belief systems that drive our behaviors and our lives. What I want to emphasize is that we *can* be choiceful about what we allow in, what we feed our minds, and how we integrate the things we expose ourselves to. Pick the things that feel good, that inspire, that generate the vibration you want to align with. And, *puhleeze*, mute the commercials.

If you really want to dig in and play with this, you can do a test. You know how elimination diets are meant to cleanse your body of various substances—gluten, dairy, sugar (oh my!)—and then you gradually add them back in to see what makes you feel like crap or not? Well, you can apply the same concept to what you feed your mind: a two-week *media* elimination "diet." Take out the soap opera and see how you feel. Stop watching the news (or limit it to a quick check online) and notice how it affects your view of the world. Listen only to music with a happy beat, calming vibe, or positive lyrics and see what life reveals to you. Again, this is just a self-check to discover which of your choices are optimizing your life experience or detracting from it. You don't have to do it forever. You can always go back to your favorite talk-and-interview. Just try it and see.

MAINTAIN A NO GOSSIP/NO COLLUSION/NO COMPLAINING POLICY

As social beings, we need each other. We rely on one another for survival, which means having a solid sense of belonging is imperative. Feeling validated is a big part of that. Back in the day, Dr. Freud made a case for talking about problems. Yup: talk therapy, baby. While it may have had its usefulness, talk therapy led to open venting which exacerbates colluding and gossiping, which leads to reinforcing the drama neural pathways in the brain while also keeping the crap you don't want active in your vibration. Sorry, but it's true. What you focus on expands, so when you think you're getting something off your chest and seeking social support, you're not only amplifying it within yourself, but you're also getting other people on board, adding their energy to the mix. Furthermore, you're also giving them *your* negative vibration and sharing its harmful effects.

When we have crap we don't like or stuff that isn't working, we can go into **grieve** mode to get the emotion out, with or without the support of another person. We all have this choice; in the midst of a growth opportunity, the sooner we can process and move on, the better life flows. When something shows up that you want to complain about, instead of pinging your BFF with a kvetchfest you can instead: hit a pillow, scream in your car, write a letter and then tear it up, have a good solid cry—whatever purges your system. Once you **recover** you can focus on what the unwanted thing led you to desire instead. Then begin telling the new story of what you *do* want. Infuse it with positive feelings. Convince yourself to the point of absolute certainty that this new story is the truth as you live it. Some people would call this self-deception, touting it as "not being realistic." Me, on the other hand, I would call it creatively using your imagination to generate the vibrational match to what you want so it can come into your experience. I would call it accessing the flow of life to let it be easy and fun. I would say, "Rock on!" The idea is that the new story in your mind generates new images and fuels your vibration with better-feeling stuff so you can sooner attract what you desire, in one form or another.

The other reason to practice a No Gossip/No Collusion/No Complaining Policy is because, from a relationship standpoint, those validation-seeking tactics have a viral effect, spreading the drama to no end. They impact you, the recipient, the person or issue that is the subject of focus—in short, they affect everything. Once you open that door it's like Pandora's Box. Better to keep it simple; keep the drama contained. There are other ways to seek validation and connection, as per Chapter 4.

This will take some practice, restraint, and focused intention to implement. I was working with a client, Rachel, for several years. One day, during our session, Rachel proudly announced that she finally, effectively *chose* not to collude. She had an unpleasant exchange with Colleague A at work and promptly called Colleague B to kick off a kvetchfest. As the phone was ringing she rapidly decided *not* to proceed with her initial plan and purpose for the call. As Colleague B answered, Rachel immediately shifted gears to ask about a project rather than fall into the water-cooler chatter.

All this being said, there is a distinction to be made between validation-seeking and solution-seeking. Talking through life's issues can be beneficial when it's used as a processing approach, seeking advice or help, and holds an expansion-oriented intention. In this case, we need to be sure we tap into a source who will *not* go into drama with us, but will stand with us compassionately, knowing that there is transformation and growth available in the undesirable circumstance. I recently had an unpleasant exchange with a colleague (whom we'll identify as #1). We had a difficult phone conversation that triggered me *big time*, fired up all my defenses and launched me into limbic chaos. I couldn't think clearly, I couldn't respond constructively to their arguments, nor effectively represent myself. I had to discontinue the call and reschedule for the next day. Now immediately after I got off the call, I wanted to dial up another colleague-friend for support. I wanted to do a brain-check to see if I was thinking rationally, and I basically wanted to get a third perspective to help clarify things so I could revisit the issue and resolve it on the call with Colleague #1 the following day. Now I had two options of whom to call: Colleagues #2 and #3, who both knew Colleague #1 and would have a reference point to give their perspective. In that moment of my upset, I knew that Colleague #2 would love to roll around in the drama of it with me, colluding and amplifying my justification and my arguments. While Colleague #3 would be able to access a place of wisdom and love for us *both* without taking sides or validating any drama; they would just give it to me straight. So that's who I called. As a result, I was able to clear my head, be heard in an honoring, drama-free way, and take an honest look at my part. The next day I was able to resume the conversation with Colleague #1 from a space of clarity, respect, and an authentic desire to resolve the issue, which we did cleanly and effectively.

Living the DRAMA-free way means not pulling other people's minds and focus onto your complaints or into your camp in a dispute. They have their own minds to contend with; they don't need your meshugas in there as well. When appropriate, useful, and solution-oriented, accessing support can be effective when the intent is not to spread the drama but to gain another perspective to learn what we can do better and ultimately help things go right.

Take a deep breath. Meditate. Burn off some steam. Recite your Personal Invocation. Find something else to engage with and help you feel valued. Keep it simple, clean, and above the line.

I remember a number of years ago, when I was first considering this shift myself (which admittedly I *still* have not made 100 percent, though it is vastly improved), I asked a mentor of mine, "What do you talk to people about if you're not gossiping or complaining together?" At that time, I didn't know how to connect with certain people without it. She told me you talk about what you're doing, things you're planning, the good stuff that's showing up in your life. I believed her and still felt fearful of losing some friendships. I mean, if my life looked too *good*, would they still accept me or want to be around me? What would we have in common? As it turns out, some of the people I had in mind did fall by the wayside. We still keep in touch, but we do not get together weekly to drink wine and commiserate. The people who are my true friends are still in my life and *happy* for every success that I have. I even have new amigos and positive people I am attracting to me, who I really enjoy and can share all the great stuff of life with, minus the drama conduit. Which is a great lead-in to . . .

SET HEALTHY BOUNDARIES WITH KINDNESS

Like most good addicts, we tend to surround ourselves with co-conspirators who indulge in the drama with us. When making changes in how we are operating and interacting, if others are not ready to do so themselves, we can come to a crossroads where we need to set healthy boundaries to "maintain sobriety," as it were. Take a smoker for instance. How successful will they be at quitting if they continue to hang out around their friends who smoke? The allure, the temptation, the shared point of connection is so magnetic that it can be irresistible and easily lead to relapse. It's the same thing with drama thinking. Listening to other people's drama, and witnessing it in the world around us, can lead us to relapse into worthlessness, anxiety or irritation, raging, and even bullying.

In order to live a *thriving* life, we have to surround ourselves with people who operate from the higher levels of consciousness. We especially need that "good energy" during the transition period when we are getting used to decreased drama and elevated levels of feeling good. In general, a *thriving* life involves surrounding ourselves with people of a similar mindset and emotional focus. As you take charge of your thought patterns, feel better, and begin to shift your vibration, the Law of Attraction will gradually deliver new people into your life with whom you will have a beautiful cohesiveness.

But what about the people you care for, who you recognize are not a match to the new next level of best that you are growing into? Since you don't want to reject or miss them, what you can do is find ways to love them without overexposing yourself to them or otherwise making yourself too vulnerable. You can structure the time you do spend together to include other additional people or be occupied with feel-good activities. If their drama does crop up, you can validate their experience with compassion and then quickly change subjects. You may even be as blunt as to say, "I'm sorry, but can we please talk about something else? Let me tell you about ___ (a good feeling, blah-blah-blah)." Take charge of the conversation. This is not rude; in fact, it actually does the other person a service to get them off the negative subject. The skill called "Yes, And" is very useful for setting healthy boundaries in this way while still being kind. It validates the other person's perspective and experience while providing you with a window to bring in something more positive to change the dialogue altogether. If you're not familiar with "Yes, And," here's the short version. In conversation, you can insert something along the following lines:

"What I like/appreciate/value/understand about what you're saying is this _____,

AND . . .

. . . from my perspective I see _____."

. . . my thoughts about that are _____."

. . . I have another way of looking at it. My opinion is _____."

"I hear/understand your experience was like this _____,

AND . . .

. . . I'm wondering if it's okay to shift gears for a moment because I'd like to tell you about _____."

. . . it reminds me about something funny that I wanted to share with you . . ."

. . . since I can empathize, I'd like to share something that I find helpful, if that's okay with you . . ."

This wording demonstrates that you "hear" and "see" the other person, and that you value who they are through acknowledging their experience. It also allows space for you to have a completely different opinion or to redirect the conversation away from drama and toward *thriving*.

You can also set healthy boundaries and shift the space of the dialogue with humor, or by excusing yourself physically altogether. When you come back to the conversation you can interject a whole new topic. I recently did this with a very dear girlfriend of mine who can at times get very animated about less-good-feeling things. We were at dinner with a third friend and the drama topic was starting to pull me down. I excused myself, went to the rest room, and when I returned—they were still on the topic, but more adamant about it now—I brought in a wacky and funny question. It was something about people not wiping the public toilets clean when they make a mess. Totally irrelevant. Nothing to do with their ongoing commentary. And yet, a total energy shifter. We were joking and giggling in no time. In this instance, I did not have to point fingers or highlight anything about how the conversation was affecting me. I simply took charge and refocused our time to be light, goofy, and playful.

As another example, I have a client, Candy, who finds that conversations with her sisters tend to pull her into drama mode, in particular when they discuss their parents. They collude and seek validation from one another regarding their mother's antics. Now, as a result of her personal growth and also of our work together, Candy is ready to let go of that and step into a more powerful, choiceful way of interacting with her mom. Part of what this requires from her is learning new ways of engaging with her sisters in order to not lapse back into old drama patterns. One thing that's working for her is being cognizant of the drama triangle archetypes of Victim, Villain, and Hero and how the roles are played out in her family dynamics. In our coaching together, we built a mental image for her of stepping off the "triangle stage" (where the drama plays out) and removing herself from the drama, so that at any given moment she can respond to her sisters with compassion and self-management, setting the emotional boundaries with kindness and respect for all.

FOLLOW YOUR FEELINGS

Perhaps the ultimate aspect to a *thriving* lifestyle is learning to live in a self-honoring way, from the heart and the gut more than from the head. In fact, science is showing that these two physiological systems are perhaps more intelligent and savvy than the organ of the brain. But because they communicate to us through the right hemisphere of the brain, the left side that houses logic and reason will often dismiss the feelings, images, music, metaphors, and urges we receive as being invalid or irrelevant. In our empirically oriented society, we have valued reason above sensing, which has taught us that what is logical and provable is what is most legitimate. This negates the importance of inspiration and spiritual guidance, which can come to us through words, but is largely found in how we feel. This feeling system is not an accident; it was built into our hardware to serve us, so we can fulfill our purpose, be connected with ourselves and others, get our needs and desires met, and have a whole lot more fun along the way.

Allowing our feelings to guide our choices is really about following intuitive impulses, listening to urges, acting on the things that feel exciting and compelling. This is the essence of self-honoring, one of the most healing energies there is. It can be applied in any context from the nursery to the classroom to the boardroom. Our urges mean there is something needed within ourselves or in the collective space between us humans that we are being called to respond to. When we miss those opportunities, because we second-guess ourselves or we play polite, not only are we negating ourselves, but we are robbing others of the gift we have to bring or the leadership we offer in that moment.

Our feelings are also indicators that guide what we are meant to do next in our day or in our life overall. In the most obvious ways, when we feel hungry we need to eat and when we feel tired we need to sleep. We know how to follow our body's signals and sensations, but because we have such shrewd minds we easily and chronically talk ourselves out of following the feelings that would perhaps answer our Constructive Question or lead us to get our needs met in unique, fulfilling ways. What oftentimes gets in the way is that during our development we learned to follow what pleased *others* first—parents, teachers, peers, siblings, etc.—and so following our own guidance became a secondary means of operating. Today, as empowered adults, we need to return to listening to our feelings in order to allow the Universe to lead us not only where we need to go to fulfill our purpose, but also where we will embrace all that we can in this human experience.

I'm drafting this chapter on a sunny January morning in the midst of a "writing retreat" in Las Vegas. Who takes a writing retreat to *Las Vegas?* Okay, let's call it what it is: the-cheapest-place-I-could-go-for-alone-time-and-a-sanity-recuperation. A spade is a spade. I recognize that taking care of my energy, doing things that provide relief, and following my impulses toward what excites me is precisely how life directs us toward where we are meant to go. On Tuesday this week, I had such an impulse. I was having a hard time concentrating at home to get this book finished, with no private designated workspace in our home and an office that requires schlepping through the hypothermic Minnesota winter. So, voilà! Thanks to last-minute deals, I followed the urge and here I am, sipping my PERQ coffee and typing away for you, dear reader. I manifested a getaway, and it feels *great!* The writing is flowing better than it has in weeks, which, for me, is clear validation that following my urge to create space and time specifically for this was actually imperative. While this example may be a touch on the extravagant side, it illustrates well the lifestyle principle of following your feelings toward joy and relief to get you where you are meant to go.

In daily living, when you are in the flow of whatever you're doing, rock on. When you start to get cranky or distracted or worried, it's your feelings guiding you to do something else. You have an unmet need that requires your attention. Pause and ask yourself, "What do I feel like doing right now?" or "What would feel good to me right now?" It might be any number of things: getting out for a walk, having something to eat or drink, taking a power nap, finishing a project, calling someone, drafting an email, singing a song, getting an early jump on your taxes (hey, *anything's* possible), partaking in a hobby like painting or playing music, or whatever is relevant in *your* world. Asking the question, again, gives your brain something to work with and allows your spirit to communicate more clearly and effectively with you.

Lifestyle Paves the Road

"Bad habits: easy to develop and hard to live with.
Good habits: hard to develop and easy to live with."

—ORRIN WOODWARD

Our habits undoubtedly determine how our lives unfold: habits of thought, habits of action, habits of emotional state, habits of companionship. When we indulge in the drama we will get more drama. When we focus on *thriving* we will get more of the things that please us, more feeling *good*. I have to admit, this is hard work; but it's really the *only* work to be done. It requires commitment, diligence, perseverance, and patience, like anything worth doing. If you want to be lean and fit, you have to have a lifestyle of healthy foods and exercise. If you want to be a scholar, you have to have a lifestyle that involves a great deal of reading and study. If you want to be attuned to your spirit and live in the flow, you have to have a lifestyle that supports and facilitates the consciousness of *thriving*. Once we make the effort to build the practices and develop the lifestyle that will get us the results we desire, life can truly become easy, joyous, and wealthful in all senses of these terms.

"Sow a thought and you reap an action;
sow an act and you reap a habit;
sow a habit and you reap a character;
sow a character and you reap a destiny."

—RALPH WALDO EMERSON

Key Concepts

✳ Feeling good is a sign that we are in alignment with our Higher Selves, in the strength and truth of *thriving* consciousness. The key to a *thriving* life is managing our energetic states so we feel good most of the time, and when we don't, to consciously recover to feeling good through the GRATE-full process.

✳ Our energetic state determines the quality of our vibration, which in turn influences the kinds of experience we attract. To effectively fulfill our desires, we must first emit the vibrational match that puts us on the same wavelength with them. Following what feels good or provides a sense of relief will achieve this in the most simple and easy way.

✳ The *thriving* lifestyle requires that we adopt certain habits that raise our vibration, keep us in alignment with our Higher Selves, and feel good most of the time. The components of the Daily Alignment Practice are as follows:

- Meditation—Meditation allows us the space for communion with the Divine that resides within us. Close eyes. Sit up. Breathe. Stay awake. Allow your mind to focus on being present or daydream of pleasurable things. Practice good-feeling states. Keep it simple and relaxed.

- Journaling Gratitudes and Appreciations—Daily writing about what we're grateful for and/or what we can find to appreciate. Gratitudes involve finding things that we already feel good about. Appreciations connect us consciously with the *value* inherent in anything, whether we perceive them as "good" or "bad."

- Acknowledging "Miracles, Magic, and Manifestations"—We write these down to acknowledge the Universe's fulfillment of our desires through identifying the "coincidences" in life and the unexpected gifts we receive. They are the evidence that we are creating the life we want. Consciously recognizing the *positive evidence* of our inner work in the outer world brings us more of it, while helping our logical brains see how randomly the non-linear world of energy works. It reinforces the concept that "the how is not up to us."

- Asking Constructive Questions—Constructive Questions are the way we "put in our order" with the Universe. Pose the questions and then *don't* try to answer them. It's the job of the Universe to figure out "how," not yours. Ask and then stay open to receiving by keeping yourself in a good-feeling zone, which allows you to be the vibrational match to your desire or solution. You can also use Constructive Questions to shift gears if you catch yourself in the drama zone and need to **get out**.

  - The basic way to determine whether a question is "constructive" and will take you in the direction of *thriving* is whether it elevates or drops your energy.

  - Constructive Questions should be open ended, positively oriented, and good feeling.

- Spending Time in Nature—The energetic field of nature holds an inherent ease and flow. It is a powerful access point for coming into alignment with the truth of Who We Really Are, and it connects us to abundance, beauty, peace, joy.

- Body Movement—The brain needs oxygen to generate new connections and build new neural pathways, to support new thoughts, new emotional states, and a new point of vibration. This is essential to making a shift to authentic *thriving*.

- Diet of Whole and Brain-Power Foods—In addition to fruits and vegetables, we need ample hydration and high-quality nutrition rich in protein, complex carbohydrates, and healthy fats to optimize brain functioning. Having a diet of whole foods and brain-power foods empowers our ability to manage our thoughts, which in turn generates our emotional states and our vibration.

- Connecting to Universal Energy through a Personal Invocation—The Personal Invocation aids our connection to Universal Energy, reminding both our conscious and unconscious minds of the inherent power we hold. Through this we amplify good feelings, become conscious of the infinite abundance available, and trust in the flow of life. Practice the Invocation aloud in front of the mirror, speaking in the present tense, using "I AM" statements and positive-feeling words. It may also include language that connects us to a higher power: God, the Universe, Mother Nature, etc. Pair this energy with a physical body movement to create an "anchor" that can help recover this positive state at will, when needed.

✳ Additional practices for a *thriving* lifestyle include:

- Keep Your Media Consumption in Check—A drama-free lifestyle involves conscious choice regarding engaging with the media. Notice how you feel when you are exposed to various forms of media stimulation. Which ones feel good and which do not? Be aware of what your tolerances include.

- Maintain a No Gossip/No Collusion/No Complaining Policy—These connection tactics have a viral effect, spreading the drama rather than resolving it. There is a distinction between validation-seeking and solution-seeking. Talking through life's issues can be beneficial when it's used for processing experiences to serve growth and expansion. A DRAMA-free, *thriving* lifestyle means not tainting other people's minds and energy with your complaints and ain't-it-awful stories.

- Set Healthy Boundaries with Kindness—Listening to other people's drama, and witnessing it in the world around us, can lead us to relapse. We can set limits on our exposure to it by structuring the time we spend with them in deliberate ways, or validating them and quickly changing topics.

- Follow Your Feelings—Allowing our feelings to guide our choices involves following intuitive impulses, listening to urges, and acting on the things that feel exciting and compelling. Our feelings are also indicators that guide what we are meant to do next in our day or in our life overall.

✳ Our habits of thought, habits of action, habits of emotional state, and habits of companionship all determine how our lives unfold. When we indulge in the drama we will get more drama. When we focus on *thriving* we will get more of the things that please us, more and more feeling *good*.

Application and Integration

Below are the Daily Alignment Practices. In the spaces provided, write out the ways you can begin to apply these tools to your own life. Consider what you need to have in place, the time of day it will work for you to do these things, and so on so you can make the *thriving* real for you.

Meditation

Time of day that's best for me:
Other thoughts:

Journaling Gratitudes and Appreciations

Time of day that's best for me:
Other thoughts:

Acknowledging "Miracles, Magic, and Manifestations"

Where I will write them:

How I will keep track of them throughout the day:

Asking Constructive Questions

Where I will write my CQs:

Time of day that's best for me:

Spending Time in Nature

Nature locations near me:

Best time of day for me to go out:

Supplies I need (as relevant) to enjoy my time in nature:

Diet of Whole and Brain-Power Foods

Foods I will eat and enjoy:

How I will be sure to have them available when I need them:

Body Movement

Body movement I enjoy:

Time of day that's best for me to exercise or get some movement in:

Connecting to Universal Energy through a Personal Invocation

Write out your starter invocation here:

I _____ (insert your name) AM . . .

CHAPTER NINE

Your Very Own Personal Cheat Sheet for Authentic *Thriving*

"Everything you want is on the other side of fear."

—JACK CANFIELD

his chapter is the one you've been waiting for, a selection of brain tricks and strategies to get you to "the other side" of anxiety, worthlessness, rage, or whatever version of drama you are hooked on in a given moment. The purpose here is for you to discover and begin to apply inner alignment strategies to shift your energetic states, recover quickly, and consistently return to *thriving* any time you do get pulled into drama. More simply put, the target is to learn to feel good and gain relief *at will.* The implementation of any of these methods will generate changes in your brain's neurological connections by way of doing something different and breaking old patterns, giving you new thoughts to work with so you can effectively change how you feel and more easily go with the flow of life.

Getting ourselves to be able to think new thoughts is kind of like undergoing new road construction. When the same highway is traveled day after day, it becomes so familiar you could almost trek it blindfolded. Then one day, to your dismay, you suddenly realize it's *not* the most efficient route to get to your desired destination anymore. To be more timely and effective there really needs to be a new road paved. That starts with bulldozing a rough path, then leveling, then laying down the concrete, then letting it dry (surely there are more steps, but this is how the simplicity of my non-engineerical mind imagines the process). The final outcome of this investment in creating a smooth, beautiful new roadway is driving on it consistently and arriving at your target destination more quickly and effectively than ever before. But it *still* took the time to pave. Likewise, in the brain, new neurological pathways have to be created in order to allow for new thoughts to travel through the roadways of our minds.

The brain is obviously an extraordinarily complex organ. However, working with it can be very simple and user-friendly. To do that, it's important to identify a few key functions, or ways we experience the brain at work. For one, the brain "thinks" primarily in pictures and sounds. It also thinks in touch (kinesthetics), taste, and smell, but most of our internal experience while we're living life on the fly is in the images we "see" in our minds and the sounds or self-talk we "hear." These thinking modalities generate emotional and energetic states within us.

To illustrate, you could be having an argument with someone. You could see the expressions on their face, and hear their words, and even feel your own angst building—and then you finish washing the dishes. The mind can drum up mega drama while you are doing mundane things like taking a shower, folding laundry, or driving in the car. Nothing is *happening* in the moment, but you get worked up because the brain can't tell the difference between thinking something (making the pictures and the sounds) and having it actually happen. The same biochemicals are released. The same emotions are generated. Which is precisely why we need to reign those thought-puppies in.

Now, in the same vein, the mind can also be used in very helpful ways. Like the other day when I was performing a concert. I was on stage with thousands of adoring fans all around. I danced like J-Lo and wore a spectacularly bedazzled bodysuit. I shook my shugah and sang my heart out; my dance moves were *on*, and they were *hot*! The arena was going *wild*! The whole stage was *vibrating* with the energy of the music—and then the dentist stopped drilling my tooth and put in the new filling.

This power of imagination is something we're born with and it's truly a gift that can transform our experiences—for better or for worse. We can catastrophize or we can fantasize. Either way, we are generating powerful emotional states that infuse our vibration with higher or lower—*thriving* or drama—energies. Most people have been sort of "trained out" of purposefully using their imaginative, resourceful brains when it comes to shaping their world and managing their emotions. In school we learn scads of logical, analytical, and reason-based methods for using our brains so we can get a good job someday and be "successful." We are taught that the creative mind is useful, but not necessarily for engaging with "reality." The seemingly secondary function of pure imagination is left undirected. As a result, we allow our thoughts to run wild inside us, which is perhaps the reason why you have this book in your hands.

It's important to learn specific tools and develop strategies to resume *intentional* use of your imagination and creative brain power, so you can take charge of your beautiful mind and discover the ways that are most effective for *you* to recover from drama and shift into *thriving*. Let's get started.

Essential Inner Alignment Tools

"She stood in the storm, and when the wind did not blow her away, she adjusted her sails."

—ELIZABETH EDWARDS

We all need "sail adjusters" or tools to effectively navigate our internal worlds. Some of these tools are adapted from various coaching methodologies, such as the Co-Active Model and Neuro-Linguistic Programming (NLP), which are highly effective practices for creating lasting change. Others come from a mindfulness approach. Then there are some random game changers thrown in there just for your energetic pleasure. As you are reading through the descriptions, I invite you to pause and give them a try or at least consider which might be *most* effective for you. There's a lot here, so don't let it overwhelm you. The variety of tools is meant to provide you with choices, since every brain operates a little differently. Don't worry about having to remember them all. Just pick the ones you like best and start with those.

Here's the overview:

- Truth or Opinion
- Flip It
- Volume Control
- Imagery Direction
- Spinning the Feelings Within
- Get Some Perspectives
- The Squirrel in the Tree
- Just Sit with It
- State-Breakers
- Make It Up
- Self-Check
- Clarify Assumptions
- Get into the Groove

TRUTH OR OPINION

Our drama thoughts are largely based on faulty or limiting beliefs that were programmed into us rather than on absolute truth. When we get triggered into drama, we have to stop and examine how true those drama thoughts are. You can start with the very simple question, "Is it true?" Byron Katie has a brilliant method of "inquiry" for exploring the veracity of our thoughts with her approach referred to as "The Work," which leads people through a series of questions to get in touch with the authenticity of Who They Really Are and allow the illusions of drama to dissolve in the presence of Truth. I highly recommend her well-structured, easy-to-apply approach. In the meantime just start examining whether your thoughts are actually a reflection of truth or opinion. You brain will probably say, "Yes. Of course they're true!" That's because you have some sort of belief system in place to support them. Usually your bad-feeling stories are complete fictions and you are the author, using pieces of old wound-based experiences to plug in and formulate the present picture in your mind, telling yourself a not-very-good-feeling story. One way to identify truth versus a personal opinion is to check for whether there's a "should" in your story; if you're "shoulding" on someone (even yourself), it's probably opinion oriented, rather that truth based. For example, if I think, "My stepdaughter should always put her dishes in the dishwasher," that's an opinion, not necessarily a hard-core fact. Yet, I could get myself very stressed about it if I were to obsess about every time she leaves her coffee spoon on the counter.

We want to look at our angst-generating stories, our *shoulds*, and ask, "Is this absolute truth or is it more of an opinion I am holding?" I always tell my clients that, for a reference point, one thing we know to be of absolute truth is gravity. No one argues about the fact that gravity exists. It's not an opinion; it's a universal law. Truth is what's eternal and unchanging. When we can get out of our own way—let go of our hard-and-fast rules and personal dogmas—and instead open up to new perspectives based on truth, we can see the infinite beauty in the souls around us and in the natural flow of life. But we have to ask the question first.

FLIP IT

We opine to no end. When we get fixated on how we see or feel about a certain experience, we are confined to the walls of our minds. That gives us no wiggle room to work with to see things in new, more *thriving* and empowering ways. When getting in touch with truth is feeling too hard, another option is to "Flip it." Turn your negative thoughts to their literal opposite to stretch the range of thoughts available to you on any given topic.

When you are met with an opinion or behavior in another person that you think is "wrong," flip your perspective to the exact opposite. See them as "right" for a change. If you hear yourself saying, "I hate this," flip it to, "I love this." It's probably not going to feel like that right away; it'll feel like a lie because it's too big of a leap. In making that leap to the opposite side, you stretch your brain into a fuller range of what's possible in terms of ways to experience the situation. Once you have some middle ground to work with you can look for something truer than your original limited stance that also feels better. If you can't find it in the actual circumstance, then just make it up in your mind—you're doing that anyway. (More to come on "making it up.")

The key is understanding that there is no one right way to do most things in life, and there is certainly no one right opinion. Most people cannot immediately go from one end of the spectrum to the other, but in flipping it they all of a sudden have access to the in-between range, and now there's something to work with. Now there's someplace productive to go that will move you toward *thriving* consciousness, which ultimately leads to more effective solutions.

As I mentioned before, the mind thinks predominantly in images, sounds (self-talk), and feelings/kinesthetics. When generating powerful changes from the inside out, we have to address each of these modalities. There are a variety of ways to work with these internal processes, many of which require an outside person to lead you through them. The approaches I've outlined here are a few basic exercises you can do on your own to get started.

VOLUME CONTROL

Imagine a control panel in your mind. On that panel, you have a large dial that says Volume. This is your mental access point to adjusting the internal auditory volume on the things that are detracting from your experience and stirring up drama, and also things you *want* to hear, things that serve you. To use this tool, begin to adjust this dial to turn down, and ultimately mute, your negative internal dialogue, and then turn up (crank up!) the positive reframe.

Doubt is a great ooga-booga to use this on. Whatever the doubt "voice" says, listen for the theme and then simplify it to one line, like, "This book is stupid and no one will ever want to read it." (Really, this is just a random example.) Listen to it once and evaluate what level, on a scale of 1 to 10, the dial is set to. Play it again at that level—say it's a 6. Then begin to turn down the dial—to a 5 or a 4—and listen again. Hear the line go softer and softer—6: "This book is stupid and no one will ever want to read it" . . . 4: "This book is stupid and no one will ever want to read it" . . . 3: "This book is stupid and no one will ever want to read it" . . . 1: "This book is stupid and no one will ever want to read it" . . . 0: . . .

. . . until it's essentially muted, imperceptible. Then, replace it with a new, more empowering line. Start from the same low volume and crank it up past the original level you started the doubt thought with—1: "This book is life-changing and readers will get immense benefit from it!" . . . 3: "This book is life-changing and readers will get immense benefit from it!" . . . 6: "This book is life-changing and readers will get immense benefit from it!" . . . 8: "This book is life-changing and readers will get immense benefit from it!!!"

Make it as loud as you can and allow it to saturate your senses, and then see how you feel compared to when you started. What you have to keep in mind is that *both* of these lines are stories; they are fictions. They both live exclusively in your mind. It's up to you to decide which one you want to have fuel your emotional, vibrational state. This method is super easy to apply. Try it first with something that does not have too much of a charge for you, just to get the hang of it. Then you will be more prepared to apply it to the tougher stuff when you get triggered into drama.

IMAGERY DIRECTION

Imagery direction is similar to what we just did with the auditory adjustment, but it utilizes your visual mind instead. In order to dial down drama, begin by watching the pictures you are making in your mind. Notice that you are simply making images of a particular scene that drags you down into a negative emotional state. If you come into the present moment and look around, you'll see no one is there and nothing is actually happening. It's really, truly, all in your head. Annoying, I know, because it *feels* so real. If we're running the movie and making the scenes that produce the feelings, why not pick some better cinematics?

Life is in the mind. When you feel like super crapola, you're in drama mode, making shitty pictures and life-degrading audio effects. When you're feeling rockin' awesome, you're *thriving* by making inspiring, fun, pleasurable, fulfilling images and sounds. We can use our brains either way. Now that you know there's a choice, which way will you pick?

Here's how to work with your mental pictures:

1. Start by identifying the negative feeling and seeing what your thoughts are doing.

2. See the picture you are creating and then notice: are you in it, like real life? Or are you watching yourself, like a movie?

3. If you are not already watching it, step outside yourself and witness the scene from a third-party, removed perspective.

4. Put a border or a frame around the scene, like it's on a TV, and then shrink it down to make it smaller and smaller, and notice how you

feel. Allow the emotional charge to die down with the reduction in image size. Then get ready to shift to something that feels better.

5. Get your mind onto something else. It could be what you would prefer to experience compared to the original picture. Or something completely different. Make up a whole new scene (like my concert appearance). Plan a vacation. Immerse yourself in thinking about anything that feels fun or gives you pleasure.

The most important thing in all this is that you shift your vibration from drama to *thriving*. Once that's taken care of, each time, as you build a habit of this, you will gradually vibrate at incrementally higher levels, which, by the Law of Attraction, will bring you more and more of what you desire and less and less drama.

SPINNING THE FEELINGS WITHIN

Spinning the feelings within is a very fascinating concept. It's something I originally learned through coaching I received that utilized NLP techniques. I find it to be very powerful and useful for amplifying positive emotional states or shifting out of negative emotional states. The concept is that our feelings have movement or a kinesthetic activity inside us. If you tune in to where your feelings reside in your body, you will probably notice some sort of physical sensation in your torso area. It may be somewhere else, but for most people kinesthetic feelings present themselves physically somewhere within their neck, chest, and abdominal areas. These feelings can have a momentum that spins backward like it's tumbling into you, or forward like it's tumbling out of you; they can also spin clockwise or counterclockwise. I've found in working with clients that they sometimes take on alternate shapes, but fundamentally focusing on these four directions can help keep the identification process simple for the linear brain. Feelings can spin at different speeds and with different intensities. They can be big or small in size.

The interesting thing about this is that when you notice a negative feeling originating from drama thinking, you can identify which way the feeling is spinning and actually start to spin it in the opposite direction. This is an abstract, non-linear concept and thus a way of harnessing the right brain wisdom to manage your emotional states. This exercise will make it significantly easier for you to shift gears and start moving in a more positive direction. It is a kinesthetic process, and here's how it works:

1. Notice your drama emotions, pay attention to where they show up in your body, and feel the direction they're moving inside you.

2. Stick your hand out and start moving it in sync with how the feelings are spinning. Move it to match the direction, speed, and size of the feelings spinning within you. This creates an external expression of the feeling you can begin to tangibly change.

3. Start to physically slow your hand down, and perhaps make the size of the movement a bit smaller.

4. Gradually come to a halt and start spinning your hand in the *opposite* direction, slowly increasing speed and increasing size. Stay present and relaxed and allow your system to flow with this turn-around.

5. Notice how your internal feeling changes. *Something's* going to happen. It's up to you to discover what that is for you and whether this process is an effective tool for you to employ.

Similarly, if there's a certain feeling state that you want more of, you can use this process to amplify it. That means when you have a feeling you like—it could be peace, passion, joy, or any other feel-good state—you can enhance it with this same process, but instead of slowing it and spinning the opposite direction, you want to intensify what's already present. Notice the direction the feeling is spinning and how big it is, then make it *bigger*; notice how bright it is, then make it *brighter*; notice how fast it's spinning, then make it spin *faster!* Make it feel really, *really good* inside you. Take it and run with it. Empower the feeling to fill up your whole system and saturate all of your neurology. Make it spin so big that the sensation is exuding out of your body; it's filling up the room, it's filling up the whole building. Now it's spinning throughout the city, the state, the continent, consuming the earth, flowing through the galaxy and all the way out to the edges of the Universe!

Now doesn't that feel good? And remember: feeling good is the primary goal.

GET SOME PERSPECTIVES

Perspective is the way we view things, how we think about them. There are a thousand bazillion different perspectives we could take on any given subject. The perspective that we take will influence how we feel about it. If you're having an argument with your significant other or a difficult conversation with your boss or a colleague, your perspective in those instances is going to be limited to your own viewpoint based on past wounding and influential experiences. Now if you put your pet (yes, Fluffy or Fido) in your shoes during that argument, they would have an entirely different perspective on the way the other human being was interacting with you.

You can basically take on the perspective of any person, animal, or inanimate object around you. Toothpaste is going to "say" something totally different about a circumstance than the moon is. Pondering what Mahatma Gandhi would think about the matter gives you access to completely different thoughts than considering what Lara Croft's stance might be. Employing a wide variety of perspectives is a highly creative way to use the imagination to open up your thought patterns and find more effective solutions to whatever the drama scenario is.

When you get caught in drama and need a new point of view, *any* perspective will do as long as it's empowering, grounded in *thriving* consciousness, and as long as it feels good in the sense that it provides you with relief. You can use this powerful technique to shift how you feel about *anything* in life. It takes a little practice and it's definitely worth developing the skillset if you want to live the most *thriving* life possible.

THE SQUIRREL IN THE TREE

Playing the Squirrel in the Tree is kind of like what we did in the Image Redirection earlier, when you looked at yourself from the outside instead of being *in* the picture. It's basically a spin on viewing things from the "observer" perspective. This idea came to me one time when I was having an intense conversation with a former boyfriend. We were sitting out on his back deck, and in the middle of the heated discussion I actually paused inside myself to wonder what would a squirrel in the tree looking down on us think about this whole goofy human interaction? It was almost laughable. From that point on I've always called this the Squirrel in the Tree.

In the NLP world, this process is called dissociation. It's a way of stepping outside ourselves to witness instead of being in the intensity of the drama of whatever's going on. The opposite of dissociation is *association*. That's when we were thinking of ourselves from the perspective of being in our body, or in the movie. It's looking from the first-person perspective rather than a third-party perspective.

From an associated viewpoint, emotions are always more intense. We take on the feeling state of whatever we are thinking, because again, the brain cannot make the distinction between imagining and actually experiencing. Employing this strategy of dissociation and playing the Squirrel in the Tree is a really valuable tool when it comes to shifting out of the drama. When we step outside of our typical stance and look at things from a distance, it allows our brains to be freed up to find new, more empowering thoughts that are embodied in the *thriving* consciousness.

JUST SIT WITH IT

Just Sit with It is about actively *feeling* any uncomfortable emotional states that arise in life in order to process them and move through them quickly and effectively. It's basically the tool that we employ in the **grieve** step of GRATE-full living. What it allows is for the negative emotional states, whatever the discomfort is, to flow through us in meaningful, self-honoring ways. When we suppress negative emotions they end up coming out sideways, frequently having an undesired, regret-worthy impact.

Fundamentally, emotions are energy and energy is continuously in motion, no matter how small the movements. When negative emotions build up from recycling drama thoughts or having our wounds activated, it has to have a place to go, calling for a release. Bottling up or repressing unwanted emotional states is kinda like sticking a soda can in a pressure cooker; eventually it will implode while having an explosive effect on the environment that it's in.

There's nothing inherently wrong about having negative emotions. They're *just* emotions, which means they're *just* energy. Our job is to consciously allow their release, directing and processing them in ways that transform the energy into something useful. This is what it is to be in a state of allowing.

It takes a certain amount of self-love and self-compassion in order to accept our drama feelings. We need to know that they are *not* the truth of Who We Really Are; they are simply a reflection of our past wounds and unmet needs. When we can see those parts of ourselves with tenderness and forgiveness, we can more quickly recover to the energies of *thriving*. Even though it's not the most fun or the most comfortable, Just Sit with It is actually a very powerful tool. It is probably one of the most efficient tools for recovering to *thriving* consciousness, like ASAP.

What does that really mean in practical terms? How do we Just Sit with It? Start by slowing things down. Stop trying to cover up the emotions. Stop trying to escape. Sit down and *feel*—actually literally take your mind's focus to the inside of your body. Get really present in the moment with your feelings; even if it's painful, it's not going to last. You might need an outlet for expression, such as crying or screaming into a pillow or writing out all your woes and then manually shredding the paper. That's all okay; it can be an effective part of the release process so you can recover.

What Just Sit with It does require (that most people resist) is that you're going to have to put down the cigarette or the glass of wine or the family-sized bag of potato chips and jumbo Butterfinger. It means you'll have to turn off the TV and shut down your phone. It means no longer distracting or numbing the discomfort, but instead paying exclusive attention to the way you *feel*. I think that's a challenge for most of us, because we learned how to suppress our feelings, not only to resist the pain, but also to avoid making other people uncomfortable around us. Going headlong into them is counterintuitive. And it is seriously, truly, the most efficient way to get through to the other side.

With courage and practice, we can develop the awareness and the ability to feel . . . *feel* . . . *Feel* . . . *FEEL* exactly where we are in our dark moments. Then we can express or respond to ourselves in healthy, loving ways—a crucial component of self-honoring.

STATE-BREAKERS

Here's some good news: we don't always have to "just sit with it." Sometimes what the drama needs is a state-breaker to get out. A state-breaker is something that interrupts your current thought flow and takes you into a totally, completely different state of mind and emotion. What this accomplishes is interrupting the unwanted thought pattern that's screwing with your positive, aligned vibration. A really great example of a state-breaker is laughter. For example, remember back in Chapter 4, the story of Terrence acting shocked when I exclaimed, "I'm white!"? The laughter that emerged from the surprise of his unexpected quip was an incredible state-breaker. There was no way I could continue my catastrophizing and emotional drama after the laughter came into play. It shone an instant spotlight on the ridiculousness of my self-imposed story.

You can use state-breakers with yourself or you can use them with other people. In certain cases, just changing subjects is also a great state-breaker. You may recall that from Chapter 8, when I interrupted my girlfriends' conversation with a comment about people keeping public toilets clean. It was such a ridiculous topic to bring into the mix that it instantaneously shifted the energy that the two of them were steeped in. Stimuli that are ridiculous, shocking, silly, gross, or out of context in any way are all powerful state-breakers.

Moving the body around is also a state-breaker. Take a deep breath and exhale with an audible sigh; shift positions in your chair; get up and walk into another room or a different corner of the one you're in. Listening to certain music, watching a funny YouTube clip, reading a book, or making goofy sounds with your voice—any of these can function as state-breakers. Not to mention, the majority of the Daily Alignment Practice will serve the state-breaker purpose as well: asking Constructive Questions, meditating (sometimes), speaking your personal invocation, or focusing on appreciations all have the potential to do the trick.

The power of the state-breaker is that it interrupts the neural pathway that you are used to coasting along in your drama thinking. When we want to create change in the brain we have to interrupt old thought patterns and create new ones. (This is what we use the five D's for in dealing with addiction, especially "distract," "depart," and "dance.") Unfortunately, when we get hooked into wound-based triggers, the patterns and beliefs that get activated can be so powerful and so dominating that it feels almost impossible to think about or do anything else. That's why we become a slave to them; it's why drama is addictive. State-breakers are an imperative tool for your authentic *thriving* kit. As you break your state (repeatedly over time), those old neural connections will gradually unravel allowing you to establish new, more positive associations to link up with your old drama triggers. When you do that, you have a new choice of how to respond. This is a powerful step toward freedom.

MAKE IT UP

In my days of training to become a coach, I heard one of my instructors say to the class, "What I make up about that is . . ." Those words roused a vague memory of Mister Rogers' Neighborhood of Make-Believe from deep among the cobwebs of my mind. To bring the concept of *making things up* into adult life was a whole new framework for me, one that took a little adjusting to. The reality is we're making everything up all the time. We're inventing the world around us *constantly*. That being the case, why not make up things that feel *good*, things that are reflections of Who We Really Are, that take us to the next level of best? Perhaps we never really think that this is an option. That's only because we didn't learn it, witness it, or have it modeled for us by adults applying it to adult life. Very few individuals among the generations before us knew how to imagine and feel things into being once they crossed the threshold of puberty. Obviously there were some who passed on the wisdom of the ages, but it's only in recent years that the broader collective consciousness has become ready to receive this concept. I hope that its reaching you today will lead you to reflect on and acknowledge what you are making up in your own life.

Most of us have shitty-feeling stories about certain aspects of our lives. We have good-feeling stories too and that's great! But it's the crummy ones that get us hooked into drama. Those are the assumptions that are disempowering, reactive, maladaptive, and addictive, which we believe so wholeheartedly that we allow them to drive the ship of our lives. The trick is to write yourself a better-feeling *story*. It might seem like a whole bunch of bull-a-baloney at first, but if so, that's okay. It just means you have a normal brain.

Writing a new story consists of telling yourself how you want things to be, but in the present tense. It's really that simple. You may have a complaint about your workplace not giving you opportunities to grow, about how you're not valued, your talents or skills are not being well utilized. Even writing those words now starts to feel depressing to me. Start to tell a new story about how you have endless opportunities in your workplace, how people are constantly approaching you for your wisdom and the expertise that utilizes your capacities and skills. You're constantly being challenged to grow and you love it! As a result of your growing you get promotion after promotion until you're in the most perfect role and you can't imagine having a better job fit ever! You can hardly believe that you get paid for doing the work that you do, because it's so pleasurable and rewarding that you would do it for *free*. Do you get the feeling of this? Better than the old depressing story, eh?

Something also to notice as you're making up new stories is the mental images and auditory self-talk that comes to your mind. You probably have different pictures displayed on your mental screen compared to what appears when you focus on the unwanted current version. You can play with the images, volume control, and spinning feelings to make the new story even more powerful! Once you develop the new story, then start to really let your imagination go deeper into it. "What else does my ideal reality include?" (Note: that's a Constructive Question.) If this new, better-feeling story were already the truth for you, how would you feel? When you can get into the feeling state of *that*, your work for the moment is done. At that juncture, you're out of the drama and into the *thriving*. You're back to feeling good—your number-one goal!

The bottom line: we might as well make up stuff that feels good and create stories that are in alignment with where we want to go. Have fun with this one!

SELF-CHECK

Self-Checking is about taking 100 percent ownership of our experience. We are constantly co-creating our realities with others and with the world around us. When drama gets stirred up we need to check in with ourselves to see in what ways we are responsible and how we can best respond to the situation. This can be applied to our overall life circumstances, workplace happenings, and interpersonal dynamics. If we perceive that something or someone *out there* is "doing it to me," there must be some version of doing "it" to myself (or others) *in here* as well, which is being brought to our attention at this time so we can heal and resolve it. Self-Checking involves tending to our wounds and making sure we are self-honoring, seeking effective ways to get our needs met. If there are things that activate drama within us, things we "don't like," it points to something in our resonant field that is drawing those circumstances toward us. This is not to say it's our "fault," because so much of what we embody is unconscious or part of a collective energy. Our job, however, is to identify what we would prefer and what we need in response to external happenings in order to grow, expand, maintain alignment, and feel good. When we Self-Check we are looking for ways we can take personal responsibility and influence change on the things that are within our domain. It reminds us that our job is *us*—managing *our* thoughts and our emotional-vibrational states. The question to ask is, "What will be most self-honoring in this circumstance?"

With regard to relationships, we walk around the earth innocently, as if *we* never hurt or "wronged" anyone. That's virtually impossible in our wound-based, self-focused, drama-prone age. While we are all doing the best we can, sometimes our words or actions have an unintended negative impact. Ideally, in learning that we hurt someone's feelings or otherwise inadvertently "wronged" them, we would be willing to acknowledge them, take stock of our own behaviors, intentions, and motives, and apologize as needed. Yet, when our blunders are presented to us, we oftentimes feel our security is threatened, activating a drama response. In this instance, most people tend to justify their actions, ascribe blame to the one who was hurt, or dismiss the issue altogether. Any of these responses will only exacerbate the drama in the relationship and continue its perpetual effects.

When we become aware that someone is upset with us or has felt hurt by something we said or did, a Self-Check will help us evaluate our involvement in the matter. It will slow down our reactions, let us hit the pause button, and ask, "What's my part in this?" Sometimes it is another person's projections and meshugas that has them upset, which has very little or nothing to do with us. We can still acknowledge their experience without having to agree with them. Other times we really have "done something" that needs examination and "cleaning up" on our end. This is why we need to Self-Check, to identify where we can make amends, learn, and grow, or where we can "let go and let God." Either way, a useful question to ask is, "What will be most honoring for this relationship?"

CLARIFY ASSUMPTIONS

Clarifying assumptions is about checking in with others, connecting with their reality rather than acting only on our story. Because we see through limited lenses based on our experiences, we automatically draw certain assumptions when we're given particular information. We think that the world operates according to *our* views. Sometimes it does and sometimes it doesn't. When it comes to getting stuck in drama, we need to clarify our assumptions with other people. It looks like this: you check in with them and say, "I have an assumption that _____ blah, blah, blah." Let them know that you recognize this is *your* assumption and it may not be true for them. Also emphasize that the reason you're checking in on it is because you *want* to understand their viewpoint and their reasons for their choices.

Clarifying assumptions is about getting to the heart of the matter. It's about seeking to understand. It's about asking questions first before deciding whether or not to "shoot." Since drama is clearly oriented around assumption-based thinking, clarifying assumptions is actually a really important technique to bring into your *thriving* lifestyle. It's a specific tool that you utilize when you recognize that you're doing some guesswork in your mind; it's not necessarily a habit or lifestyle as much as it is something that you can employ as needed.

You may want to develop your own list of general assumptions about life, about people, and even about yourself before you start practicing this with others. This exercise will help your brain to identify what your overarching themes are. I used to have an assumption that "people think women

211

are most attractive when they have tiny bottoms and skinny legs." That's because the people I grew up around held that view, which of course was shameful to me since I am *not* built that way. I've come to learn that out in the big, wide world there is a range of preferences and varying perspectives on what defines attractiveness. That assumption is actually invalid when it comes to certain cultures and even individuals who appreciate women with rounder shapes and thicker statures, finding *them* to be most attractive.

Our assumptions are usually grounded in the stories that we develop through witnessing others, the beliefs we adopt, the opinions that were imposed upon us, and the values and morals that we were taught. Since there really is no one right way of doing anything in life, letting go of our assumptions allows life to become so much easier and more peaceful.

Assumptions are the bane of authentic connection. Check in, clarify, get the real scoop. The same goes if you notice other people making assumptions about *you*. It's always okay to step up and let them know the truth of who you are, how you're thinking, and the values you hold. Whatever they're projecting onto you is nothing to take offense over. It's simply a human mechanism for trying to relate, and we all do it. Here we see why transparency is so important for deep connection and true *thriving*. When we limit people to our viewpoints of them we objectify them, whereby we hold ourselves in the space of separation. And separation kills. It's painful, it's useless, it's totally unnecessary, and it's a cornerstone for drama.

GET INTO THE GROOVE

Last but not least, music is a powerful tool for shifting how we feel. Get up, get your body moving, sing, connect with the lyrics. Anything that has a personal empowerment message, feels soothing, or enlivens can do the trick. This can help you utilize the Dance of the Five D's. What's on your *thriving* playlist? Put it together and keep it handy on your MP3 player or your smartphone. Identify specific songs that are funny or calming. Know what your go-to music resource is before the drama hits, so you can click

PLAY and just let the music take you away.

Applying the Tools to Your Life

In order for these tools to work, you do actually have to use them. A hammer does not smack a nail of its own accord—furthermore, one strike is not usually enough to drive the nail all the way home. You have to take charge of the hammer, line it up, hold focused intention, and drive it in. Same deal here, especially if you are working with a human brain. You have to try these guys on for size, which can be a great thing to do with a partner, ideally someone who is understanding and encouraging. Practice utilizing them when you are not in an overly stressed drama state. That way you can familiarize yourself with them and have an idea of how to work them *before* you get triggered into a reactive, defensive survival mode, in which case you will not be able to remember your own name, much less how to make up a new story or change the images and sounds in your mind. Get it into your system first when all cortical cylinders are firing properly and efficiently.

Always remember to let it be fun and easy.

"Through consciousness, our minds have the power to change our planet and ourselves. It is time we heed the wisdom of the ancient indigenous people and channel our consciousness and spirit to tend the garden and not destroy it."

—DR. BRUCE LIPTON

Key Concepts

＊ To live an authentically *thriving* life we need to begin changing our stories to feel better, shifting our energetic states at will, recovering quickly, and consistently returning into alignment when we go below the line. The implementation of any of these methods will generate changes in your brain's neurological connections and give you new thoughts to work with so you can effectively change how you feel, as well as influence your external experiences.

＊ Essential inner alignment tools to recover from drama:

- Truth or Opinion—Evaluate whether your thoughts are based on absolute truth or if they are just an *opinion*.

- Flip It—Take the main theme of what you are thinking and flip it to its complete opposite. Allow the juxtaposition to provide you with range to shift into a better-feeling direction.

- Volume Control—Listen for negative internal dialogue. Sum up the message in one line. Notice the volume setting in your mind. Begin to turn down the volume on that voice. Once it's muted, replace the line with a positive one, start from mute, and gradually turn up the volume on the better-feeling dialogue and even surpass the original volume setting of the original disempowering voice. Let it feel good!

- Imagery Direction—Notice the pictures in your mind when you are in a drama state. Remove yourself if you are in the picture, shrink the picture down, and put a frame around it, like you're watching TV. Let it shrink smaller and smaller and notice how you feel about the scene as you can see it less and less. Be intentional about getting your mind onto something else in the present moment of your real life in order to recover and feel good.

- Spinning the Feelings Within—When feeling bad, notice where the hub of the energy is in your body and what direction it is spinning: forward, backward, clockwise, counterclockwise. Move your hand in rhythm with that feeling, then begin to make it smaller and slow it down until you reach a halt. Then slowly begin to spin your hand in the opposite direction to instigate a reverse of the inner feeling to something more positive.

- Get Some Perspectives—Play with finding another way to see things. Everything in life offers an alternate perspective on your drama: a tiger, Mother Teresa, the sunrise—a different viewpoint will give you space for relief and recovery to *thriving*.

- The Squirrel in the Tree—This is a fun play on the Observer concept. It involves an internal dissociation from the drama images and thoughts we conjure up, freeing ourselves to witness instead of being *in* the intensity of the drama. Watching how you're managing your thoughts is the key here.

- Just Sit with It—Here we process the emotion. Tolerate it. Feel it. Go deeper into the energy of it and the recovery will come quickly and effectively.

- State-Breakers—Interrupt the energetic states of drama, and shift into a totally, completely different state of mind and emotion. This is an intervention to cut off the stuff that's screwing with your *thriving* so you can get back into it.

- Make It Up—Invent new stories with your creative imagination for the sake of nothing more than feeling good. Instead of making up the drama stories, make-believe things are exactly as you want them to be and all systems—mental, emotional, physical, spiritual—will follow in accordance with what you envision and how you influence your energetic states through this method.

- Self-Check—When drama gets stirred up we need to check in with ourselves to see in what ways we are responsible and how we can best respond to the situation. Self-Check is simply looking for how we can take personal responsibility and influence change on the things we *do* have control or influence over to get our needs met. It reminds us that our job is *us* and managing *our* thoughts and *our* emotional-vibrational states.

- Clarify Assumptions—When getting stuck in relational drama we need to clarify our assumptions with other people. We see through limited lenses based on our experiences, and automatically draw certain conclusions when we're given particular information. Checking in with others allows us to understand their reality, rather than acting only on our story.

- Get into the Groove—Music, music, music! It's good for the brain! Good for the mood! Make your feel-good playlist and turn to it when you need a positive vibe injection.

Application and Integration

Tools I think will work best for me:

My drama tendencies that I will apply them to are:

Simple ways to remind myself to use these tools are:

My additional thoughts and reflections are:

CHAPTER TEN

The Universe Was Built for You to *Thrive*

"No amount of reading or memorizing will make you successful in life. It is the understanding and application of wise thought that counts."

—BOB PROCTOR

Being lifelong Earth Dwellers, most of us have an inherent understanding of gravity and how it works. At the very least, we unconsciously discovered its existence when we began to walk. If we did not succeed in taking those first few steps, we didn't float up; we fell down. Even at that age, without us intellectually knowing what gravity is or how it works, it still exerted its force upon us. This is because it is a Universal Law; it applies to all things even in the absence of our awareness of it. It is exactly the same with other laws, which you may not be aware of but are still influencing your life.

We humans are exceptionally adept at making life much more complicated than it needs to be. We overthink the reasons that underlie our experiences and constantly search for meaning to figure it all out. We end up not trusting life and feeling as though we are victims of an "angry God." Part of the reason for all of these difficulties is that we simply lack an awareness of what the Universal Laws are and an understanding of how they work. Because we understand gravity, we expect to go down if we stumble. We expect that if we're holding an object and then let go, it will fall to the floor. While in certain instances this can be a bummer, it's not a surprise. We know what to expect, so we know how to watch our step or adjust our grip to stay upright and keep things in one piece. When it comes to other Universal Laws, we don't know how to work *with* them until we learn what they are and identify how they influence the creation of our lives. In the absence of that, the frustration and anxiety we build up from our lack of understanding makes us highly drama-prone. This is why thought-management is so important. Having an understanding of how the Universe works in our favor when we let it helps us to direct our thoughts and choices in a manner that works with these Laws, leading us to be much more powerful and effective with significantly less struggle or concerted effort.

A Snapshot of the Universal Laws

This chapter offers a high-level overview of the Universal Laws and provides tips on how to apply them to change old drama patterns into authentically *thriving* consciousness. Let's take a look at the ones that are essential to dialing down the drama and really stepping into authentic *thriving*. They take some time to understand and apply, so keep reviewing these pages and processing them through your beautiful brain. Here's what we'll cover:

- The Law of Perpetual Transmutation
- The Laws of Gender and Gestation
- The Law of Attraction
- The Law of Polarity
- The Law of Relativity
- The Law of Rhythm
- The Vacuum Law of the Universe

THE LAW OF PERPETUAL TRANSMUTATION

The Law of Perpetual Transmutation basically says that things are always coming into, and going out of, existence or form. Since everything in life is made up of energy, and energy is constantly moving, anything we can imagine, all the things that we see or know, are somewhere in the process of becoming or receding, of converting from one form to another—including your ideas. Your ideas are a form of energy flowing as thoughts. Before you had an idea of something you desired, you had some sort of experience that brought to your awareness a kind of "lack." Out of this lack emerged the idea of what you would like to have, and you innately knew that the fulfillment of that idea would feel great and be preferable to your current experience. This is what we call "contrast." An idea held with belief and *thriving* energies empowers the assimilation of the desire at the quantum level, which can then emerge into physical reality.

For example, you're going about your day, busy with tasks. Your mind is occupied with whatever you're focused on doing when all of a sudden you have an experience of hunger and the accompanying desire to eat. You don't dismiss the hunger or the desire as something you can never ever achieve or as a need you'll never get met. You instead get an idea of what you would like to eat, of what would feel good to you in that moment.

You get the idea that having a salad would satisfy your need for food and it would feel great, taste yummy, be nourishing. Now, until you actually go to the fridge, pull out your veggie kit, and mix the greens, your salad is still in the idea phase of the "becoming" process. You don't think "salad!" and it instantaneously appears. There is a bit of processing and assembly that is required for you to ultimately get that meal into your belly and quell the hunger signals. This makes logical sense when you know the components of the salad are in the fridge and you understand that making the salad is just part of being able to have it manifest into your experience and fulfill your desire. You don't dismiss the possibility of having a salad just because you can't see the unassembled items that compose it, hidden in the fridge.

Then, while you're washing and chopping the veggies, you don't begin to doubt having a salad just because you don't see it on the plate in front of you immediately. You believe, unquestioningly, that through your actions the salad *is* coming.

You don't get annoyed that the salad is only on the plate and not in your belly as you walk it to the table to sit down. Instead, you feel good—happy, grateful, eager, excited—that it's almost time to eat.

Finally, you get to enjoy the physical reality of eating, chewing, swallowing, and feeling your hunger dissipate as your body is nourished. What was once your idea, your desire for food, has become your experience of consuming a salad. Eventually that salad will also convert its form, transmuting into the breakdown of nutrients and waste, and eventually getting burned as energy or going back to the earth, so to speak.

When it comes to something as simple as salad, we get this whole process. We understand the steps. What I want you to also "get" is that it's pretty much the same with anything else we want to manifest; we just usually don't know what all the "salad components" are and we don't see the way they are going to reach the plate or how they'll make it into our bellies.

The Law of Perpetual Transmutation is, like gravity, constantly working in relationship to us, and delivering to us (or not) based on our thoughts. The desire, focused attention, belief, and gratitude-in-advance are all essential components of the manifestational process. They are the elements we can "see" or know along the way. As soon as we inadvertently dip into doubt or grow impatient, annoyed that our stuff isn't here yet, we unfortunately reverse the energetic process. Since what we focus on is what we get, our negative feelings push away the object of our desire, and it will no longer manifest for us but will retreat back into the ethers. The image on the next page illustrates this process and how this law works.

THE LAWS OF GENDER AND GESTATION

All things in life house the dual energies of the masculine and the feminine.

Law of Perpetual Transmutation

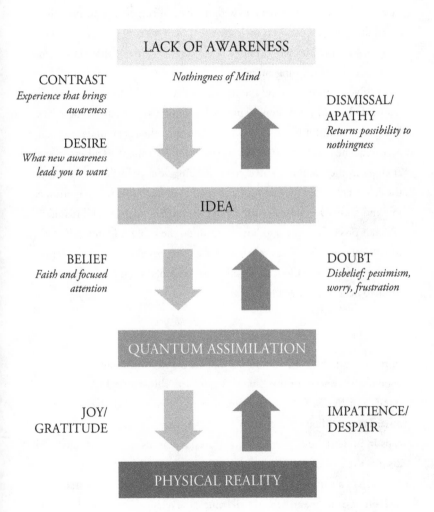

The Law of Gender basically reminds us that in order to manifest what we want, we have to have both the "seed" (the idea) and the "fertile soil" (the energetic state). In order for our ideas to grow, we have to nourish them with focused attention, belief, and high-vibrational energies like joy and appreciation. The Law of Gestation reminds us that all things that come into manifestation take a certain amount of time to do so, including our ideas. These laws work in tandem with the Law of Perpetual Transmutation. Since the gestation period is basically the time it takes to go from "Idea" to "Physical Reality," it's our job in the meantime to cultivate those idea-seeds with effective, nourishing energies.

If you wanted to grow a tomato plant, you would not keep it in a pot in the dark, cold cellar, pour some toxic chemicals on it, and expect it to bring you beautiful fruits. You would plant it in the earth, under the sun, and frequently feed it water. When you hold your mental and emotional energies in the realm of drama, you're keeping your beautiful idea-seeds in the cellar, fed with toxic chemicals, instead of in the fertile soil of gratitude, joy, and faith. Our ideas need such an environment to grow and manifest, which is precisely why it's so important to do the Daily Alignment Practice to cultivate *thriving*. The consciousness of *thriving* alone will help deliver what you desire—without much effort on your part even—when you continue to believe and live GRATE-fully.

THE LAW OF ATTRACTION

In recent years the book and movie *The Secret* introduced audiences worldwide to the concept of the Law of Attraction. This is a vital law to understand, and by itself, is incomplete. It works synchronistically with these other laws. Without awareness of them, many people have been left with gaps in understanding that the brain uses as reasons to get frustrated and dismiss the Law of Attraction as invalid or as "woo-woo."

The Law of Attraction simply states that like energies are attracted to each other. Since we are vibrational beings, the quality of the energies we are emitting through our thoughts and emotional states will attract people and circumstances that match them. Whatever you're experiencing in your life is a perfect reflection of how you're managing your thoughts (or not) and the kind of emotional states you're generating. I know this is really annoying to think about in the beginning, because it seems like it is "all our fault." In a way it is, because we are always co-creating with the Universe. We are 100 percent responsible for everything in our world, but it's not like we're intentionally creating the relationship conflicts, the job loss, the car crash, or the illness. While these things may on some level be divinely ordained or appear as "fate," in many cases they are reflections of the quality of energy that we are embodying and emitting by virtue of how we are directing our thoughts day in, day out.

When we recycle the same old thoughts, perpetuate the same old themes, and reactivate the same old wounds, we will surely attract people and circumstances that match the same vibration we are emitting, and then we say, "See! This always happens to me!"

The challenging thing, however, is the paradox of being where you are in any given experience, and empowering the feeling state of where you want to go. We live in a co-creative Universe, so anything we need to pay attention to within ourselves, perhaps an area that is ready for conscious growth, will become highlighted for us through our experience with the outer world. Said differently, anything we are complaining about is an area of *opportunity*. Drama is what gets us stuck in negative internal patterns and inhibits the process of creating new life experiences and opportunities. Once we can heal the drama, we can be with the contrast in a way that allows a natural flow of harmony in our lives.

Regardless of what's going on in your life, don't make yourself "bad" for it. What you've manifested is the result of a *past vibration* anyway. *Do* use what's going on to draw your attention to the kinds of things that you are thinking about. If you're spending most of your time in DRAMA consciousness, you're probably spawning a vibration that is attracting unwanted stuff. Carrying on with the kinds of patterns that you developed in the past, based on how you learned to operate in the world, will continue to perpetuate similar experiences simply because you have not updated your current vibration to align with your desires.

Fortunately, you don't live there all the time. Sometimes, you *are* above the line in the energies of *thriving*, thinking thoughts that feel good. This is why you also attract great things, evidenced in the experiences you do enjoy. Enter the Daily Alignment Practice: miracles, magic, and manifestations. The conscious external acknowledgment of the good stuff amplifies it in our vibration, moves us up the spectrum of consciousness to feel better and better, and to also attract more and more of what we want.

More cool news: the stuff that shows up in our experience that we don't like *automatically* leads us to identify what we would prefer, even if it's not on a conscious level. The "bad stuff" provides the "contrast" we need to generate new ideas that we can grow into, by practicing belief, joy, and gratitude. Living in *thriving* consciousness nurtures them to come into our physical reality. When the Law of Attraction brings to us unwanted stuff, it is really our call to grow into the next level of who we are capable of becoming. That growth comes through managing our thoughts and being deliberate about our emotional states, in spite of the circumstances—AKA: keeping pace on the physical plane with the soul's expansion. Once we can bring the *thriving* energy forward, no longer in pain from the drama or the lack, the Universe, by Law of Attraction, must deliver on our desires. Again, this navigation of the chaos of contrast and resulting manifestation of our desire is what the DRAMA-free, *thriving* lifestyle is designed to empower, to make easier for us, so we can really, truly let life be so much more easy, joyous, and wealthful.

You'll notice in the illustration on the next page that the contrast from experiencing the "bad stuff" of life and the desire that emerges from it results in an idea of what we would prefer. That idea can then be responded to with positive or negative energies. There is a distinction made between

Law of Attraction

CONTRAST

DESIRE

IDEA

THOUGHT PATTERNS:
Positive, thriving consciousness

THINKING
Generating new ideas and images

BELIEF
Faith and focused attention

FEELING STATE

JOY/GRATITUDE

THOUGHT PATTERNS:
Negative, DRAMA consciousness

REMEMBERING
Recycling old experiences and memories

DOUBT
Disbelief: pessimism, worry, frustration

IMPATIENCE/DESPAIR

PHYSICAL REALITY

PHYSICAL REALITY

thinking and remembering in the process of attracting our experiences. The Law of Attraction is working, like gravity, whether we are aware of it or not. When we are in drama mode, many times we are recycling past memories or catastrophizing based on our old wounds. When we are in *thriving* mode, we are thinking new thoughts, *telling the new story as we would like things to be*, and allowing it to feel really, *really* good, even just in the imagining process. Hold the belief, infuse a little joy and gratitude, and voilà! You have a new physical reality. Stay in the drama, do the doubt dance, and feel like crap, and you'll probably get more of the same-old-same-old. You see, you always have two paths you can take from the same contrasting experience and the same idea-seed of your desire that results from it. You can go DRAMA or you can choose the DRAMA-free way.

Part of the catch to the Law of Attraction is being able to live in the Vibrational Time Paradox. As seen in the next illustration, Physical Reality always follows Vibrational State. This means you have to practice the energy of having what you want in the absence of it *first* in order for it to manifest. This is where telling new stories and using your imagination to generate a positive emotional state come in. We need to use any excuse we can to feel good—rich, loved, valuable, peaceful, connected—because it is this feeling that allows the Law of Attraction to line things up and deliver the match to our vibration. Said differently, what you are experiencing in any given moment is the result of a *past* vibration. What you are emitting now determines what will come in the future. The challenge is to feel *good* regardless of the present lack of what you desire. We can do this when we understand the Laws of Perpetual Transmutation, Gender, and Gestation.

We can know that it's comin', baby, so start gettin' *excited*!

THE LAW OF POLARITY

As the name implies, everything in the Universe has an equal opposite: inside and outside, up and down, hot and cold, back and front, dark and

Vibrational Time Paradox:
Feeling Things into Reality

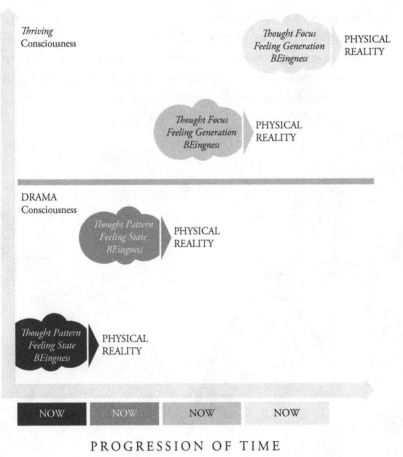

light, etc. The opposite is equal in measure; the distance from New York to Los Angeles is the same as the distance from Los Angeles to New York (when measured in a straight line). What this means in the non-physical world of our thoughts and vibrations is that all things we call "bad" also inherently have an equal opposite "good."

Our life experiences, in general, are neutral. They have no meaning until we assign meaning to them. There is a collective consensus about the "goodness" or "badness" of various experiences, which are usually based on how they make us feel. The Law of Polarity is here to remind us that little annoyances also hold little opportunities. Those things that appear most traumatic or devastating also yield the greatest gifts and blessings. This Law is what we connect with in the *thriving* tool Flip It, which is the brain's way of stretching into the full opposite so we can move in the direction of discovering the "good" concealed in the "bad."

Law of Polarity

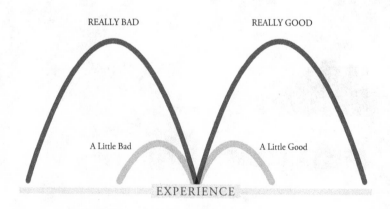

THE LAW OF RELATIVITY

Distinct from Einstein's *Theory* of Relativity, the Universal Law of Relativity illuminates that all things in life have a comparison point; everything is relative. We use this language in our vernacular all the time, but I'm not sure how many of us really utilize the gift delivered in this law. All things are measured by point of comparison. Your household income is probably not as high as Donald Trump's, but also probably not as low as that of a homeless person on the streets of Calcutta.

Nothing is good or bad, high or low, without a relative comparison point—including your vibration. You can tell whether your vibration is high or low based on how you *feel*. This is why we make feeling good *on purpose* so important.

We can best utilize this law as a tool to enhance the positives in our lives by focusing on something comparatively "worse," in order to highlight the blessings we already enjoy. Instead of doing what your drama thinking implores, which is comparing yourself to those who are what you would consider "better off" than you—smarter, richer, taller, shorter, thinner, curvier, older, younger, etc.—compare yourself to those who are "worse off"—less smart, less advantaged, less capable, less wealthy, less attractive, less well-fed, etc. The purpose is not to live in a better-worse world; it is to alter your point of reference so you *feel better*. It's to give you easier access to gratitude, appreciation, joy, calm, and love. One effect of shifting your point of comparison when evaluating yourself is the enhancement of your positive self-regard, which automatically aligns you with your Higher Self and inherently increases your vibration to the levels of *thriving* consciousness. This process then works in tandem with the aforementioned laws to improve your life experience.

THE LAW OF RHYTHM

The Law of Rhythm states that there is an ebb and flow to all things and experiences in life. There is a season for all things, and to every action there is a reaction. Our physical, mental, and emotional energies have rhythmic fluctuations. In order to expand we must first contract. This is the pulsing of life. Nothing is static; it's always in movement. Being in sync with our own rhythm can help reduce confusion and enhance ease and joy in life. A prime example: women who know their menstrual rhythms can better tend to their emotional fluctuations during certain days on their cycles. Listening to our rhythms helps us follow what feels good in any given moment.

The Laws of Polarity and Relativity show us that there are good days and bad days, comparatively high and low moments. We can expect that the down times will come. What the Law of Rhythm states is that *an up is on the way* when we are down. Being able to *allow* our emotions to flow exactly as they are, even (especially!) in the energies of sub-*thriving*, is what helps us maintain alignment with our Higher Selves. It's what following our rhythms and keeping pace with the soul's expansion is all about. At times that may mean seeking relief through the release found in crying, punching a pillow, or yelling in your car, which energetically takes us into the momentum of the upswing. When we resist the "downs," we perpetuate the lower drama states. So the stage of **grieve** in GRATE-full living, and the tool of Just Sit with It, is what allows us to deliberately swing the pendulum the other direction and let the Law of Rhythm (and Attraction—because thoughts attract like thoughts) move us back into the higher states of *thriving*.

What the Law of Rhythm helps us be aware of and prepared for is something called the "breakdown before the breakthrough." The breakdown before the breakthrough is essentially a complete emulsification of our internal energetic structure at the spiritual level, breaking everything down completely and then rebuilding it to exist on a new, higher level of who we are capable of being. This is similar to what a butterfly—nature's epitome of transformation—does in its cocoon. Entering as a fugly little larvae, the soon-to-be-butterfly completely breaks down over time and rebuilds its physical structure to emerge as a strong yet delicate-winged beauty. As humans, we experience the "ebbing" of life as what we would call "downs," "hitting bottom," or "dark times." What we fail to realize is it is precisely the experience of those lows that launches us to the next new high. The breakdown before the breakthrough is that darkest moment that comes before our brightest dawn. When we come out on the other side, we embody a more refined, improved version of ourselves. By understanding the Law of Rhythm and knowing that resistance or difficulties often increase *right before success*, we can be prepared to *allow* it and then ride the rhythmic wave of *thriving* rather than being beaten down by the lows and subsequently getting stuck in the drama.

THE VACUUM LAW OF THE UNIVERSE

Life doesn't do "voids." This law states that if there is an absence found in an otherwise "occupied" space, *something* will be pulled in to fill the space to maintain hemostasis or preserve the status quo. If you want something new, you have to purge the old to make space. If you want a fulfilling partnership, you need to leave an unhealthy relationship behind first. If you want a new physical body, you have to give up some TV time to make room for a workout routine. Likewise, if you want to get rid of something that is no longer effective, you have to replace it with something new or else risk going back to the old. When making the decision to live consistently in *thriving* consciousness, it means you have to go drama-free to make room for new thought patterns and better-feeling states.

When you determine what you want—in any area of life—take the time to identify what you're holding on to that's keeping you from it. It could be beliefs about security or thought patterns of victimhood. It could be a fierce need to be seen as "independent" or "successful." To release the old, ineffective ways, first know where you're going and what you'll be replacing them with. If you don't identify what to fill the void with you'll be subject to falling back into old patterns, simply because the Universe will fill the space with *something*, and usually that's the default to what we know or are already familiar with.

At the beginning of 2015, I determined to lovingly release two thought patterns that keep me from what I truly want: inferiority and scarcity. To declare that I'm letting these patterns go is great, but it's not enough. I need to know what I'll be focusing on, practicing, implementing, and believing *instead*, otherwise my brain will automatically default to what it has practiced for decades. My replacements: "I am enough" and "There is always more than enough." These are the basic go-to thought themes to start, and then I can build from there: "I am enough, and where I am is absolutely perfect. The gifts I bring and the talents I share offer infinite value. I am always growing into more." "The Universe is infinite in possibilities and in abundance. There is always more than enough of everything I want and need. It's easy to share and be generous because I am in the infinite flow of abundance and well-being. I am gratefully receiving endless wealth of all kinds *now*." By the way, did you notice that this is "making it up" and telling the new story? This new framing and belief stance generates better-feeling images in my mind, and each thought attracts another like-thought that builds up my momentum and leads me into higher and higher vibrational states. Wahoo!

Knowing where to go helps us shift gears when we get triggered into the old drama internalogue, so we can continue to grow into an ever-more *thriving* consciousness.

Conscious Use of the Laws of the Universe

Now that you have a high-level understanding of the Universal Laws, and some ideas of why they are important and how they work, start to develop your own unique way of engaging them. Keep it simple. Have patience. Know that if you embrace GRATE-full living, do the Daily Alignment Practice, and employ the tools for DRAMA-free thinking, you will automatically be working with these laws to your favor. Let it be simple, easy, and always let it feel good.

"Everything is energy and that's all there is to it. Match the frequency of the reality you want and you cannot help but get that reality. It can be no other way. This is not philosophy. This is physics."

—ALBERT EINSTEIN

Key Concepts

✳ Having an understanding of how the Universe is designed to work in our favor helps us direct our thoughts and choices in a manner that works *with* these Laws, leading us to be much more powerful and effective with significantly less drama. These laws work harmoniously with one another to support our ability to live in alignment with our Higher Selves and have the best experiences possible. The Laws of the Universe we can apply to navigating the chaos and authentically *thriving* are:

- The Law of Perpetual Transmutation—All things in life are made up of energy, and that energy is perpetually coming into and going out of various forms. This includes our thoughts and our ideas, which can come to fruition or not based on quality of energy we use to fuel them.

- The Laws of Gender & Gestation—The creation of all things requires a seed, a fertile environment for the seed to grow to its full expression, and a requisite amount of time for that process to complete itself. When it comes to having a *thriving* life, the seeds are our ideas of what we desire, the environment in which they flourish or wither is the mind and energetic state, and the gestation period is influenced by our alignment with our Higher Selves and trust in Divine order.

- The Law of Attraction—Like energies come together. Things, people, experiences all have a vibrational quality to them. The vibration we emit as a result of the energetic state we embody by way of our thoughts determines what we attract into our sphere of experience. The time paradox of this law is that our present moment circumstance is the result of a *past* vibration. Anything we want to move into the future must first be "vibrated" within.

- The Law of Polarity—All things have an equal opposite to them.

When looking at "bad" experiences we can rest assured, knowing that there is an inherent "good" in them as well, a blessing of sorts, even if we can't see it yet.

- The Law of Relativity—All things have a point of comparison that we can use to feel good or feel bad, depending on whether we are focusing on something "worse" than our conditions or "better" than them.

- The Law of Rhythm—Life has a natural ebb and flow, a season for all things. This is a contraction-expansion dynamic that we experience in order to grow. Flowing with the rhythm allows for *thriving*; resisting it leads to drama.

- The Vacuum Law of the Universe—Nature avoids "voids." If there is an absence found in an otherwise "occupied" space, *something* will be pulled in to fill the space to maintain hemostasis or preserve the status quo. A shift from drama requires intentional "filling" with something positive or more useful.

Application and Integration

Ways I see the Universal Laws at work in my life:

How I will apply knowledge of these laws to be drama-free:

How I will utilize these laws to be intentional about *thriving*:

CHAPTER ELEVEN

Interacting with OPD—Other People's DRAMA—and Championing Change

"If we could look into each other's hearts and understand the unique challenges each of us faces, I think we would treat each other much more gently, with more love, patience, tolerance, and care."

—MARVIN J. ASHTON

This chapter is written primarily for those folks who bear witness to OPD—other people's DRAMA—and are not sure how to support them and encourage the shift to *thriving*. Perhaps you are somewhat less drama prone, in terms of your own negative emotional intensity and the acting out it can produce. You may not know how to relate or respond to the drama behavior you witness in others. It's a fine line to walk, wanting to be supportive but not enabling, seeking to be a catalyst for improvement without shaming. You want to stay off the Drama Triangle, not playing Hero and not victimizing or vilifying the other person by saving, enabling, or criticizing them, because that only perpetuates the cycle. So then, what do you do? You're in a relationship with this person, be it personally or professionally, so how do you engage and respond in effective ways? That's what this chapter is about. You can apply these concepts to any of your people, regardless of the role they play in your life: workplace relationships (boss, coworkers, or employees), significant others, friends, children, teenagers, club comrades, religious associates, and so on.

This chapter is still also for those who struggle with drama and are wanting to commit to the world of *thriving*. You will want to learn how to remain immune from "catching" OPD and also identify what kind of support is most effective for *you* when you are triggered into drama, so you can ask your people for help, educating them about what works for you. As loved ones, we always reach out to do what we *think* is most supportive, but we may not be hitting the mark. It's important to have the conversation in a drama-free moment about what's helpful and what's not, regardless of which end of the spectrum you tend to be on.

A few years ago, I had a drama episode around food (which you know by now has been one of my trigger-point "issues"). In this particular instance, I let myself get way too hungry and then started to catastrophize and panic about eating, terrified that it would "make me fat." In a meltdown moment on the kitchen floor, my husband tried to help by thrusting pictures of literally starving people in my face. Although his intention was good, and he was instinctively using the Law of Relativity to get me to snap out of it, I was already so deeply in the throes of drama that it had the *opposite* effect, plummeting me desperately into humiliation, making matters worse. What would've been more helpful in that moment would have been to just let me ride it out, while remaining present and loving.

Drama needs love, consistency, predictability, and strong but unattached compassion. I recently had a conversation with a lady who worked in a hotel shop where I was staying. She was sharing with me an instance when her husband had a drama episode in the car, getting flustered and worked up into a heightened negative state (I don't know what the topic was, and it's irrelevant anyway). He screamed at her something to the effect of, "Do you wanna fuckin' drive?" And—*BAM*—she got yanked right into *his* drama state. She then started yelling too, getting *reactive* in return, which only fed the beast.

When we witness OPD, we need to take charge of our own energy first and *not* get suckered into the drama zone. This is why it's so important to know what our options are in advance. I told her, she could've responded calmly, lovingly, with something more along the lines of, "Oh sure, baby, no problem. You just rest, relax, and I'll drive." The thought never occurred to her. Because she was so trained into their marital dynamics, which involved this kind of repartee, she fell into the auto-response mode that they both knew: yelling and amplifying the drama.

It can be very easy for us to get sucked into another's emotional energy. We take it on, as if it were a contagious virus (which it kinda is), and we quickly become disoriented, losing ourselves in the chaos of what they want or need or are screaming about. Since our brains learn what to expect from others, and since we engage behaviors that fulfill our biochemical needs, beginning to make changes in pre-established dynamics will likely take some persistence, time, and patience—both with yourself and the other person. It's really important to know how to engage in ways that remain neutral and loving, honoring both the other person *and* yourself. Over time, and especially when you can talk about these things in calmer moments, claiming the opportunity to heal one another's wounds, you can move together into *thriving* living.

Responding to a DRAMA Episode

*"What is not Love is but a **call** for Love."*

—MARIANNE WILLIAMSON

If you've noticed, I've used this quote a few times throughout this book. That's not a mistake or an editorial mixup. It's intentional, because it succinctly identifies the purpose of drama ("a call for love") and we need constant reminders of that. When we see others in distress, we often have the tendency to want to "fix" it or "save" them. But we are all fine precisely where we are; we are all just in our process of life. Rushing in as the Hero can have the opposite effect of reinforcing the "drama addiction," although it may calm things in the moment. Acting the Hero is ironically joining in on the drama, as a Hero needs a Victim to feel valuable. The rush in to "save" the person can also continue to perpetuate their needs—for security, to matter, to be loved—being met *via* drama, which does not serve their improvement or recovery. This is what's called "enabling."

We need alternative responses we can choose from to interact with drama effectively. First and foremost is to know, at your core, that drama is *not* the truth of who the person is. It is simply a series of biochemical and behavioral reactions to unhealed wounds getting activated and/or essential needs not being met.

Apparently wedding planning provided me a number of opportunities to learn about drama, because here's another example from that time period. In a moment of misalignment with my Higher Self one night (okay, total alienation), I was in full-blown drama mode, crying and then getting irritated with myself for being so upset. I had just about had it with my own tantrum when I blared at my (now) husband, "How can you stand me? How can you love *this*?"

He pulled me into his arms and soothingly said, "Because I know *that's* not you." (I think that comment alone guaranteed him my pending, "I do.")

In that instance, he was able to see past the drama, through the haze, to remember the truth of who I am, at the heart of me. His comment gave me permission to just let go of the struggle and the turmoil, which provided relief and the opportunity to move toward calm and recovery. It also reminded *me* of the truth of my Spirit, a reconnection that in and of itself is healing.

I have a very close friend who uses a similar approach with one of her loved ones. When he gets into his drama zone and lashes out, she says to him, "Come back to me, So-and-so! This is not You! Please come back to me." She told me this helps, even if it does not break the spell completely. It only takes a small shift to start with, and then another, and then another, and then the Law of Attraction will aid the momentum toward recovering to *thriving*.

The other thing to know when you witness OPD is that the drama episode is temporary. Gradually the person will "sober up" and **recover** to **align** once again with their Higher Self. The unknown variable is what the duration of the episode will be. While you don't really have a choice in that matter, there are certain things you can do to help move the process along. How much momentum they already have built up around their drama in the moment will undoubtedly influence how quickly they'll be able to recover and what kind of approach will be most effective.

The following passages offer various approaches to interfacing with drama. The most important element is not what you *do*, but the *energy* you bring into the interaction. People will always sense whether you're bringing faux niceness or genuine compassion, and that makes all the difference in the world to drama. As the adage goes, *it's not what you say but how you say it.*

STAY "OVER HERE" WITH YOUR SELF

First things first: manage your own energy. This is like putting your oxygen mask on before assisting others. In the moments Terrence is able to soothe me, it's because he has kept his energy steady and stable and not been sucked into my drama. Therefore, he can meet me from a higher energetic place and quell my angst—or at least not feed it. It's like the rocks of the shoreline remaining steady while the waves of the sea crash upon them in a storm. They don't stop the storm, but they also do not fuel it or amplify it.

Drama can have a viral effect. Developing drama "immunity" will help you to remain calm, solid, and connected with your Higher Self. You develop the immunity (or at least a resistance) by cultivating your Daily Alignment Practice and committing to this as a lifestyle. It'll help your brain significantly in staying "over here" with yourself, and being less susceptible to what's happening "over there."

I was recently in an airport and asked a question to a TSA agent who was somewhat unpleasant in her response. Her tone was rude and the expression on her face looked annoyed that I was even asking, and then disgusted when I went a step further to want to understand why she gave me the reply she did. I felt myself almost immediately taking on a drama demeanor. I wanted to get nasty back or go into victim mode. I had to re-direct it before the urge totally took me, talking myself out of going down that pathway. I told myself, "I don't need to catch her bad mood. She must be having a bad day. I'm sure there's a reason for her answer and I'm just not seeing the whole picture. I hope she feels better soon. In the meantime, I'm responsible for how I feel and something like this will not ruin my day." Now, along with practicing a *thriving* lifestyle, I have some experience with recovering to above the line, so this happened pretty quickly for me. It takes some practice to recognize when we take on other people's drama moods. Sometimes we just get hooked so quickly it's remarkable how one moment we can be going about our day feeling good and the next we're swirling in someone else's turmoil. Yet we can work consciously to stay "over here," inside ourselves.

LET THEM KNOW THEY'RE SEEN AND HEARD

Remember, the reason drama behavior develops is to get our needs met and to guard our wounds. When we witness OPD, we can remember this and find ways to validate their experience without reinforcing the drama. Start with listening. There is tremendous healing power in just tuning in to what another person is saying. Another simple skill to apply is articulating what you are witnessing, literally.

"I see you are really upset."

"You appear to be trembling."

"You're crying on the floor."

"You are yelling really loudly."

"You aren't talking to me right now."

"You don't look like you're feeling too good."

"Your face is getting red."

"I see tears forming in your eyes."

Simply state what you are observing. What this does is acknowledges the person in an unemotional way, and lets them know they matter—they are seen, heard, and on some level, understood—which meets the need without indulging the drama. You may have to repeat the articulating over and over, and that's fine. Just remain neutral and caring and the drama energy will eventually subside.

ASK QUESTIONS

The brain can rebel against a lot of comments or dictates, but it has a hard time rebelling against questions. Questions will switch up the neural pathways the person is using and open up the channels of connection with their Higher Self, as long as the questions are:

- Open ended

- Positively oriented

Stick with "what" and "how" questions; avoid using "why" as it can activate defensiveness. Ideally, you want your questions to move the person incrementally up the scale of consciousness, but that can take practice and training. Just do the best you can to start and see what happens.

"What would feel better to you right now?"

"How can we resolve this together?"

"What if this issue were just temporary?"

"What if this problem were already solved?"

"From another perspective, what do you think Fluffy (pet's name) would say about this?"

"Would it help you to have some time to yourself for this?"

You can also pose a question as an "I wonder . . ." statement.

"I wonder what the opportunity in this is."

"I wonder what would happen if we set this issue aside for a minute."

"I wonder if having a snack would help."

"I wonder what this moment will look like when we reflect on it tomorrow."

OFFER THE BIG PICTURE

Rage- and ego-based drama are founded in the tunnel vision and rigidness that the left-hemisphere of the brain gets into while in drama consciousness. What helps to alleviate them, bringing the mind back into balance, is the right hemisphere's ability to see the big picture. Highlighting the broader view will help the person shift their thinking toward *thriving*. Both questions and statements that focus on the big picture will help.

"In the grand scheme of things, how important is this to you?"

"How will the whole of your life be affected by this?"

"If we look at the big picture, I wonder what size this piece of the puzzle is."

"I wonder how things would look from a bird's-eye view."

"I wonder what God/Jesus/the angels/the Universe would have to say about this."

PROVIDE STRUCTURE

Anxiety, depression, and worthlessness drama are the opposite. They emerge from the emotional and wide view of the right-hemisphere—which shows up as chaos and emotional overwhelm—so they require the logic and narrow focus of the left-hemisphere to come back into balance. Again, questions or statements that establish such a thought path will help.

"What's the best action step we can take right *now*?"

"If there were a strategy to solve this, what would be the easiest part to start with?"

"What do you think is the most logical solution?"

"What can you count on right now?"

"What's the most predictable aspect of this scenario?"

"What's the plan, Stan?"

USE STATE-BREAKERS

A good state-breaker can trump drama in a heartbeat. One of the best to utilize is humor, especially if that's an easy access point for you. Make them laugh. Say something completely ridiculous, like my husband did through his feigned shock at my squawking, "I'm white!" It highlighted the absurdity of my drama and broke the spell on the spot. Be sure not to confuse humor with sarcasm, as sarcasm is a behavior that creates and activates the wound of shame.

Any benevolent attention-shifter will work. Get up and move around in strange ways or make funny voices to shake up their visual and auditory processing and put some alternate stimuli into their brains. Questions rock for shifting gears. You can use them to refocus the other person's attention toward something positive, like planning a vacation, inquiring about their kids or a new pet, or how they like the project they're working on. Ask what they think of the Vikings' new quarterback (enter relevant team/interest), or if they saw the trailer for a new movie that's out, or what their opinion is on a current event. Any different, neutral, or better-feeling topic will do. Again, the momentum of drama they have already built up will influence their recovery time, but just getting the ball rolling by interrupting their present-moment pattern will allow their biochemistry to resolve and return to balance.

JUST SIT WITH IT IN LOVE AND COMPASSION

It goes without saying that love and compassion are powerful, healing energies, which drama will respond to positively in most cases. Sometimes we don't actually have to *do* anything. We don't have to pass the tissue or rush over to hug or touch them. Just sitting with someone, in their presence, witnessing their angst without running away or trying to "clean it up," while maintaining a feeling of love and compassion, is the most curative care we can give. It is the healing power of commitment and honoring. In silence, as we focus our loving attention on another, they can feel it, and it will soothe them. We are spiritual beings having a human journey, and it's messy. It's not perfect. In fact, more often than not, it's downright grubby. And that is the essence of the journey. Get messy. Sit in the muck. Clean it up. Learn from it. Grow into more. Get messy again. Even muckier. Clean it up when you're ready. Learn something different. Grow to the new next level of best. That's just what it is. When we can have someone be with us, witness us, love us through all that, without hastening our process, we can truly heal and expand and live out our purpose on Earth.

While you observe the world around you, start to identify when you are seeing drama in the works so you can familiarize yourself with how it looks and sounds as it emerges and unfolds. You can find it *everywhere*. Even if you don't know the person, as you witness the drama you can still wish them well. As a simple example, a few months ago I heard a sound bite on the radio of an interview with a famous athlete. He was perfectly delightful in the discussion until the host brought up one of his past foibles. There was a stark and immediate change in how the athlete engaged in the conversation: indignant and defensive. The drama was *audible*, clearly grounded in what sounded like the wound of shame. It saddened me to see how that reaction was then played upon to drum up more attention and hype about the interview itself, rather than evoking understanding or compassion for the humanness demonstrated in the exchange—a humanness we all have in our unique ways. I was moved to mentally send out some positive vibes to the athlete and hold the vision of his healing and well-being.

When wounds are prodded, people will react—they just will. It's a social survival mechanism. Attune your senses to this so you are better prepared to respond in effective ways when it shows up in your personal sphere. When we witness OPD live and up close, the goal is to maintain our own balance while activating our curiosity, compassion, and an effort to see and acknowledge the other person. If you don't know the person exhibiting drama, you can still say a silent prayer for them. The guy who flipped you the bird on the highway or the stressed-out mom who berated her kid in the grocery line ahead of you, they need your positive thoughts. Wish them peace. Send them blessings. Every thought we think matters; your kindness makes a difference, even if it isn't overtly applied.

When It's *Not* Your Job to Champion Change

"Not my circus, not my monkeys."

—POLISH PROVERB

In some cases, it's not up to you to do the change championing. With certain people, you are better off not doing anything at all, not having any particular response to OPD. Some people will amplify their drama no matter what we bring. In these situations, the best thing is to keep it clean, clear, and straightforward. Make your responses brief and to the point. *Just the facts, ma'am.* Reserve emotion, remain neutral, and simply state information. Speak what's true for you in ways that do not (logically) provoke more. Set your limits and step away.

I have a client who experiences chronic drama interactions with the mother of his child. No matter how kind, agreeable, or patient he is, she responds with more drama. We discussed this being a reflection of her wounds, which he could effectively see. Too much compassion and the desire to smooth things over—to fix things—became the problem. No matter how he tried to be helpful to her, she could not receive it. In this kind of case, he is clearly *not* the person to champion change or support her emotional process. By altering his approach to keep things neutral, factual, and brief, the drama between them has significantly died down if not resolved itself altogether.

Remember my family member FM from Chapter 7 who sent the text messages accusing me of trying to control things because I offered to bring cake to Bepa's birthday? Well, I eventually discovered the same was true with them. That situation resolved itself, but when another issue came up, FM turned to ranting emails. I quickly discovered that no matter how I explained myself or offered to help, there was always an e-tirade response. Even an authentic "I love you" didn't help, because the drama on their side was so thick my good intentions could not penetrate it. I had to take charge and say, "Here are the facts. This is how it will work for me," and let everything else go. In some cases, it was even best to not reply at all.

We all have certain people like this in our lives—family, friends, or colleagues—for whom we are not the "right" person to take care of them in their drama episodes nor champion change. In fact, we may be the very source of enabling their drama when we indulge in responding to them with repeatedly explaining ourselves and our intentions, through pleading or begging, or in overly accommodating ways.

When nothing we do makes any difference, especially if the relationship is already stressed, fractured, or wounded, it's a good sign we are not the one to encourage their drama-free process or recovery. To engage with these folks, we want to keep it clean, short, to the point. Don't give them too much interaction as they will convert it into ammunition or fuel to amplify their drama. For engaging, a great, simple one-liner is, "That just doesn't work for me." You can repeat this one as often as needed. "I understand what you are saying and that just doesn't work for me." Another is, "Here's my choice, and I ask you to respect that." Or, "Thank you. I'll give that some thought." You can deliver anything along these lines with kindness and neutrality and then politely complete the interaction—hang up the phone, discontinue the email or text correspondence, leave the room.

Remember It's Not about You

One of the keys to championing someone toward the DRAMA-free way and coming into alignment with their Higher Self is *your* knowing that it's not about you. In the moment drama hits, we need to be able to see each other for the truth of Who We Really Are, and when we make it personal we can't do that, because we are separated from ourselves and the relationship.

OPD is not your fault. It's not your responsibility to take care of. Your job is *you*. Yet, as you are in relationship with others, you will inevitably run into drama somewhere along the line. When that happens, remember it's not personal. This knowledge will help you stay "over here" and respond thoughtfully from a place of love and compassion, without enabling, while reminding the other person that the drama is not Who They Really Are; it's just what they learned. And they can learn something new too, like how to live the easy, joyous, and wealthful life that's waiting for them as they practice GRATE-full living and choicefully embody the energies of *thriving* consciousness.

In the face of OPD, you may have moments where you feel like you need an exorcist. The person in front of you has been consumed from the inside

251

out, mutated into the blighted character you witness who seems to have overtaken the beautiful Spirit you know and love. Be patient. Stand in love. Hold compassion. Trust the problem has already been solved; the transformation will unfold.

"It is one of the most beautiful compensations of life that no man can sincerely try to help another without helping himself."

—RALPH WALDO EMERSON

Key Concepts

✱ Drama needs love, consistency, predictability, and strong but unattached compassion. When we witness OPD, we need to take charge of our own energy first and *not* get suckered into the drama zone.

✱ We take on other people's emotional energy, "catching it" as if it were a contagious virus, quickly becoming disoriented and losing ourselves in their chaos. Beginning to make changes in pre-established dynamics will likely take some persistence, time, and patience—both with yourself and the other person.

✱ Ways to engage with Other People's Drama are:

- Stay "Over Here" with Your Self—First manage your own energy. Developing your Daily Alignment Practice will help you stay present and be less susceptible to what's happening "over there."

- Let Them Know They're Seen and Heard—Validate the person's experience by articulating what you are witnessing, literally. Acknowledge the person in an unemotional way.

- Ask Questions—Open-ended and positively oriented questions will help the brain shift gears and recover from drama.

- Offer the Big Picture—Highlight the broader view with both global questions and statements. This is ideal for rage- and ego-based drama.

- Provide Structure—Anxiety, depression, and worthlessness drama need logic and narrow focus with questions or statements that establish practical steps or logical sequencing.

- Use State-Breakers—Make them laugh. Ask questions. Bring up a totally unrelated subject.

- Just Sit with It in Love and Compassion—We don't actually have to *do* anything. Just sitting with someone, in witness to their drama

253

while maintaining a feeling of love and compassion, is exceptionally healing.

✳ Sometimes it's not your job to champion change.

✳ When any response you bring is evoking more drama, keep your interactions brief, neutral, and simply state facts.

✳ All of these techniques should be employed with conscious attention to the impact on the other person. They are most effective when selected with clear, positive intentions, delivered from above-the-line energies of *thriving*.

Application and Integration

What I now understand about OPD is:

OPD I am most susceptible to "catching" is:

How I can manage my own energy and thoughts when I am exposed to OPD:

Strategies I will apply to situations where I witness OPD are:

Additional reflections I have on my own drama or the drama I witness in specific people in my life are:

CHAPTER TWELVE

Ditch the DRAMA and *Thrive*!

Bravo! You made it this far in the book, which tells me you're ready to live the DRAMA-free Way! Your *thriving* life is available to you in any *and every* given moment. Your spirit is calling you from within, imploring you to flow without resistance, to reach for the better feelings, and to grow with what life has given you. There is always a new, next level of your best Self available to you. It's your job to decide you want it and to claim it! Grab hold and don't let go. It is your birthright. Know that there will be ups and downs on this journey, and the ride is so worth it. Be patient with your glorious Self. Whatever is happening in your world right now is for your benefit and your growth; it is in the interest of your highest good, even if you can't see it yet.

Confusion as the Birthplace for Transformation

"Oh, benevolent Mother Nature, who invented love as a motive for personal growth! Under the pretext of loving someone else, she cajoles us into loving the person we happen to be."

—UNKNOWN

In 2007, I woke up. Not like from a nap, but from the lack of awareness of who I was as a spirit having my human experience. I woke up to the drama I was creating in my own life. I started the process of becoming aware of the ways I defer my power to win approval and gain acceptance. I was in chronic good-girl mode, attempting to live up to external expectations and who I thought I *should* be. I was fundamentally frightened, untrusting of the world, and I did not believe I was capable of providing for or sustaining myself. Above all, I didn't know that the power to change any of that lay within *me*. As with any large-scale transformation in life, I had to have my world crumble and all my beliefs challenged in order to take the leap into who I was (and still am—it's a process, after all) capable of becoming.

It was in 2007 that I got all shook up, turned inside out and upside down, as I was faced with one of the most difficult decisions of my life up until that time. I was engaged to Dr. Perfect, whom I had been dating for four years. He was the too-good-to-be-true husband waiting to happen, and a genuinely kind, beautiful person. Everyone in my family loved him and all signs pointed to a perfect life ahead. Then, out of the blue, the most wretched thing chanced itself upon me—I fell in love with *someone else*. And not someone with whom I was likely to build a positive future. Mr. Irresistible-But-Impossible was ten years my senior, freshly divorced with two kids, living at home with his mom, and carrying a boatload of debt. Not exactly my picture of provider-ship or harmonious family. But the heart knows no reason. I mean, it's not like I tried to meet or fall for him; I certainly wasn't looking for it. I was planning a wedding for crying out loud. But somehow all the circumstances mysteriously aligned themselves to orchestrate our working together and repeated social exposure, which yielded an intense connection with a fierce gravitational pull toward one other.

When I look back on it now, I can see that the Universe recognized the limited, closed-off, self-negating direction I was headed with my life and decided to intervene. The reason why I say this is because at the time I believed that I *needed* a man to take care of me and that I was too stupid to support myself or have any meaningful career of my own. The whole focus of my young adult life had been geared toward finding a husband who would be "a good provider" and then adjusting myself to be everything *he* wanted or needed me to be—just like I was taught. I was prepared to settle right into the safety and security of life with Dr. Perfect, keeping myself nice and small. But then Mr. Irresistible-But-Impossible dropped into the picture. All my ideas and dreams for my perfect life were thrown into massive upheaval. What was I to do? Continue on course with marrying the super-great guy who did truly love me and would've provided a very comfortable life for me, OR do the honest thing and follow my heart—even though I knew I was walking into a relationship that was the antithesis of all I had desired for myself? Needless to say, that decision was *really hard.* At the end of the day, though, it was not about the men or the marriage or any of that business. It was about the confusion and upheaval serving my personal evolution, forcing me to reevaluate my values and who I was capable of being, which led to the ultimately crucial result of awakening to my Self. This experience launched me in the direction of authentic empowerment and conscious spiritual growth, taking me down a completely transformed life path that, today, allows me to serve my higher purpose and keep pace on the physical plane with the expansion of my Soul.

I did have to get through it first, however. I certainly couldn't see or recognize any of these insights at the time, but the Universe helped me along the way. While in the midst of the turmoil, shame, and doubt, a surge of opportunities for learning and discovering the true Jennifer presented themselves to me. I got unsolicited books—both audio and paperback—in the mail from various relatives. A stranger I met at a church I never go to turned me on to *The Secret* and thereby the Law of Attraction. A coworker randomly brought me a workbook for personal development, introducing me to the spectrum of Universal Laws. The therapist I was working with at the time presented me with information about the new theories of quantum physics and the concepts that thoughts are things and that we co-create our reality by how we focus our thoughts.

Through these resources, I learned that everything in my world and my experience was *my* responsibility. That was a tough pill to swallow. Prior to that, I spent most of my mental and emotional energy projecting, blaming, rationalizing, catastrophizing, resenting, worrying, and regretting. I spent a great deal of my social energy kvetching and complaining, ain't-it-awful-izing, gossiping, and colluding. I bounced around on the drama triangle, largely inhabiting the Victim role, but also spending plenty of time as both Hero and Villain. Once I was inundated with the new thought paradigms that were coming into my sphere, I could feel the truth in them. The resonance that reverberated through me was undeniable; I had to get honest with myself as well as change my ways of viewing and interacting with the world.

This whole awakening journey began with massive confusion and a cancelled wedding, (yes, I did in fact call it off). It subsequently took me through two-and-a-half years of crazy love and stubborn pride, trying desperately to make the Mr. Irresistible-But-Impossible thing work. That relationship eventually disintegrated as it had served its purpose and was no longer in alignment with who I was becoming or the direction I was headed. Finally, I moved into my own self-awareness, independence, sense of purpose, meaningful career, and a sweet marriage with Terrence. This era of my journey was basically a full life overhaul. The whole kerfuffle, which seemed to be a low point, actually set me on a completely different trajectory toward becoming the woman I am today: a *Soulapreneuress*, teacher, leader, author, mentor, and a humble servant of the higher energies that guide us along the way.

Oftentimes, life utilizes—even mobilizes—such turbulence in order to invite us into higher levels of being, new realizations, and increased expansion, but we still need to choose which path to take: the path of the "shoulds," of what's known and familiar, or the path of conscious growth.

We're seeing this happen now in humanity as a whole. We're being challenged and pushed to our edges. When we reach the threshold where what's familiar is becoming too painful or intolerably constrictive, it's time for a shift toward something that will bring relief. In my case, following the passionate entanglement rather than the intended marriage generated the confusion that would launch me into my new, next level of expansion. When we take the leap and trust life, we will then naturally be guided along toward the things that will be more fulfilling and more pleasurable for us at each next stage of our human experience.

That particular phase of my personal maturation to consistently *thriving* and living in alignment with my Higher Self took a solid seven years, and there is still (plenty!) more work to be done. During those years, I recognized how I let myself live a drama-filled life, and how I actually even craved the chaos. Without my own unique direction independent of a man, and without a sense of purpose in my life, I lusted after the false aliveness "kick" I got from making mountains out of molehills and from needing perpetual rescue. I can go on and on about that former lifestyle, but you really have the bigger scope of it embedded in the content of this book. While I'd love to say that my drama days are over, the truth is that my particular wounding and learned reactions still account for some of the threads that are woven throughout my inner fabric. In some areas of my life the drama is pretty well resolved and in others it's just beginning to come into my awareness as needing healing. I would like to think some sort of epiphany will befall me and I will have complete transformation and total peace and joy *all the time*. While I'm waiting for that moment to arrive, what I *can* do is consciously navigate my interior space of thoughts and feelings, ride the emotional waves, be intentional about my inner alignment, and follow what feels most self-honoring at any given instant—the quintessence of authentic *thriving*.

My desire is that the discoveries and tools that emerged from my struggles will help you and your loved ones set out on the voyage of inner alignment to really own the *thriving* life that is your birthright. Everyone has their own experience of this journey; there is no singular "right way." Expect the best, because any way you slice it, this is the most rewarding, fulfilling, and authentic way to live as a spiritual being having a human experience.

DRAMA Does Not Resolve Itself Overnight

Change takes time and practice. Traversing the DRAMA-*Thriving* paradigm timeline does not happen in one fell swoop. The emotional revamping and brain rewiring processes are truly a progress-not-perfection kind of journey. If you are a support person, a witness to the external emotional drama, it's essential that you stay balanced and focus on your love or compassion for the other person—even when their "issue" *appears* to be with you. Remember it's actually about their wounds being activated and their need to be seen and heard, to feel valued and understood, to *matter*.

Making changes in our own drama patterns requires patience and compassion with ourselves. It *is* happening, even if incrementally, on a micro scale. At the moment that I was shriveled on the floor in my eating petrification and shame (from Chapter 11), I could also actually *see* what was happening. I was able to play the Squirrel in the Tree. I knew it was drama, and yet the intensity of the chemical release was already there. It was so powerful and consuming I couldn't stop it; I had to just ride it out. It was as if I'd already taken the hits of cocaine or shots of tequila (plural on each, 'cause this was strong stuff) and I just had to wait for my body to metabolize it. Now, several years further along the path, I've found that sometimes I can interrupt this flow earlier in the process and recover more quickly. That's what this journey is about. It's not about never having bad moments. The Law of Rhythm (and our life experience) tells us the "downs" or the "ebbs" are just gonna be there. We can expect it, not in a negative way, but in a wise and preparatory way. Learn what helps you dial down the intensity and interrupt the biochemical flow *before* it gets so strong that you have to just wait for it to be over.

When we bring our negativity into any given environment where we are exposed to other people, there is the potential of passing it along. Take responsibility for your thoughts. Let's stop spreading the drama. To do so we each have to choose the softer path. We have to be willing to overcome the addiction and let go of the cheap thrill. That calls for following what feels good, moving in the direction of meeting our needs for aliveness by fulfilling our greater purpose and living based on our passions.

Sometimes we can know in our brain-minds what we need to do and still not be able to take action or effect change. This does not mean we are weak or that we cannot change. It simply means we are not there yet in our journey or that our current circumstances are presenting a next level we can grow into (which there always will be). *All in good time, my Pretty, all in good time.* Take heart. When we do launch into a drama episode—for whatever reason—and it has a negative impact on others, we need to come back and clean it up. Be aware of how your words, actions, and behaviors affect those around you and apologize as needed. Taking ownership for our energetic impact requires courage and an awareness of our effect on others. It's a way of tending to our relationships in an honoring manner while we're diligently working on making changes and healing our personal patterns of drama.

We need to be accepting and apologetic with ourselves as well. Inner alignment and consciously directing our energetic states is some of the hardest work we can do. We have to counter subconscious programming that was installed in us not of our own accord, but based on someone else's circumstances, wounds, and beliefs. We have to navigate the chaos of the outer world that envelops us. Each time we go below the line and consciously recover to our Higher Selves we experience a mini death and rebirth, the process required to expand into who we are capable of becoming. This is the most rewarding work there is. With application of the concepts and practices in this book, you *can* heal your wounds and resolve your DRAMA.

Our DRAMA-Free World

"Thoughts increase by being given away. The more who believe in them the stronger they become. Everything is an idea."

—A COURSE IN MIRACLES

While drama is manifested in countless forms throughout our culture and the world, I have hope for the human race and life on Earth. Frankly, I think it's a miracle how *well* we live together on this planet. When I reflect on the intensity of DRAMA I've experienced in myself and witnessed in others—a microcosm of the macrocosm—I marvel that we've been able to get this far without completely obliterating each other. The only explanation I can make up is that the power of love and the innate proclivity of the spirit to evolve and transform exceeds—or at the very least balances—the ego's petty ways. The outlook for humanity and the natural world is bright when we focus on the pockets of good—expressions of authentic *thriving*—seen in spiritual, humanitarian, and ecological movements across the globe, as well as in emerging inspirational entertainment and motivational messages circulating about the social media sphere. It's *there*, it exists in myriad forms, and we can strengthen that positivity with our own focused attention. We can each contribute in small and unique ways through how we focus our thoughts and maintain our individual alignment with our Higher Selves, adding to the collective *thriving* energy on the planet. Every thought we think, every intention we hold, every action that manifests from our being *matters*. I matter. You matter. We *all* matter. If we each honor ourselves and take charge of our own energy to feel good most of the time—and stop worrying about what anyone else is thinking or doing—together we will create an infinitely more harmonious home for our Soul-selves here in this human realm. We will achieve our *pivot* and set the Earth upon a higher trajectory for generations to come.

The Universe is unfolding itself in the most perfect ways, and we are all a part of that process. Our job in the co-creative effort of life is continuously recovering to Who We Really Are, to the truth of our Souls. Reach for the higher energetic states at will, in spite of your circumstances. Get out of the drama. Grieve as needed. Feel the feelings so you can move through them and integrate them in meaningful ways. Come back into alignment with your Higher Self. Grow into the new expansion your Soul has moved toward.

Know also that growth can come through love and joy, not always pain and suffering. Just be your beautiful human self and nurture your spirit along the way. Love. Forgive. Practice your daily alignment. Feed your positive self more than your negative self. Get help. Keep it simple. Have fun. Laugh as hard as you can, as often as you can. Let it all be fun and easy. And give yourself and the world the gift of being, authentically, the truth of Who You Really Are.

"You can totally rely on the flowing harmony of the interactions of your energy and the energies outside of you to continuously give you more than you need to be happy. ... By getting rid of our emotion-backed addictions, demands, and expectations that reject what is ... we at last find more security, more delightful sensations, more powerful effectiveness, and more love than we could ever need... And so, hand in hand, we journey down the river of our lives toward the vast Ocean of Oneness that is our source and our destiny."

—KEN KEYES, JR.

Epilogue

As I'm wrapping up this project, there are a few illustrations I want to share with you. When I began the journey of writing this book, I never would have imagined that I'd be completing the edits and finalizing the manuscript from a nursing home guest suite. In the last few weeks, my beloved Bepa, who is now ninety-one, has determined she is ready to pass. As her Healthcare Power of Attorney and closest family member, I gladly embrace it as my job to be part of that process with her. A couple weeks after she started clearly articulating, "I'm ready to go. I miss Paka (Grandpa) too much," she landed in the emergency room with a bleeding ulcer and no desire for treatment. Approaching that time, she had begun the natural end-of-life withdrawal process, accompanied by a loss of interest in things she previously enjoyed and a complete loss of the healthy Dutch appetite she prided herself on for decades. We spent two nights in the hospital and upon her arrival "home," she was admitted to hospice care.

It has been nearly three weeks since that occurred, and Bepa has "rallied" to resume eating, enjoying various activities, joking around, and telling family stories. I'm told this is a common occurrence once hospice gets involved, since the person is getting more personalized attention. I myself have been literally living in the nursing home with Bepa for at least half the time (since I live ninety miles from her), which means she has someone who cares for her tending to her frequently and consistently. What's more, other family members have been showing up to pay their respects and say their goodbyes. Some are interested in capturing family history before it's gone. There are also additional visitors coming just because they like her. All in all, this lady went from spending her days alone in a nursing home bed, dining with a few "table mates," and one weekly visit from me, to having me practically move in, doing fun activities together, as well as seeing multiple visitors throughout the week. She's a brand-new Bepa as a result.

This experience is a testament to the imperative need to be seen and heard, to feel valued, to *matter*. In my estimation, Bepa has regained a sense of mattering. She's experiencing love and connection. The nursing home can provide well for her physical needs; it's her community who meets her mental, emotional, and spiritual needs. And that is life-giving.

On my end of things, amid all the travel, the emotionality of this experience, running a business, and navigating a stepfamily at home, I've had to consider the financial expense of my commitment to being by Bepa's side as much as I can during this transition. It's a lot of work to stay engaged on a conscious spiritual level and not get caught up in the drama. I keep recovering to the idea that the Universe will meet all my needs in perfect timing and Divine order, that I am safe and provided for in all ways, and that this experience holds the highest good for all involved. But I have to admit I have my fearful scarcity moments to weed through. A couple weeks ago it randomly occurred to me that I can just *ask* for what I want and need. (Duh.) This all-powerful, infinite Universe *is* capable of providing, after all. It's my job to ask.

So I posed the Constructive Question: "Where will the income come from to easily and richly stay here [in the nursing home guest suite] for as long as I like, as many nights as I need?" The next day, Terrence told me he got an unexpected $700 bonus check from his employer and he suggested I put it toward the nursing home guest suite expense. What's more, when we re-signed our apartment lease around that same time, the office told us we'll get $1,000 off our renewal month's rent. That $1,700 will cover almost a full month with Bepa if I stay over every single night. Now, that's what I call a miraculous, magical manifestation.

This is how authentic *thriving* works. I allowed myself to let go of figuring it all out, asked the question, and let the Universe take care of the HOW. Even though this is an emotionally tumultuous time and my energetic state has been all over the place, by practicing GRATE-full living and honoring *everything* that shows up, even in the sub-*thriving* zone, I maintained alignment with my Higher Self, which has allowed for all my needs and desires to be effortlessly met. My brain would never have come up with this solution, because that wasn't my job. My job is to "be," yield, ask, receive, serve, love, sit with it, process, grieve, recover, align, take action, evolve. That's all our jobs ever are. We can trust life. When we choose to be DRAMA-free, life will take care of the rest, allowing us to authentically *thrive* in the coolest possible ways.

Author's Invitation

Dear Reader,

It is my passion and my life's work to provide transformational experiences for the up-leveling of humanity and the evolution of our Earth. Writing, teaching, speaking and mentoring are a large part of that, as well as creating unique, Soul-connection events.

If this book has resonated with you, there are additional resources for you to make these concepts actionable and get *real* results in your own life. At the time of this publication, there are several options available. Start with whatever is best suited to you:

- *The Drama-Free Way* online course, a companion to this book. It takes you deeper into the concepts, offers additional explanations and tools for authentic thriving and provides updated perspectives not available in the book alone

- The *Daily Alignment Practice* online course (currently for women only), where you receive deeper learning about how these practices elevate you and empower your authentic thriving. Along with this, you receive membership to a private Facebook group where each day I craft unique practices based on the energy of the day to help you attune to the natural rhythms of life and flow of the Universe

- Customized training or a keynote talk for your organization, group, conference or event. See reviews section at the end of this book to discover what other audiences have experienced

- Read *The Drama-Free Way* in your book club and host a live virtual Q&A with the Author

You can access these options or contact me for more information when you visit: www.JenniferALLY.com

You can also stay connected with me on Instagram @Jennifer.Ally and Facebook @JenniferALLYKern

It is my absolute honor and privilege to serve your elevation, awakening and up-leveling along your life path. My intention is for you to be empowered to thrive authentically and bring your beautiful Soul's truth, wisdom and gifts to make our world a better place. *We need you now!*

It's time to release the old drama—for good. I believe in you and your ability to *rise*. And I'm right alongside you in that journey, as much or as little as you desire.

I look forward to meeting you soon.

With sweet reverence and wild blessings,
Jennifer ALLY

ABOUT THE AUTHOR

Jennifer Ally Kern has a BBA in International Business and a Master of Psychology. She is a world traveler and polyglot, communicating in four languages. Before starting her business Intrinsic SOULutions in 2009, she began her career as an addictions counselor at the Mayo Clinic.

Jennifer has studied with top minds in the areas of higher consciousness, Neuro-Linguistic Programming, behavior change, Universal Laws, and spiritual wisdom. She has multiple certifications in the field of coaching, extensive training in leadership development, and is a certified Akashic Records Master Healer. She is the creator of the Inner Alignment Model and the *Lead in Alignment* system, and in 2018 she founded THRIViesta: Soul-centric Events. She is an advocate and champion for human evolution, authentic connection, the spiritual awakening movement, and manifesting the "new earth" in our lifetime.

When she's not busy enjoying her work, Jennifer loves traveling, Latin dancing, running, strength-training, singing, painting, time with loved ones, and lounging about doing absolutely nothing.

Connect with Jennifer at: www.JenniferAlly.com.

Acknowledgments

I t is with great honor and deep gratitude that I want to devote a few lines to thank those who went before me: the great thinkers, the idea machines, the diligent researchers, the experienced professionals, the wise souls. I do not consider myself to be an academic, neuroscientist, researcher, anthropologist, theologian, medical professional, or psychologist. I think of myself more as one who interprets, translates, and repackages wisdom to make it tangible, relatable, and especially *applicable*. I have been able to stand on the shoulders of giants, as it were, to compile the various concepts and tools presented in this book, in the hope that it offers a succinct and user-friendly approach to living a more effective, *thriving* human life. Many of the exquisite minds I've learned from are noted in the bibliography. I thank you all for your generous and profound contributions.

In the original version of the book, there are many names mentioned and that gratitude still holds true today. For this revised edition, I want to offer a special thanks to the readers of the 2016 *Drama-Free Way*. You showed me the value in these pages and how much of an impact it made. And more importantly, you applied it to your lives, in your process of growth and evolution, and that makes all the difference. The world is literally a better place because of it.

A few more names of teachers and supporters I've worked with personally and received from directly: H. H. Sai Maa Lakshmi Devi Mishra, Brynne Dippell, Bob Proctor, Roger Love, Rich Anderson, my cousin Kecia, my F3 sisters, and my family. Great thanks to my dad for your support, belief in me, and gifting your editorial talents to this edition. And a special shout-out to my mom, who has truly lived the drama-free path of authentic thriving—and continues to model patience, love, courage, innovation and the freedom of being Who You Really Are.

Glossary of Terms

Alignment—The synergistic state of one's human-self and Soul-self merged together and operating harmoniously on the Earth plane, to grow, contribute, connect, and enjoy the process of life.

Alternatives—New thought patterns or ways of responding to DRAMA thinking that redirect the response to drama-potential stimuli in order to short-circuit the drama, to feel better, and to maintain the energies of *thriving*.

Core Human Wounds—Three mental-emotional-spiritual wounds resulting from interactions that inhibit or violate our essential needs to be seen and heard, to matter, and to be valued just as we are, posing a direct threat to our sense of belonging. The wounds are:

- Shame

- Abandonment

- Betrayal

DRAMA—A wound-based social survival mechanism that seeks to meet our needs to be seen and heard and to feel that we matter. The energies of drama are the ineffective, distorted versions of sub-thriving. Drama energies always have the element of struggle and resistance to them, grounded in the falsehood and weakness of the ego. DRAMA is an acronym for thought patterns that are: Disempowering, Reactive, Assumption-based, Maladaptive, Addictive.

- Disempowering—Disempowering thoughts disconnect us from our Higher Selves, or defer our choices and our emotional states to circumstances or other people in a self-negating way. They are thoughts that involve self-shaming, abandonment, and betrayal, and that originate from the lower energies of drama.

- Reactive—Drama thinking has a survival fight-flight-freeze compulsion that comes from our wounds being activated or "poked into" through our own internal dialogue, triggering circumstances or interactions with others.

- Assumption-based—Drama comes from the assumptions we make that are not grounded in truth, but are based on past wounds and the way we see things as a result of them. When something resembles what we know to be hurtful, we will naturally make relevant assumptions in order to stay safe.

- Maladaptive—Something that is *mal*adaptive has the fundamental inability to alter its structure or functioning to better survive in a given environment. Old behavioral modifications become outdated when we reach new circumstances and relationships that no longer warrant the old defenses and justifications.

- Addictive—Drama *thinking* is the misuse of *thought substance* in a manner that is destructive and yet difficult to stop. It can come from mentally re-living wounding experiences, perpetuating wounds with behavior and self-talk, and amplifying stories that create the chemical and emotional states of DRAMA consciousness. It stimulates a sense of "aliveness" we may not otherwise be experiencing in life.

DRAMA Episode—the overall experience of being trigered into DRAMA thinking, the resulting biochemical flood, feeling the lower energetic states of DRAMA, then acting out with its resulting impact on others, justification, satisfaction, social reinforcement, and potential remorse.

GRATE-full Living—The process of managing our internal worlds of thoughts, emotions, and motivations through the steps of: Grieve/Get Out, Recover, Align, Take Action, Evolve.

- Grieve/Get Out—Grieve represents a conscious naming and allowing the emotions found in the energetic states of sub-*thriving*. Involves identifying and actually *feeling* the true emotion, then directing the release of the energy through self-honoring, kind means of expression. Get Out is the alternative when there is no emotional experience to process, but the drama is stirred up from unnecessary stories and ruminations that are not relevant to current circumstances.

- Recover—Coming back to center after a drama episode, getting grounded in the present moment, settling into the balance and neutrality achieved once negative emotions have been allowed and integrated. The crossover energy is Willingness, which empowers the shift to the higher energetic states of *thriving*.

- Align—The experience of resonance with one's Higher Self that ensues from being in the energetic states of *thriving*, marked by relief, feeling good, clarity, presence, calm. It is generally found in the energetic states of Contentment, Curiosity, Reverence, and Harmony.

- Take Action—Meaningful and effective action (which could be *in*action) comes from the place of alignment, allowing our human experience to keep pace with our Soul's expansion.

- Evolve—Growing with the new experience that the action takes us into, reaching a new "next level" of expansion and development, growing into who we are capable of becoming, and establishing a new normal.

HALT—When on the brink of a drama episode, check to see if one of these triggers could be the culprit: Hunger/Hormones, Alcohol, Loneliness/Boredom, Tiredness.

OPD—Other People's Drama, what we witness as externalized expressions of wounding in others; the "acting out" behavior in others that seeks to meet their essential human needs.

Recycled DRAMA—Drama thinking that ruminates in the past and tells the same old story over and over again, even if there are new characters or circumstances in the version du jour.

Sub-thriving—Lower energetic states that are essential to our growth and development when honored and processed effectively; they are the ebb or the contraction that allows the flow and expansion of our Souls in the human experience.

The Law of Attraction—Like energies come together by way of matching vibrations.

The Laws of Gender and Gestation—The creation of all things requires a seed, a fertile environment for the seed to grow to its full expression, and a requisite amount of time for that process to complete itself.

The Law of Perpetual Transmutation—All things in life are made up of energy, and that energy is perpetually coming into and going out of various forms.

The Law of Polarity—All things have an equal opposite to them. Every "bad" has a "good," like an up has a down.

The Law of Relativity—All things have a point of comparison that we can use to feel good or feel bad, depending on whether we are focusing on something "worse" than our conditions or "better" than them.

The Law of Rhythm—Life has a natural ebb and flow, a season for all things, a contraction-expansion dynamic required to grow.

The Vacuum Law of the Universe—Nature avoids "voids." If there is an absence found in an otherwise "occupied" space, *something* will be pulled in to fill the space to maintain homostasis or preserve the status quo.

Thriving—Living in alignment with one's Higher Self and keeping pace on the physical plane with the expansion of the Soul. *Thriving* energies are grounded in truth and strength. They exhibit the resonant space of the spirit operating effectively in the human realm.

Triggers—External stimuli (circumstances, people) or internal focus on a subject that activates DRAMA thinking or initiates a DRAMA Episode.

Wound-based Living—Operating from—thinking, feeling, and acting from—places of residual core wounds, activating the worst parts of the self rather than the best.

Bibliography

Arbinger Institute. *The Anatomy of Peace: Resolving a Heart of Conflict.* San Francisco: Berrett-Koehler Publishers, 2006.

Arntz, William, Betsy Chasse, Matthew Hoffman, and Mark Vicente. *What the #$*! Do We (K)now?* Directed by William Arntz, Betsy Chasse, and Mark Vicente. Captured Light, 2004.

Bandler, Richard. *Get the Life You Want.* Deerfield Beach: Health Communications, 2008.

Brown, Brene. *The Gifts of Imperfection: Let Go of Who You Think You're Supposed to Be and Embrace Who You Are.* Center City: Hazelden, 2010.

Byron, Katie. *Loving What Is: Four Questions That Can Change Your Life.* New York: Harmony Books, 2002.

Canfield, Jack and Janet Switzer. *The Success Principles: How To Get From Where You Are To Where You Want To Be.* New York: Harper, 2005.

Dispenza, Joe. *Evolve Your Brain: The Science of Changing Your Mind.* Deerfield: Health Communications, 2007.

Ford, Debbie. *Dark Side of the Light Chasers: Reclaiming Your Power, Creativity, Brilliance, and Dreams.* New York: Riverhead Books, 1999.

———. *The Shadow Effect.* Directed by Scott Cervine. Hay House, 2009. DVD.

Gomes, Jean, Catherine McCarthy, and Tony Schwartz. *The Way We're*

Working Isn't Working: The Four Forgotten Needs that Energize Great Performance. New York: Free Press, 2010.

Gottman, John and Nan Silver. *The Seven Principles for Making Marriage Work.* New York: Crown Publishers, 1999.

Hawkins, David. *Power vs. Force: The Hidden Determinants of Human Behavior.* Carlsbad: Hay House, 2002.

———. *Transcending the Levels of Consciousness: The Stairway to Enlightenment.* West Sedona: Veritas Publishing, 2006.

Hicks, Esther and Jerry Hicks. *The Astonishing Power of Emotions: Let Your Feelings Be Your Guide.* Carlsbad: Hay House, 2007.

Hay, Louise. *You Can Heal Your Life.* Santa Monica: Hay House, 1984.

Householder, Leslie. *Hidden Treasures: Heavenly Help with Money Matters.* Ebook.

Karpman, Stephen. *The Drama Triangle.* 1968.

Karpman, Stephen. "KarpmanDramaTriangle.com." 2010. www.karpmandramatriangle.com.

Kimsey-House, Henry, Karen Kimsey-House, Phil Sandahl, and Laura Whitworth. *Co-active Coaching: Changing Business, Transforming Lives.* Boston: Nicholas Brealey, 2011.

Lipton, Bruce. *The Biology of Belief: Unleashing the Power of Consciousness, Matter and Miracles.* Santa Rosa: Mountain of Love/Elite Books, 2005.

Martinez, Mario. *The MindBody Code: How to Change the Beliefs that Limit Your Health, Longevity, and Success.* Boulder: Sounds True, 2014.

Myss, Caroline. *Self-Esteem: Your Fundamental Power.* 2002. Audio lecture.

Neuroscience and Transformational Coaching Training Series. BEabove Leadership.

Wager Smith, Karen. *Stress, Inflammation, and Depression.* Neuroscene, 2010. Podcast.

Wikipedia article: Noosphere. https://en.wikipedia.org/wiki/Noosphere

Zukav, Gary. *The Seat of the Soul.* New York: Simon & Schuster, 2014.

Reviews

The Drama-Free Way Speaking, Training, and Courses

Since the release of the first edition of *The Drama-Free Way*, Jennifer Ally Kern has spoken on this subject in numerous conferences and a wide variety of organizations, including: The Mayo Clinic, Best Buy, WeightWatchers, Buffalo Wild Wings, the University of Minnesota, the International Coach Federation, Women Entrepreneurs of Minnesota, and more. While the participant feedback is generally anonymous, the following are a collection of reviews from these engagements:

"Jennifer was recommended . . . and we were NOT disappointed. Her presentation style was informative, engaging—kept everyone involved and interested throughout her 90 minutes (which could have gone longer, as our feedback survey suggested). Our group walked away with techniques to help them stay centered through the onslaught of drama from others. Jennifer also shared tips on how to manage your feelings when you might bring some drama to yourself or others. All great information that can be used both at work and in life. She was wonderful to work with and we would definitely have her speak at a future event."

"Wonderful class! I didn't know what to expect and it was GREAT. Real life stories and examples were extremely relevant and they clearly showed the root of the problems we encounter in relationships. There is a LOT of drama in my area at work—one person is the source of most of the drama. I can better understand why she behaves the way she does and how I might be able to help her feel heard and validated."

"I left with a new understanding of using positive energy and a willingness to change and take personal responsibility to make my workplace more productive."

"Great presentation style! Jennifer was very knowledgable. She kept the presentation moving and thought provoking. Materials were clear and well presented. Jennifer was very open and receptive to questions and comments. Very good introduction to new thought/thinking paradigms! I'd love to see a 'part two' and go deeper!"

"Jennifer is amazing! I wish everyone in my department could have the opportunity to hear her speak. Absolutely fabulous class. I wish it had been longer. There was a lot of material to cover and I would have loved to learn even more."

"I enjoyed Jennifer's training and style. Real life examples, group activities, PowerPoint slides, handouts, and she even had her own book to draw from! All relevant and applicable training tools and resources to enhance learning. I especially appreciated the Energetic State Spectrum, Energy-Based Brain Functioning & recovering to higher energetic states. That was fascinating and 'clicked'. I'd love to see her speak to a bigger group at our organization."

"Jennifer's information was impactful and thought provoking. She generated a lot of conversation and was able to help the group understand how our 'way of thinking' impacts our relationships and productivity at home and work. The meeting evaluations were very positive and we are looking forward to having her back."

"This was by far the BEST course I have taken. I was thoroughly engaged and have immediately started applying the information I learned."

"Jennifer Kern was amazing. I felt that both the content and the presenter were tuned into the work we do and the culture we are working in. I went and purchased her book as soon as I got back to my desk."

"This was definitely a different take on drama than I was expecting. We need more topics like this—workplace culture, drama, change, and bullying. I'm motivated to read her book and have the rest of my team read it as well!"

"While the content was not what I necessarily expected it to be, I felt it was interesting, self-reflective and beneficial for me. It could be longer. I will be looking into getting further details on this topic and hope to read her book!"

"Jennifer Kern is an engaging speaker who compassionately invites us to look at the role drama plays in our lives. She creates a safe space for exploration and tools for under- standing and moving beyond the drama and into the lives we want to be living."

The *Daily Alignment Practice* Course and Group

"This has been a tremendous journey and it came at a time in my life when I needed it the most. The *Daily Alignment Practice* allows me to center, ground myself and reconnect with my peace and calm. Now, I'm confident, regardless of the type of day I'm having, I have resources at my disposal when I need them. And when I see others in the group 'rocking' their Alignment, I cheer/celebrate silently."

"This Alignment practice has been really important and really awesome, especially watching for 'magical manifestations'. So many amazing opportunities have come my way since I started! I feel like things are falling into place within my business, which is great because I was feeling stuck and unclear about my offerings to the world. Focusing on my Alignment is a beautiful process."

"The *Daily Alignment Practice* is helping my inner knowing. I'm experiencing more depth, as there are topics covered here that I haven't come across in other places. Jennifer Ally is a superstar kicking vibrational ass . . . and I love it! I'm so glad for the doors opening to endless possibilities. I appreciate the beautiful energy of the community. Together we get to collaborate for a better world. I am beyond thankful."

"About a week before I found the *Daily Alignment Practice* and the Facebook group, I was praying to find a group of high-vibing people, so this was really a gift for me. What I discovered was the power of Appreciation. I was already doing my Gratitudes and it came easy to me, so this was new. It helped me to grow, to appreciate myself, to appreciate things as they are and let go of trying to make them different."

"I started the *Daily Alignment Practice* group during a time when I had a lot of transition—a new relationship, moving and looking for a new job. It's amazing how many times the daily practice coincides with exactly what I need to work on: manifestation, abundance and remembering magic (that's a big one for me). It's been great to remember to come at my manifestations from a place of self-worth, feeling great, excitement and enthusiasm. It's helping me focus on how I want things to *feel*, who I want to meet and the opportunities I want to have, rather than my old way of stressing and worrying if I'm worthy enough. Now I feel like 'I own this . . . I got this . . . I'm worthy of this.' I'm really grateful for this as a support network and modality in my life right now."

To get involved, visit: www.JenniferALLY.com

CPSIA information can be obtained
at www.ICGtesting.com
Printed in the USA
LVHW092056070821
694083LV00002B/9